Accelerated Computing with HIP

Yifan Sun, Sabila Al Jannat, Trinayan Baruah, and David Kaeli

December 2024

Editorial Project Manager: Timour Paltashev
Project Manager: Timour Paltashev
Cover Designer: Tyler Webb
Copy Editor: David Kaeli
Copyediting: Editage Author Services

Notices:
Knowledge and best practices in this field are constantly changing. As new research and experience broaden our understanding, changes in research methods, professional practices, or medical treatment may become necessary. Practitioners and researchers must always rely on their experience and knowledge to evaluate and use any information, methods, compounds, or experiments described herein. In using such information or methods, they should be mindful of their safety and the safety of others, including parties for whom they have a professional responsibility.

ISBN: 979-8-218-57657-8

Contents

1 Introduction   **1**
    1.1   Parallel Programming 3
    1.2   GPUs 5
    1.3   *ROCm* 7
    1.4   *HIP* Framework 9
    1.5   What This Book Covers 10

2 Getting Started with *HIP* Programming   **11**
    2.1   Introduction 11
    2.2   *"Hello World"* in *HIP* 11
    2.3   Process Data with HIP – the Vector Add Example 12
       2.3.1   Parallel Execution Opportunities 13
       2.3.2   Organizing Threads 13
       2.3.3   Data Movement with HIP API 16
       2.3.4   Error and Correctness Checking 18
       2.3.5   Putting It Together 19
       2.3.6   Summary 21

3 HIP Kernel Programming   **23**
    3.1   Calling Functions within HIP Kernels 23
       3.1.1   ___global___ Function in HIP 24
       3.1.2   ___device___ Function in HIP 24
       3.1.3   ___host___ Function in HIP 25
       3.1.4   Combining ___host___ and ___device___ functions 26
    3.2   Using Templates in HIP Kernels 27
    3.3   Using Structs in HIP 28
    3.4   Conclusion 33

4   HIP Runtime API   **35**

   4.1   HIP Memory Management   35

      4.1.1   Pinned Memory   35

      4.1.2   Unified Memory   37

   4.2   HIP Streams   39

      4.2.1   The Basics of Streams   39

      4.2.2   Key Stream-Based APIs   40

      4.2.3   Default and Non-Default Streams   41

      4.2.4   Concurrent Kernels   42

      4.2.5   Overlapping Computation and Communication   43

   4.3   HIP Events   45

      4.3.1   Creating *HIP* Events   46

      4.3.2   Recording *HIP* Events   46

      4.3.3   Calculating Elapsed Time using *HIP* Events   47

      4.3.4   Coordinating Operations Using *HIP* Events   47

      4.3.5   Releasing Memory Using *HIP* Events   48

      4.3.6   Creating Event with Specific Flags   48

      4.3.7   Ensuring Consistency between the Two Processing Units . .   48

      4.3.8   Vector Add with *HIP* Events   49

   4.4   Conclusion   51

5   GPU Programming Patterns   **53**

   5.1   Two-dimensional Kernels   53

   5.2   Stencils   58

   5.3   Multi-Kernel Example – BFS   61

   5.4   CPU-GPU Computing – KMeans   64

   5.5   Atomic Operations – Histogram   68

   5.6   Conclusion   70

6   AMD GPU Internals   **73**

   6.1   AMD GPUs   73

   6.2   Overall Architecture   75

   6.3   Command Processor and the DMA Engine   77

   6.4   Workgroup Dispatching   77

   6.5   Sequencer   79

   6.6   SIMD Unit   80

   6.7   Thread Divergence   82

   6.8   Memory Coalescing   83

   6.9   Memory Hierarchy   84

6.10 AMD RDNA GPUs 87
6.11 Conclusion 88

7 *HIP* Tools   **91**
7.1 *ROCmInfo* 92
7.2 *ROCm SMI* 95
7.3 *The ROCm* Debugger 98
7.4 *ROCm* Profiler 102
    7.4.1 ROCTracer 102
    7.4.2 rocprofiler 104
7.5 ROCm Profiler V2 106
    7.5.1 Application Tracing 107
    7.5.2 Kernel Profiling 108
    7.5.3 ROCSys 111
7.6 Porting *CUDA* Programs to *HIP* Using Hipify 114
    7.6.1 *Hipify* Tools 114
    7.6.2 General Hipify Guidelines 119
    7.6.3 Hipification of Matrix-Transpose 120
    7.6.4 Common Pitfalls and Solutions 123
7.7 Conclusion 124

8 *HIP* Performance Optimization   **125**
8.1 Highly Parallel Workload – Image Gamma Correction 125
8.2 Fixed-Sized Kernels—Image Gamma Correction 128
8.3 Reduce—Array Sum 131
8.4 Tiling & Reuse – Matrix Multiplication 135
8.5 Tiling & Coalescing: Matrix Transpose 140
8.6 Conclusion 143

9 *ROCm* Libraries   **145**
9.1 *rocBLAS* 146
    9.1.1 Using *rocBLAS* 146
    9.1.2 *rocBLAS* functions 149
    9.1.3 Asynchronous execution 149
    9.1.4 *rocBLAS* on MI100 150
    9.1.5 Porting from the legacy *BLAS* library 152
9.2 *rocSPARSE* 152
    9.2.1 Sparse data representation 153
    9.2.2 *rocSPARSE* functions 154

9.3   *rocFFT* 156

       9.3.1   *rocFFT* workflow 157

       9.3.2   FFT Execution Plan 159

9.4   *rocRAND* 160

9.5   Conclusion 164

10 Multi-GPU Programming   **165**

10.1   *HIP* Device APIs 165

10.2   Stream-Based Multi-GPU Programming 167

10.3   Thread-Based Multi-GPU Programming 169

10.4   *MPI*-Based Multi-GPU Programming 171

10.5   GPU–GPU Communication 175

10.6   *RCCL* 179

       10.6.1   *Broadcast* 179

       10.6.2   *AllReduce* 182

10.7   Conclusion 184

11 Machine Learning with *ROCm*   **185**

11.1   *PyTorch* on *ROCm* 186

       11.1.1   Installing PyTorch 186

       11.1.2   Testing the PyTorch Installation 187

       11.1.3   Image Classification using Inception V3 188

11.2   *TensorFlow* on *ROCm* 190

       11.2.1   Installing Tensorflow 190

       11.2.2   Testing the Tensorflow Installation 190

       11.2.3   Training using TensorFlow 191

11.3   Conclusion 192

12 *ROCm* in Data Centers   **193**

12.1   Containerized *ROCm* 193

12.2   Managing *ROCm* Containers using Kubernetes 194

12.3   Managing *ROCm* Nodes using *SLURM* 197

       12.3.1   *SLURM* interactive mode 198

       12.3.2   *SLURM* batch submission mode 198

12.4   Conclusion 199

13 Third-Party Tools   **201**
  13.1 *PAPI* 201
    13.1.1 Introduction 201
    13.1.2 *PAPI* utilities and tests 203
    13.1.3 *PAPI* support for AMD GPUs 204
    13.1.4 Preset Events and Counter Analysis Toolkit (*CAT*) 205
  13.2 *Score-P* and *Vampir* 206
    13.2.1 Overview 206
    13.2.2 Tracing with *Score-P* 207
    13.2.3 *Score-P* Usage 209
    13.2.4 Profiling the *Quicksilver* Application 209
    13.2.5 Summary 211
  13.3 *Trace Compass* and *Theia* 211
  13.4 *TAU* 218
    13.4.1 Profiling *HIP* Programs Using *TAU* 218
    13.4.2 Tracing *HIP* Programs Using *TAU* 220
    13.4.3 Using *APEX* to Measure *HIP* Programs 222
    13.4.4 Summary of *TAU* 224
  13.5 *TotalView* Debugger 225
  13.6 *HPCToolkit* 230
    13.6.1 *HPCToolkit*'s Workflow 230
    13.6.2 Analyzing *PIConGPU* with *HPCToolkit* 231
    13.6.3 Collecting and Analyzing Profiles and Traces 231
    13.6.4 Measurement Using Hardware Counters 234
  13.7 Debugging and Profiling with Linaro Forge 236
    13.7.1 Linaro DDT 237
    13.7.2 Linaro MAP 237
    13.7.3 Linaro Performance Reports 238
    13.7.4 GPU Debugging Using Linaro DDT 238
    13.7.5 GPU Profiling using Linaro MAP 242
    13.7.6 GPU Performance Reports 244
  13.8 *E4S* - The Extreme Scale Scientific Software Stack 245

A ROCm Installation   **249**
  A.1 Prerequisite 249
  A.2 Understanding the ROCm Packages 250
  A.3 Installation 251
    A.3.1 Installer Script Method 251
    A.3.2 Package Manager Method 252

A.3.3 Verification of the Installation Process 253
A.4 Upgrading ROCm 254
A.5 Uninstalling ROCm 254

B *CDNA* Assembly   **257**
B.1 Using *CDNA* Assembly Code 257
    B.1.1 Retrieve *HIP* Kernel Binary 258
    B.1.2 Disassembling a *CDNA* Binary 258
B.2 *CDNA* Registers 258
B.3 Instruction Types 259
B.4 Memory Access Instructions 260
B.5 Example: Shifted Copy 261
B.6 Example: Branching 262
B.7 Comparing CDNA2 and CDNA3 264
B.8 Conclusion 266

C OmniTools   **267**
C.1 Omnitrace 267
    C.1.1 Omnitrace Configuration File 268
    C.1.2 Collect Traces 268
    C.1.3 Output and Visualization 270
C.2 Omniperf 270
    C.2.1 Profiling Programs with Omniperf 271
    C.2.2 Analysis with CLI 272
    C.2.3 Analysis with Web-Based GUI 274
    C.2.4 Analysis with Grafana 274
C.3 Summary 275

Foreword

The world of high-performance computing has recently witnessed a milestone: achieving, for the first time, exascale performance with the Frontier supercomputer deployed in the Oak Ridge National Laboratory. Frontier was superseded as the fastest supercomputer in the world by the El Capitan supercomputer deployed in the Livermore National Laboratory. These two world's fastest supercomputers are powered by AMD's CPUs, GPUs, and APUs.

Given these advances in computational performance, a new class of applications can now be pursued, including:

- Weather and climate forecasting,
- Biomedical research,
- High-end equipment development,
- New energy research and exploration,
- Animation design,
- New material research,
- Engineering design, simulation, and analysis,
- Remote sensing data processing, and
- Financial risk analysis.

AMD has enabled these advances by delivering a new class of high-performance CPUs and GPUs and a rich open-source software stack supporting HIP and ROCm execution. This emerging programming ecosystem offers many novel features, including interoperability of hardware accelerators (i.e., AMD and NVIDIA GPUs), as well support for key high-performance compilers (e.g., LLVM), cluster deployment, and essential application frameworks (e.g., Raja, Kokkos, TensorFlow and PyTorch) and key high-performance libraries (rocBLAS, rocSparse, MIOpen, RCCL, rocFFT). To complement these advances, the high-performance computing community has also contributed to these milestones by providing state-of-the-art third-party tools for performance monitoring, debuggers, and visualization tools.

The second edition of Accelerated Computing with HIP, co-authored by Yifan

Sun, Sabila Al Jannat, Trinayan Baruah, and David Kaeli, provides the high-performance computing community with an informative reference to guide programmers as they leverage the benefits of exascale computing. The text comprises 13 chapters and three appendices, providing a concise yet complete reference for HIP programming. Beginning by reviewing the basics of graphics processors and parallel programming for these devices, it then introduces HIP kernel programming and the HIP runtime application programming interface (API). In the following chapters, HIP programming patterns and AMD GPU architectures are covered. Next, HIP debugging and profiling tools, as well as performance optimization are presented. This is followed by an examination of ROCm libraries. Multi-GPU programming, machine learning frameworks, and data-center computing are discussed subsequently. Finally, several third-party tools are introduced, and the appendices cover ROCm installation, AMD GPU CDNA assembly code, and OmniTools. Several HIP and ROCm programming examples are included, helping the reader quickly master HIP programming.

The textbook is a well-structured introductory approach to accelerated computing with HIP. Users interested in learning more about scientific computing may refer to the official documentation website at https://docs.amd.com. While the textbook helps novice users of HIP acquaint themselves with step-by-step HIP programming, the ROCm documentation website helps users transition to more complex APIs, programming models, and development tools. An advanced developer could find extensive, useful details on the actual implementation of the HIP programming model and related libraries in the following open-source repository: https://github.com/ROCm-Developer-Tools/HIP.

Jack Dongarra

Professor Emeritus in the Electrical Engineering and Computer Science Department at the University of Tennessee
Distinguished Research Staff member in the Computer Science and Mathematics Division at Oak Ridge National Laboratory
Founding Director of the Innovative Computing Laboratory at the University of Tennessee
Recipient of ACM A.M. Turing Award (2021).

Preface

If artificial intelligence is the steam engine of the Fourth Industrial Revolution, GPUs are the fuel that powers it. In contrast to a CPU, which is typically designed with a few or tens of cores, a GPU typically has thousands of cores that can complete trillions of calculations in a fraction of a second. This incredible power makes the GPU an extremely popular processing device for processing vast amounts of data present in a wide range of computing tasks. Moreover, it allows users to efficiently compute expensive artificial neural network operations. Tasks that were previously considered impossible because of their high computational costs (e.g., real-time facial recognition and autonomous driving) have now been made practical, thanks to the capabilities of GPUs.

There are fundamental differences between CPU and GPU architectures that prohibit GPUs from simply reusing and improving upon the CPU programming model. Although CPU programming is taught in most high schools and universities, only a few institutions offer courses on parallel computing. To harness the power of GPUs, programmers must learn parallel programming languages and frameworks. Notably, AMD has provided the ROCm platform and HIP programming language that allow programmers to leverage GPUs from AMD and other vendors to accelerate their applications.

The goal of this book is to provide helpful guidance to GPU programmers looking to develop HIP programs for the ROCm platform using GPUs. The reader of this book will learn how to reason through real-world problems and break them down into independent parts so that GPUs can be used to solve them efficiently. This text is designed to take programmers on a tour of GPU hardware design and demonstrate how to effectively leverage its unique hardware features to optimize software performance. Finally, the text includes instructions on how programmers can exploit the ROCm ecosystem by invoking libraries to perform linear algebra operations, while leveraging multiple GPUs in a single application.

Audience of the Book

This book is designed for programmers who wish to use GPUs to improve application performance, and it is suitable for both AMD and NVIDIA GPU programmers, as HIP is a portable language that runs on both platforms. ROCm is open sourced, allowing other GPU developers to support this platform. This book does not require knowledge of CUDA programming, however, we highlight how HIP differs from CUDA while explaining how to port those programs to HIP, promoting interoperability such that a single application can be executed on different underlying hardware. For non-CUDA programmers, our book starts with the basics by presenting how HIP is a full-featured parallel programming language. Then, it provides coding examples that cover a wide range of relevant programming paradigms.

The reader is expected to have basic C/C++ programming skills, as HIP is an extension of C/C++. Thus, most language features (e.g., memory management and variable types) are the same. Prior experiences in parallel programming will be helpful, as they will make concepts, such as concurrent and parallel execution, easier to understand. However, this experience is not required, as the text fully explains the GPU parallel execution paradigm.

Organization of the Book

The book is organized into 13 chapters and three appendices. After the general introduction in Chapter 1, we introduce HIP and basic HIP kernel syntax in Chapter 2 and Chapter 3. In Chapter 4 and Chapter 5, we cover commonly used APIs and discuss commonly used GPU programming patterns. In Chapter 6, we provide a detailed introduction to the AMD GPU architecture. In Chapter 7, we introduce a few ROCm tools that allow programmers to debug and profile real GPU applications. We also introduce *Hipify*, a tool that can automatically port CUDA programs to HIP so that they run on AMD GPUs. Building upon the knowledge provided on the GPU architecture and associated tool support, in Chapter 8 we cover various methods of optimizing HIP program performance.

In Chapter 9, we introduce ROCm libraries that provide high-performance implementations of commonly used and well known algorithms, such as matrix multiplication and the Fast Fourier Transform. In Chapter 10, we introduce methods of leveraging multiple GPUs in a single program to boost overall application throughput. In Chapter 11, we demonstrate how to run deep neural network applications, including PyTorch and TensorFlow, on AMD GPUs. In Chapter 12, we explain how to manage GPUs in datacenters using GPU containers and SLURM, which are commonly used frameworks used to manage GPU workloads.

To ensure that the text is comprehensive, we include Chapter 13, which discusses third-party tools. Tool programmers from different organizations contributed to this chapter, and their contributions are exclusive to this text. The specific tools covered include:

- Section 13.1 was contributed by Anthony Danalis and Heike Jagode of the University of Tennessee, Knoxville. The Performance API (PAPI) is a library that tracks low-level hardware operations on CPUs and GPUs, as well as on communication networks and I/O systems.

- Section 13.2 was contributed by Bert Wesarg and William Williams of the Technical University in Dresden, Germany. This section introduces Vampire, a commercial tool used to visualize event logs, and Score-P, the preferred way to generate event logs for Vampire.

- Section 13.3 was contributed by Michel Dagenais, Arnaud Fiorini, Yoann Heitz, and Bohémond Couka of the Polytechnique Montreal, Canada. This section introduces Trace Compass and Theia. Like Vampire, Trace Compass is a trace visualization tool that targets high-performance computing use cases. Theia is an open extension cloud and desktop IDE platform that connects to Trace Compass to provide performance analysis support.

- Section 13.4 was contributed by Sameer Shende and Kevin Huck of the University of Oregon. This section introduces the Tau Performance System, a parallel performance evaluation toolkit that identifies system resources and temporal consumption thresholds per application.

- Section 13.5 was contributed by Bill Burns and John DelSignore of Perforce Software, Inc. This section introduces the TotalView debugger, which supports both GUI and command-line modes while allowing programmers to debug HIP programs interactively.

- Section 13.6 was contributed by Xiaozhu Meng, Dejan Grubisic, and John Mellor–Crummey of Rice University in Houston, TX. This section introduces the HPC Toolkit, which supports the measurement and analysis of GPU-accelerated applications.

- Section 13.7 was contributed by Louise Spellacy. A toolset used for GPU performance profiling and debugging is introduced in this chapter.

Section 13.8 was contributed by Sameer Shende of the University of Oregon. This section introduces the Extreme-Scale Scientific Software Stack, a curated collection of software products based on the Spack package manager.

Source Code for Examples

Source code examples are provided throughout the book. For brevity, we list only those relevant to the context and omit boilerplate examples. In cases where full programs are needed, we provide the code on GitLab at:

https://gitlab.com/syifan/hipbookexample.

Acknowledgements

The writing of this book would not have been possible without the support from AMD. The authors appreciate the help from each individual who organized the project, reviewed chapters, and provided raw materials. First, we would like to thank Timour Paltashev and Marc Benson. Timour initiated the project and organized meetings with the authors and stakeholders, managing the project to move it forward. Marc helped push the project via top executives' approval at AMD, so the authors could get sufficient support.

We also want to thank Roopa Malavally, who managed the ROCm documents at AMD. Roopa connected the book writing team with AMD employees to manage critical internal reviews, which helped to ensure the book has the most current and accurate content regarding its subject matter.

The chapters of this book have been reviewed by AMD engineers to ensure correctness. We appreciate the efforts of the AMD engineers who provided their insight and feedback. Here is a list of people who reviewed chapters (ordered by last name): SiuChi Chan, Dan Cyca, Jeff Daily, Diwakar Das, Wenkai Du, Rahul Garg, German Andryeyev, Joe Greathouse, Kenny Ho, Sreenivasa Murthy Kolam, Evgeniy Mankov, Laurent Morichetti, Braga Natarajan, Timour Paltashev, Christophe Paquot, Gina Sitaraman, Colin Smith, Peng Sun, and Tony Tye. The legal team at AMD, especially Suneet Gautam, has been involved with the project from the start and helped resolve multiple issues.

Additionally, we appreciate the effort provided by the contributor of Chapter 13, Third Party Tools. Please refer to the Preface for the list of contributors of each section in Chapter 13.

Again, we appreciate the support received from AMD that made this book possible. We especially appreciate Timour Paltashev, Mark Benson, and Roopa Malavally for their oversight on the development of the book and for connecting the authors with AMD engineers, so that the authors could receive support whenever needed. We thank Oleksandr Kupriyanchuk for his review of the book. We also want to acknowledge the suggestions and support from Hugo Andrade, Louise Crockett, Preethi Jayadev, and Patrick Lysaght regarding the publishing process.

Chapter 1

Introduction

Over the past 40 years, we have seen amazing advances in processing power, and microprocessor designers have regularly delivered higher performance chips by adding more transistors and scaling the processor clock, taking advantage of silicon technology's Moore's Law and Dennard scaling. However, early in the 21st century, as predicted by Robert Dennard at IBM, the clock frequency of a chip was limited. Hence, we found ourselves unable to push silicon to higher power densities as the energy accumulated would become impossible to dissipate. In response, chip vendors began looking for advancements in parallel processing using multiple cores on a single chip. Although new levels of high performance have been achieved, most extant software was written assuming a sequential processing model. This continues to pose challenges to programmers who are pushed to pursue new and innovative methods to exploit parallelism in their applications.

Recently, we witnessed the number of cores on a single microprocessor grow from a couple to many. For example, AMD's third-generation Ryzen Threadripper central processing unit (CPU) hosts up to 64 cores, with the next iteration aiming for 128. Application programmers have started to leverage the benefits of many-core CPUs because they excel at running multiple concurrent sequential threads.

Another interesting trend is heterogeneous computing, which uses platforms specialized for specific execution models. The first wave of such efforts was introduced by graphics card vendors (e.g., ATI and NVIDIA) who built the first graphics processing units (GPUs) with tailored chip designs to accelerate data-parallel graphics-heavy workloads. Notably, these designs required applications to be written using proprietary graphics languages, which presented barriers to

1

their widespread use as accelerators.

Today's graphics vendors typically exploit a single program multiple data (SIMD) model, in which computational loops are unrolled to leverage parallel execution units working in a SIMD fashion. With the introduction of programmable shaders, GPUs could be programmed using high-level languages, leveraging existing techniques from *C* and *C++*, such as NVIDIA's Compute Unified Device Architecture (*CUDA*) (June 2007) and Khronos' Open Computing Language (*OpenCL*) (August 2009). These parallel programming languages made multi-platform GPU application development fairly consistent. Notably, *C++* dialects use common syntax and data-type conversion standards. Thus, GPU programs now only differ in their low-level details.

As *CUDA* gained popularity, concerns were raised about it only running on NVIDIA hardware, which posed a problematic single-vendor source paradigm. *OpenCL*, which can run on GPUs, CPUs, digital signal processors, and field-programmable gate arrays, addressed this issue by adopting a *CUDA*-like programming model. Hence, the cost of portability was significantly reduced. OpenCL's requirement that device code being presented as a string posed unnecessary difficulties with code maintenance and debugging.

For the *Fortran* 1997 language, Open Multiprocessing (*OpenMP*) version 4.0 API started supporting GPUs. Currently, it supports the *C++03* standard. However, using anything from *C++11* onward can result in unspecified behaviors. Notably, it forces a portable multithreading procedure, even when directives dictate automatic data layouts and decompositions, resulting in serious drawbacks. *OpenMP* also requires the CPU for all processes, as opposed to *CUDA* and *OpenCL*, which outsource parts of the execution (kernels) to the GPU. Furthermore, *OpenMP* only offers the ability to create several threads and change how blocks of code are executed based on those threads. Moreover, its scalability is limited by its memory architecture. Experimental results have demonstrated that *OpenMP* code performance degrades with large data inputs [42], as opposed to that of *CUDA*.

The Open Accelerators (*OpenACC*) Heterogeneous Programming Standard appeared in November 2011. As with *OpenMP*, C, *C++*, and *Fortran* source code can be annotated to identify areas of acceleration using compiler directives and additional functions. Like *OpenMP* 4.0 and newer versions, *OpenACC* targets both the CPU and GPU for operations. Unfortunately, *OpenACC* is currently only supported for PGI and Cray hardware; thus, we cannot fairly compare it to other heterogeneous technologies.

In August 2012, Microsoft presented its massive parallelism approach as an extension to the *C++* language via its *Visual Studio C++* compiler, *C++* Accelerated Massive Parallelism (*AMP*). It was implemented on *DirectX 11* as an open specification. A year and a half later, the updated specification (version 1.2) was released. Microsoft had planned on this update becoming part of the *C++14* Standard, but the *C++ Committee* did not adopt it.

AMD introduced the Heterogeneous Interface for Portability (*HIP*) programming language in October 2016 to address both portability and performance. *HIP* follows many similar parallel programming historic conventions that *CUDA* has also leveraged. However, *HIP* can run on multiple platforms with little to no performance overhead. Using AMD's Radeon Open Ecosystem (*ROCm*) platform, parallel programs developed using *HIP* can be used for a wide range of applications, spanning deep learning to molecular dynamics.

This book introduces the *HIP* programming language and its ecosystem of libraries and development tools. Notably, it is based on *C++*, and readers of this book are expected to be somewhat familiar with the language. In the examples presented throughout this text, we target the AMD Instinct Machine-Intelligence (MI)-100 GPU, with which readers are not required to be familiar. Most code examples will run on any GPU supported by *ROCm* or *CUDA* platforms. This chapter introduces readers to the world of parallel computing with *HIP* and *ROCm*. Later chapters explore the features and ecosystem of *HIP*.

1.1 Parallel Programming

Many science and engineering problems possess parallel characteristics in terms of their solutions. With task-level parallelism, multiple tasks can be computed concurrently. Additionally, a single task may demonstrate data-level parallelism, where operations are simultaneously performed on multiple data elements. This class of parallelism is frequently encountered in applications that process large datasets (e.g., images, video, audio, and neural networks).

Several parallel programming languages and models based on the collective use of shared memory have been developed over the past few decades. The most commonly used frameworks include Message-Passing Interface (*MPI*), which supports scalable cluster computing, and *OpenMP*, which supports shared memory multiprocessing. *MPI* workflow managers monitor multiple nodes of a cluster, where each node has its own memory, but the memory is not directly addressable by remote nodes. Communication between memories is performed via message-passing. *OpenMP* adopts a pragma-based scheme that relies on the compiler to produce parallel code. Microsoft followed an alternative approach in its *C++ AMP* language, in which a parallel execution language extension is supported by the compiler.

A common high-performance parallelism method focuses on the portions of a program whose executions are the most time-consuming. For many applications, these portions involve loop bodies and nested loops. Listing 1.1 shows a common nested loop for a matrix–matrix multiplication operation.

Listing 1.1: Simple nested loop example – matrix–matrix multiplication.

```
1  // Multiplying two N x N matrices
2  for (i=0; i<N; ++i)
3    for (j=0; j<N; ++j)
4      C[i][j] += A[i][j]*B[j][i];
```

Assuming the use of row-major indexing, each row of **C**[i][j] is computed in a parallel thread, as shown in Figure 1.1. Each thread is assigned to a computing pipeline, which significantly reduces the execution time of the loop nest. This code example illustrates just one method of leveraging the power of parallel hardware to accelerate the execution of compute-intensive code.

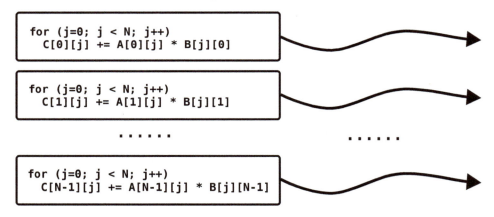

Figure 1.1: Mapping the computation of rows of matrix **C**[i][j] to individual threads for parallel execution.

The task of implementing a parallel program can be daunting. If the parallel programming environment (e.g., the compiler and *C++ AMP*) automatically identifies a parallelism opportunity, the runtime system can utilize a conservative set of schemes to accelerate execution. However, if the parallel programming environment requires the programmer to explicitly define all parallelism opportunities (e.g., *OpenMP*), correct code development may be difficult to ensure. Instead, a middle-ground is needed that will allow us to exploit the acceleration available on parallel hardware. Fortunately, *ROCm* and *HIP* provide a rich number of libraries that can be used for common parallel operations (see Chapter 9). Thus, high-performance code can leverage the power of parallel hardware without explicit calls for parallel operations.

1.2 GPUs

GPUs were originally designed to render 3D graphics, and they still do. However, in 2007, programmers and vendors reengineered their GPU programming interfaces to allow programmers to use familiar *C/C++* semantics for parallel applications. NVIDIA's *CUDA* reflected these GPU compute devices and the familiar *C/C++* semantics, as did *OpenCL* and other GPU programming interfaces.

The design of GPUs vastly differ from those of CPUs, whose architectures are optimized for single-threaded performance. Deep pipelines are used with multi-level caches and sophisticated branch prediction techniques. In contrast, GPUs are optimized for thread concurrency with shallow pipelines, programmer-controlled memory management, and little real estate devoted to managing control flow.

Although CPUs have adopted many cores in some of their more recent designs, they still differ vastly from GPUs. See Figure 1.2 to observe the architecture of AMD's MI100 GPU. There are many simple in-order processing cores on a GPU that execute in lock-step. Today's CPU designs are dominated by multiple cache levels and complex control-flow logic. As mentioned, CPUs were originally optimized for single-threaded performance. However, more recently, multi-core CPUs have expanded this paradigm to chiplet-organized cores and memory optimized for non-uniform shared memory access. The objective is to optimize memory performance through effective caching across groups of threads.

The GPU, in contrast, is optimized for memory throughput. Given the massive number of threads that concurrently access memory, GPU parallel processing is organized around wavefronts of execution.

In terms of their multithreading models, CPUs and GPUs again differ significantly. Fundamentally, CPUs have multiple cores, and each runs a different thread. However, multiple threads can be run on a single core by utilizing simultaneous multithreading [29]. GPUs, in contrast, adopt a single instruction multiple thread (SIMT) model, in which all threads execute the same code, such as how a CPU provides vectorized execution. Threads on a CPU remain under the control of a software runtime system or operating system, whereas GPU threads use a hardware-based scheduler. This difference allows GPUs to change threads in a single cycle.

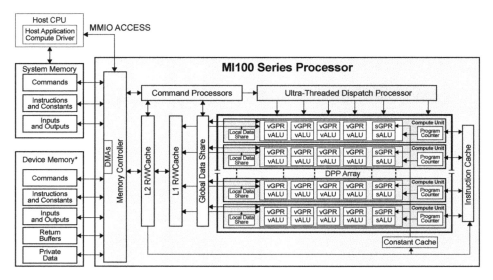

Figure 1.2: AMD MI100 microarchitecture (courtesy of AMD).

Wavefronts include a fixed set of work items (i.e., 64 for the MI100 referenced in this book). GPUs exploit data-level parallelism using thread-level parallelism. At the lowest level, SIMD units execute vector instructions. A programmer typically launches thousands of threads on the GPU as its hardware scheduler is very good at managing such thread loads. On an AMD GPU, threads are bundled into workgroups that are dispatched to individual compute units (CUs) for execution. The hardware creates a workgroup for every cycle and dispatches one wavefront to the CUs, where the parallel threads are processed. Figure 1.3 shows the relationships between work items, wavefronts, and CUs. In Chapter 6, we closely examine these concepts as they are integral to writing efficient parallel programs for AMD GPUs.

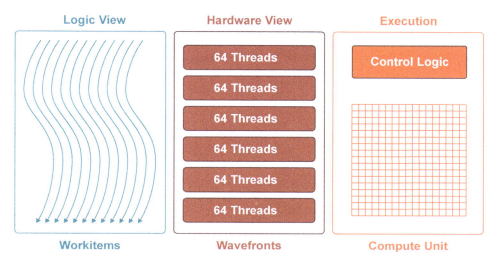

Figure 1.3: Wavefront execution.

1.3   *ROCm*

AMD's *ROCm* is an open-source software development platform that supports high-performance GPU computing across multiple hardware vendors. The run-time language was informed by earlier heterogeneous system architecture (HSA) efforts that focused on providing a flexible programming model for a rich array of architectures and application domains. As such, *ROCm* was designed to support a wide variety of popular open-source frameworks for high-performance applications targeting GPUs. The *ROCm* software stack was designed around similar principles adopted long ago by the UNIX open-source community, focusing on portability, minimalism, and modular software principles. The AMD programmers envisioned *ROCm* as an open platform for GPU-based programming that would support AMD GPUs but would also allow other vendors to support their own hardware through the *ROCm* code base [38].

Software programmers frequently reuse, port, or adapt a variety of common software frameworks and libraries to new hardware platforms to provide common APIs for programmers use. Writing code using this higher level of abstraction is desirable as it reduces the effort of moving applications between different platforms.

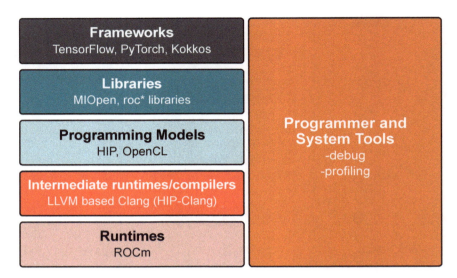

Figure 1.4: *ROCm* software stack.

Although *ROCm* was introduced in 2016, its software development community has grown rapidly, particularly in areas of high performance and machine learning (ML). Current *ROCm* support includes:

- Frameworks: *MIOpen, TensorFlow, PyTorch, Kokkos,* etc.

- Libraries: *rocBLAS, rocFFT, rocRAND, rocSPARSE, rocSOLVER,* the *ROCm* Collective Communication Library (*RCCL*), *rocThrust, rocALUTION, rocPRIM*), etc.

- Tools: *rocProfiler, rocTracer,* and *rocgdb.*

These are just a few of the several packages available from the *ROCm* ecosystem.

ROCm is the primary runtime system that supports *HIP* execution. *ROCm* supports many AMD GPUs (e.g., Instinct MI50, MI100, MI200, MI250, Radeon Vega 64, and Radeon VII), recent AMD Ryzen and Epyc processors, and some CPUs. For example, the *HIP CPU Runtime* is a header-only library that allows CPUs to execute unmodified *HIP* code. This list is expected to continue to grow as the *ROCm HIP* model is adopted by additional platforms.

1.4 *HIP* Framework

AMD's *HIP* open-source framework contains the *C++ Runtime* API, kernel language, tools, and libraries that allow programmers to create portable applications for AMD and NVIDIA GPUs from single-source code. GPU programmers familiar with *CUDA* or *OpenCL* will recognize a similar set of APIs and libraries available in the *HIP* language. *Hipify* tools, based on the *clang* frontend and *Perl* regular expressions, automatically convert *CUDA* to *HIP*, as explained in Section 7.6. Most *CUDA* API calls are automatically converted one-for-one to *HIP* API calls by the *Hipify* tools.

Software programmers are generally restricted to a specific programming model supported by their target hardware platform. However, each vendor has the choice of supporting cross-platform models, which are typically designed for a broad set of programmers to give them more flexibility and hardware choices. In contrast, *CUDA* is a proprietary model that cannot be used on non-NVIDIA GPUs, forcing *CUDA* programmers (until recently) to continue using NVIDIA hardware. *HIP* now solves this problem and allows programmers to generate source *C++* code that can be compiled for NVIDIA and AMD platforms, offering freedom of choice in terms of hardware platforms.

HIP is designed to work seamlessly with the *ROCm Runtime* (*ROCr*). Like *CUDA* and *OpenCL*, *HIP* uses two types of APIs: those that run on the CPU or host and those that run on the GPU or device. The host-based code is used to create device buffers, move data between the host and a device, launch device code, perform synchronization, manage streams and events, and more. The device-based code (kernel) is executed on the GPU. We cover the *ROCr* later in this text.

HIP marshaling libraries (e.g., *hipBLAS*, *hipFFT*, *hipRAND*, *hipSPARSE*) are analogous to *CUDA* and *ROCm* libraries in that they provide a portability layer distributed separately from *HIP*. *HIP* also offers some inherent benefits. For example, the vendor-neutral *HIP* API allows programmers to port code written for the *ROCm* environment to a *CUDA* stack, resulting in an open environment in which programmers can write code once and reuse it on NVIDIA or AMD GPUs. Notably, *HIP's* code performance on NVIDIA GPUs is the same as that of the native *CUDA*.

1.5 What This Book Covers

The aim of this book is to equip readers with the necessary tools to write efficient parallel programs for GPUs. The early chapters present the fundamentals of the *HIP* programming language, while covering GPU architecture basics. We then explain how to develop and optimize parallel programs for GPUs by leveraging various features and tools. Writing GPU programs has become easier owing to the availability of a rich set of *ROCm* libraries. We provide code examples of using several of the libraries in this book and focus on writing efficient programs for both single and multiple GPU systems. For readers familiar with *CUDA*, we take an existing *CUDA* application and explain how to convert it easily to *HIP* using *ROCm* tools. We also present a rich collection of tools available for *ROCm HIP* to enable programmers to easily and efficiently optimize their GPU applications. Finally, we discuss high-level ML frameworks and explain how to apply them using *ROCm*-based systems.

Chapter 2

Getting Started with *HIP* Programming

2.1 Introduction

In the introductory chapter, it was highlighted that *HIP* is the preferred language for leveraging the parallel processing capabilities of AMD GPUs on a *ROCm* platform. For individuals acquainted with *C/C++* syntax, *HIP* acts as an extension of *C/C++*, incorporating additional syntax and library interfaces (i.e., GPU programming APIs). Although mastering APIs might initially pose challenges, the syntax is relatively simple to grasp with some practice. A practical approach to learning *HIP* is by reviewing the syntax in example programs and tracing their operations. In this chapter, we introduce two basic *HIP* programs, HelloWorld and VectorAdd, to assist readers in comprehending *HIP* syntax, program structure, and flow. In the following chapters, we will introduce more advanced features.

2.2 *"Hello World"* in *HIP*

Many of us began our programming journey by implementing the *"Hello World"* program in various languages. Adhering to this tradition, we employ the GPU in this book to exhibit the greeting. This application triggers a GPU thread to print the *"Hello World"* message.

To initiate a task on the GPU, programmers must first develop the GPU code tailored for GPU execution. Our example is shown in Listing 2.1. The kernel, *gpuHello*, simply prints *"Hello World"*. A GPU kernel is essentially a function that returns **void** (i.e., no return data). To make a function a kernel, we must prefix the function signature **__global__** to allow the compiler to generate GPU-specific code.

Besides the GPU kernel, programmers must develop the CPU segment of the program (i.e., host program), illustrated in the **main** function. GPUs cannot operate independently and require the close coordination of a CPU. To launch the GPU kernel (i.e., GPU kernel launch), we invoke the GPU kernel function similarly to a regular CPU function. The distinct element is the **<<<>>>** sign inserted between the function name and the parameter list, which denotes the number of threads within the kernel. In this instance, we use **1, 1** to indicate that we only want to create a single thread. The necessity for two numbers is explained later.

Listing 2.1: *"Hello World" HIP example*

```
1  #include <hip/hip_runtime.h>
2
3  __global__ void gpuHello() {
4      printf("Hello World\n");
5  }
6
7  int main() {
8      gpuHello<<<1,1>>>();
9      hipDeviceSynchronize();
10 }
```

To compile this program, the *ROCm* platform provides a clang-based *HIP* compiler, *hipcc*. On a platform with *ROCm* installed, the compiler is invoked using **hipcc** from the command line interface (CLI). Appendix A provides details on how to install *hipcc*, as well as other utilities and packages. To compile our *helloWorld.cpp* source file, we would use **hipcc helloWorld.cpp -o helloWorld**. The program, similar to any regular CPU program, is run by simply entering **./helloWorld**.

2.3 Process Data with HIP – the Vector Add Example

The HelloWorld program might serve as your introduction to GPU programming, yet its utility is limited. GPUs are engineered for high throughput data processing. Therefore, in this subsequent example, we demonstrate how to use the GPU to execute element-wise addition operations on two vectors, with the results stored in a third vector.

2.3.1 Parallel Execution Opportunities

As is known, for data processing GPUs run fast because they can process data in parallel. Therefore, to use GPUs for data processing, the first step is to analyze the parallel execution opportunities.

To consider the parallel execution opportunities in the vector-add example, let us try implementing the program with CPU, as shown in Listing 2.2.

Listing 2.2: *HIP* error-checking example

```
int main() {
    int n; // the number of element in the array.
    float *a, *b, *c;

    // Allocate and initialize a, b, and c.

    for(int i = 0; i < n; i++) {
        c[i] = a[i] + b[i];
    }

    // Use the calculation results and free the memory.

    return 0;
}
```

At the heart of the implementation is a for loop. The potential for parallel execution originates from code that would traditionally be structured within a loop, as there is a need to replicate a specific action multiple times. In this instance, each iteration handles one position in the vector. Given that the iterations within the loop are not interdependent, they can be executed in any order. Here, we assert that the iterations are independent of each other, and thus, can be parallelized. The intrinsic characteristics of this problem make it well-suited for resolution via GPUs.

In the rest of the section, we will introduce a few concepts before implementing the program on a GPU. We will focus on introducing how to manage threads and memory.

2.3.2 Organizing Threads

Upon launching a GPU kernel, numerous threads executing the same kernel function are created. The ensemble of the threads generated by one kernel is referred to as a grid.

For the Vector Add example, a one-dimensional grid is likely preferable to align well with the program. Nonetheless, certain applications might necessitate processing inherently two-dimensional (e.g., matrix) or three-dimensional (e.g., spatial) data. HIP facilitates the creation of two-dimensional and three-dimensional grids. For now, our attention will remain on the one-dimensional grid.

HIP also categorizes threads into blocks, with a block typically comprising 32–1024 threads. Threads within a block can interact and synchronize amongst themselves. In this instance, thread-to-thread synchronization and communication are not required, but we will explore how to employ these features in more advanced examples later.

When a kernel is launched with the **<<<>>>** symbol, two numbers are provided, denoting the grid size (number of blocks) and the block size (i.e., number of threads within each block). The total thread count is the product of grid size and block size. HIP disallows the creation of partial blocks.

An understanding of the thread organization in HIP is necessary before we can start preparing the kernel code. On CPUs, initiating one thread to process each data point is plausible. However, the considerable CPU thread management overhead can swiftly undermine performance. Fortunately, GPU threads are lightweight, making it commonplace to designate a thread for each data point. Let us proceed by writing the GPU thread first (see Listing 2.3).

Listing 2.3: Vector_add GPU kernel

```
// HIP kernel. Each thread takes care of one element of c
__global__ void vecAdd(
    double *a, double *b, double *c,
    int n
) {
    // Get our global thread ID
    int id = blockIdx.x*blockDim.x+threadIdx.x;

    // Make sure we do not go out of bounds
    if (id < n) {
        c[id] = a[id] + b[id];
    }
}
```

The kernel function is designed for individual thread execution. In the line **int id = blockIdx.x*blockDim.x+threadIdx.x;**, a unique identifier id is generated for each thread across the entire grid of threads. This identifier is essential for distinguishing each thread and ensuring they operate on distinct data elements or perform unique operations. It used a few built-in variables to calculate the global unique identifier. The meanings of the built-in variables are provided below.

- `blockIdx.x`: This term provides the index of the current block within the grid along the x-axis. Since blocks are arranged in a grid, each block has a unique index in the grid.

- `blockDim.x`: This term represents the total number of threads per block along the x-axis.

- `threadIdx.x`: This term provides the index of the current thread within its block along the x-axis.

In this context, the suffix `.x` denotes indices on the x-axis, while `.y` and `.z` can be used for two-dimensional and three-dimensional kernels, respectively.

In a multi-block scenario, the expression **`blockIdx.x*blockDim.x`** computes the index of the first thread in the current block. This is essential because each block may contain multiple threads, and thus this expression effectively computes the "offset"of the first thread in the current block relative to the entire grid of threads.

Adding **`threadIdx.x`** to this offset produces the global index of the current thread across the entire grid. This global index **`id`** is unique to each thread, allowing each thread to know its position within the grid and operate accordingly, e.g., processing a unique data element.

Next, the add action is performed. Initially, a boundary check is conducted using the **`if`** statement. Partial blocks cannot be launched and data might not align perfectly with the blocks; therefore, there could be threads that do not need to execute any action. For example, if there are only 40 numbers in each array, we still have to launch 64 threads because only full blocks can be launched. In this case, the last 24 threads will have no data to process.

Listing 2.4: Organizing threads and kernel launching

```
// Number of threads in each thread block
blockSize = 64;

// Number of thread blocks in grid
gridSize = (int)ceil((float)n/blockSize);

// Execute the kernel
vecAdd<<<gridSize,blockSize>>>(GPUArrayA,GPUArrayB,GPUArrayC,n);
```

Eventually, in Line 11, the sum action is performed, mirroring the CPU implementation. To activate the kernel, both the block size and grid size must be specified. Let us set the block size at 64 (the rationale behind this number selection will be discussed in Section 8.1). Ideally, the total thread count should equal n. However, considering block sizes, rounding up to the nearest block boundary is necessary. Hence, the following code can be used to launch the kernel.

One thing to note is that we do not yet have **GPUArrayA**, **GPUArrayB**, and **GPUArrayC**, because the data is still on the CPU side. We will introduce how to prepare the data next.

2.3.3   Data Movement with HIP API

At the beginning of any program execution, we assume the data is maintained by the CPU. Typically, if a large data set needs to be processed, the data set is either loaded from a file or downloaded from the Internet, operations that GPUs cannot directly do. In this simple example, let us allocate some CPU data with the **Malloc** function and randomly generate the data (see Listing 2.5).

Listing 2.5: Allocation of CPU memory

```
1  // Declare all CPU arrays here
2  // Size, in bytes, of each vector
3  size_t bytes = n*sizeof(double);
4
5  // Allocate memory for each vector on host
6  CPUArrayA = (double*)malloc(bytes);
7  CPUArrayB = (double*)malloc(bytes);
8  CPUArrayC = (double*)malloc(bytes);
9  CPUVerifyArrayC = (double*)malloc(bytes);
10
11 // Initialize vectors on host
12 for(int i = 0; i < n; i++) {
13     CPUArrayA[i] = i;
14     CPUArrayB[i] = i;
15 }
```

The data is on the CPU side; we need to copy the data from the CPU to the GPU so that the GPU can process it. After the kernel execution, we also need to copy the data back from the GPU to the CPU to use the results. Furthermore, we also need to allocate memory spaces on the GPU to have buffers to receive the data. To achieve these goals, HIP provides a set of memory management APIs, as listed below.

- *hipMalloc*: This API call allocates GPU memory, and its functionality is like that of the *malloc()* function of a CPU. This API call allocates a specified chunk of memory that will be used to hold a *HIP*-specified data structure on the GPU. Note that the maximum size of this allocation is limited by the size of the GPU's physical memory, which varies from GPU to GPU. The syntax for *hipMalloc* has the form, **hipMalloc(void **ptr, size_t size)**, where ****ptr** is a pointer to our data structure, and **size** specifies the size of the memory allocation. For example, if we set a pointer to an array of single-precision floating-point values in **dev_A**, and we want to allocate 1,024 entries to hold this array on the GPU, the syntax is **hipMalloc((void**)&dev_A, 1024*sizeof(float)))**. Note that this is a blocking API call (i.e., the next line of code will not be executed until the allocation is complete).

- *hipMemcpy*: This API call transfers data from the CPU to the GPU and vice versa. The first argument is the destination array, and the second is the source. The third argument concerns the data size to be transferred, and the fourth specifies the direction of the transfer. Care should be taken to ensure that the data size fits the destination buffer and that it is in a valid range from the source buffer. Otherwise, incorrect or random values may be generated. The syntax for this API call is **hipMemcpy(void *dst, const void *src, size_t sizeBytes, hipMemcpyKind kind)**. Here, the ***dst** parameter refers to the destination buffer where data are copied. ***src** refers to the source buffer, and **size** refers to the size of the data being transferred. The fourth argument specifies the direction of the transfer, which can be (1) **hipMemcpyHostToDevice** for transferring data from the CPU to the GPU, (2) **hipMemcpyDeviceToHost** for transferring data from the GPU to the CPU, (3) **hipMemcpyHostToHost** for transferring data from the CPU to the CPU, and (4) **hipMemcpyDeviceToDevice** for transferring data from the GPU to the GPU. For example, if we have a GPU buffer **dev_A** that holds floats and a CPU buffer **host_A** that holds floats, and we want to copy 1,024 entries that currently reside in **host_A** to **dev_A**. Our *hipMemcpy* call syntax will be **hipMemcpy(dev_A, host_A, 1024*sizeof(float), hipMemcpyHostToDevice)**. This is also a blocking API call.

- *hipFree*: Like *hipMalloc* memory allocation, it is good practice to free the allocated memory on the GPU when we are done with it. This is achieved by using the *hipFree* API, whose syntax is **hipFree(void *ptr)**. For example, to free up a variable declared initially as **float *dev_A**, which has been allocated using *hipMalloc*, we simply write **hipFree(dev_A)**.

Code in Listing 2.6 demonstrates how we can use the APIs in the context of the VectorAdd example. In particular, we allocate three buffers for vectors A, B, and C, using the **hipMalloc** API. Then, we copy the input data, vectors A and B to the GPU side. After the kernel execution, we copy the output vector C back from the CPU side. Finally, we release the allocated memory.

Listing 2.6: GPU data management for the VectorAdd example.

```
1  //Declare all GPU arrays here
2  hipMalloc(&GPUArrayA, bytes));
3  hipMalloc(&GPUArrayB, bytes));
4  hipMalloc(&GPUArrayC, bytes));
5
6  // Copy host vectors to the device.
7  hipMemcpy(GPUArrayA, CPUArrayA, bytes,
8      hipMemcpyHostToDevice));
9  hipMemcpy(GPUArrayB, CPUArrayB, bytes,
10     hipMemcpyHostToDevice));
11
12 // Code related to kernel launching
13
14 // Copy data from the device to the host.
15 hipMemcpy(CPUArrayC, GPUArrayC, bytes,
16     hipMemcpyDeviceToHost));
17
18 // Use the data.
19
20 // Release device memory
21 hipFree(GPUArrayA);
22 hipFree(GPUArrayB);
23 hipFree(GPUArrayC);
```

2.3.4   Error and Correctness Checking

It is important to ensure that every *HIP* API call, whether allocating memory or copying data, is executed successfully. One common way to do this is to create an assertion macro (e.g., **HIP_ASSERT**, as shown in Listing 2.7). In the example, we can see that the *hipMalloc* call is wrapped by that assertion. Should it fail, the program will immediately terminate at this point. Moreover, if assertion checking is not performed for every runtime API call, the program may fail at a later point (e.g., kernel launch), and the source of the problem will not be immediately clear. For example, if a programmer attempts to allocate 6 GB of data to a GPU with a total memory capacity of 4 GB, the API call will appear to be successful if checking is not performed. Later, when the kernel is launched, the program may crash or produce corrupt results. Therefore, it is good programming practice to use assertions after every API call.

Listing 2.7: *HIP* error-checking example

```
#define HIP_ASSERT(x) (assert((x)==hipSuccess))
#define NUM 1024
int main() {
    float* gpuA = 0;
    HIP_ASSERT(hipMalloc((void**)&gpuA, NUM * sizeof(float)));
}
```

2.3.5 Putting It Together

We list the full VectorAdd example code in Listing 2.8). We have introduced most of the parts of the code before. The only extra line that we need to highlight is Line 63, the call to **hipDeviceSynchronize**. This line of code is inserted after the kernel launch and the device-to-host memory copy. This function call is required because kernel launching is an asynchronous process. The kernel call returns without waiting for the kernel execution to complete on the GPU. Without this explicit synchronization, device-to-host memory copy may start before the correct results are generated, copying the wrong results.

Listing 2.8: Full VectorAdd Example code

```
#include "hip/hip_runtime.h"
#include <stdio.h>
#include <stdlib.h>
#include <math.h>


#define HIP_ASSERT(x) (assert((x)==hipSuccess))

// HIP kernel. Each thread takes care of one element of c
__global__ void vecAdd(double *a, double *b, double *c, int n) {
    // Get our global thread ID
    int id = blockIdx.x*blockDim.x+threadIdx.x;

    // Make sure we do not go out of bounds
    if (id < n) {
        c[id] = a[id] + b[id];
    }
}

int main(int argc, char* argv[]){
    // Size of vectors, in number of element and in bytes
```

```
22     int n = 10240;
23     size_t bytes = n*sizeof(double);
24
25     // Host vectors
26     double *CPUArrayA;
27     double *CPUArrayB;
28     double *CPUArrayC;
29     double *CPUVerifyArrayC; // For verification
30
31     // Device vectors
32     double *GPUArrayA;
33     double *GPUArrayB;
34     double *GPUArrayC;
35
36     // Allocate memory for each vector on host
37     CPUArrayA = (double*)malloc(bytes);
38     CPUArrayB = (double*)malloc(bytes);
39     CPUArrayC = (double*)malloc(bytes);
40     CPUVerifyArrayC = (double*)malloc(bytes);
41
42     // Allocate memory for each vector on GPU
43     HIP_ASSERT(hipMalloc(&GPUArrayA, bytes));
44     HIP_ASSERT(hipMalloc(&GPUArrayB, bytes));
45     HIP_ASSERT(hipMalloc(&GPUArrayC, bytes));
46
47     // Initialize vectors on host
48     for(int i = 0; i < n; i++ ) {
49         CPUArrayA[i] = i;
50         CPUArrayB[i] = i+1;
51     }
52
53     // Copy host vectors to device
54     HIP_ASSERT(hipMemcpy(GPUArrayA, CPUArrayA, bytes,
           hipMemcpyHostToDevice));
55     HIP_ASSERT(hipMemcpy(GPUArrayB, CPUArrayB, bytes,
           hipMemcpyHostToDevice));
56
57     // Calculate grid size and block size
58     int blockSize = 256;
59     int gridSize = (int)ceil((float)n/blockSize);
60
61     // Execute the kernel
62     vecAdd<<<gridSize,blockSize>>>(GPUArrayA,GPUArrayB,GPUArrayC,n);
63     hipDeviceSynchronize();
64
65     // Copy array back to host
66     HIP_ASSERT(hipMemcpy(CPUArrayC,GPUArrayC, bytes,
           hipMemcpyDeviceToHost));
67
```

```
68    // Compute for CPU
69    for(i=0; i <n; i++) {
70        CPUVerifyArrayC[i] = CPUArrayA[i] + CPUArrayB[I];
71    }
72
73
74    // Verfiy results
75    for(i=0; i <n; i++) {
76        if (abs(CPUVerifyArrayC[i] - CPUArrayC[i]) > 1e-5) {
77            printf("Error at position i %d, Expected: %f, Found: %f \n",
                      i, CPUVerifyArrayC[i], CPUArrayC[I]);
78        }
79    }
80
81    // Release device memory
82    HIP_ASSERT(hipFree(GPUArrayA));
83    HIP_ASSERT(hipFree(GPUArrayB));
84    HIP_ASSERT(hipFree(GPUArrayC));
85
86    // Release host memory
87    free(CPUArrayA);
88    free(CPUArrayB);
89    free(CPUArrayC);
90    free(CPUVerifyArrayC);
91
92    return 0;
93 }
```

2.3.6 Summary

In this chapter, we learned the basics of parallel programming on a GPU using *HIP*. Starting from a very basic *"Hello World"* example, we worked our way up to vector addition on a GPU. We examined the basic structure of a *HIP* program, which will help us understand the more complex examples later in this book. Basic APIs, such as those involved in allocating memory, moving data between devices, and kernel launching, were also covered. Finally, we now understand the importance of using checks and assertions in the case of API call failures and for correctness verification against standard CPU implementations.

As a summary, let us review the common steps involved in GPU program execution. The steps are as follows:

- Allocate CPU memory buffers for all data structures used and populate them with the desired program values. Typically, there are two types of data structures: one to provide the input to the GPU and another to hold the data copied as output from the GPU after computation.

- Allocate similar data structures to the GPU memory buffers using a *HIP Runtime* API (i.e., *hipMalloc*).

- After allocation, copy data from the CPU buffers to the GPU buffers using the *hipMemcpy* runtime API. This ensures that the data we populated to the CPU buffers also reside in the GPU buffers before launching the kernel.

- Set the grid and block sizes of the GPU kernel. Although this can be accomplished using the kernel launch function, it is preferable to separate this step in the code for clarity. This step involves a lot of flexibility that will allow us to choose the most efficient block size. We cover this issue in later chapters.

- Launch the kernel on the GPU.

- Initiate synchronization between the CPU and GPU using *hipDeviceSynchronize*. This step is not strictly necessary as we will not perform debugging yet, and all commands are in the default stream.

- Copy the desired data back from the GPU to the CPU. This must be accomplished to access the results of the GPU kernel (e.g., storing them in a file, displaying them to standard output, or performing any number of post-processing steps on the CPU). It is important at this point to check the correctness of the code, as explained in the next section.

- After collecting the data values from the GPU, free all of the allocated memory on the GPU using the *hipFree* API.

In the following chapters, we will introduce more advanced examples, mainly to discuss extra features supported by HIP.

Chapter 3

HIP Kernel Programming

3.1 Calling Functions within HIP Kernels

In this section, we explore the function-type qualifiers in HIP, a vital concept in GPU programming that allows us to specify the type of function. Function-type qualifiers inform the compiler whether a function should be executed on the CPU, GPU, or both, enabling us to harness the full potential of heterogeneous computing.

Procedural programming (i.e., the use of functions) was originally introduced in early programming languages to eliminate code repetition. Encapsulating code in a function that is used multiple times promotes reusability and increases maintainability. The programmer can reuse previously implemented code; further, they can rely on functions to deliver the functionality promised by their names. Although a simple vector addition example may not require additional function encapsulation, real-world GPU programs often change in terms of complexity. Naturally, we gravitate towards using functions to manage this complexity. However, HIP programs require the programmer to provide explicit guidance on the function's purpose (e.g., whether the kernel is to be called by the CPU and executed on the GPU), a GPU function (to be called and executed on the GPU), or a CPU function (to be called and executed on the CPU).

Given that the GPU operates under the supervision of the CPU, the GPU does not independently initiate the execution of functions on the CPU; rather, the CPU controls and manages the overall process, including tasks performed by the GPU. HIP incorporates function-type qualifiers to address this requirement, giving the programmer the ability to specify where a function should be executed.

Understanding these qualifiers will empower you to effectively harness the GPU's heterogeneous parallel computing capabilities and unlock their full potential for accelerating your application.

3.1.1   ___global___ Function in HIP

The function-type qualifier ___global___ is a fundamental aspect of HIP programming. The ___global___ qualifier designates a function as a kernel, enabling it to be called from the host CPU and executed on the GPU. Kernels do not return values to the host CPU directly. We need to employ a memory copy API to facilitate communication between the CPU and GPU (this was discussed in Section 2.3.3). An example of a kernel that uses the ___global___ function-type qualifier is presented in Listing 3.1. In this code sample, we define a global function, with a specified return type of void, and well-defined parameter types. However, a question arises: what happens when we need to call a function from within this kernel? We will explore this scenario in the next section.

Listing 3.1: Using ___global___ function in HIP Kernel

```
1  __global__ void vector_add(float *out, float *a, float*b, int n) {
2    int id = bockDim.x * blockIdx.x + threadIdx.x;
3    if (id < N) {
4      out[id] = a[id] + b[id];
5    }
6  }
```

3.1.2   ___device___ Function in HIP

The HIP ___device___ function type qualifier allows the programmer to define functions to be called by kernels, or other GPU functions, and executed on the GPU. In HIP, ___device___ functions encapsulate small, reusable, computations that can be called from multiple GPU functions. Device functions simplify and optimize GPU programs by breaking down GPU code into smaller, reusable, components.

In Listing 3.2, we define a device function named *get_global_id*. This function calculates the global index of a thread within a block of threads and returns the computed value. Although this example may have limited practical use, it demonstrates the use of a device function. We then have a kernel function named *myKernel*, declared with the global qualifier. The kernel function is executed simultaneously by a large number of threads on the GPU. Each thread processes a different portion of the data, enabling a high degree of parallelism and overall faster computation. In this case, *myKernel* leverages the *get_global_id* device function to calculate the global index of the thread and stores the value in the *id* variable. Lastly, the main function includes the invocation of the kernel using the triple-angled brackets notation $\langle\langle\langle \ \rangle\rangle\rangle$. This launch mechanism allows multiple GPU functions to reuse the code encapsulated within the device function, leading to code reuse and program simplification.

Developing programs using this model, ___device___ functions offer a powerful means of modularizing GPU code, enhancing reusability, and streamlining complex computations. Through the usage of device functions, developers can break down their code into manageable components, resulting in improved code organization and better performance.

Listing 3.2: Using ___device___ function in HIP Kernel

```
1  __device__ int get_global_id(void) {
2    return blockDim.x * blockIdx.x + threadIdx.x;
3  }
4
5  __global__ void myKernel(int *a) {
6    int id = get_global_id();
7  }
8
9  int main(){
10   ...
11   myKernel<<<gridSize, blockSize>>>(a);
12   ...
13 }
```

3.1.3 ___host___ Function in HIP

In addition to the global and device qualifiers, HIP introduces the host qualifier. This qualifier plays a significant role in specifying the execution context of functions in HIP programming. When a function is marked with the host qualifier, it signifies that the function will be executed on the CPU.

In HIP, functions with the host qualifier must be explicitly called from the host, as shown in Listing 3.3. They are designed to carry out computations and tasks better suited for execution on the CPU, versus the GPU. It is important to note that if no qualifier is specified for a function in HIP, it is automatically assumed to be executed on the CPU by default, as shown in the Listing 3.4. Hence, the host qualifier is equivalent to not using any qualifier. The host qualifier provides clarity and specificity in terms of the execution environment for functions in HIP.

By distinguishing between host- and GPU-executed functions, developers can precisely allocate tasks to the appropriate processing units, optimizing performance and resource utilization within their programs.

Listing 3.3: Using ___host___ function in HIP Kernel

```
1  __host__ int add_numbers(int a, int b){
2    return a+b;
3  }
```

Listing 3.4: Using default function in HIP Kernel

```
1  int add_numbers(int a, int b){
2    return a+b;
3  }
```

3.1.4   Combining ___host___ and ___device___ functions

The device and host function qualifiers can be combined in HIP programming, resulting in visible and executable CPU and GPU functions. These combined qualifiers create what are known as device and host functions, which offer a valuable option for code sharing between the host and device, eliminating the need for redundant programming. In Listing 3.5, the function *myFunction* is designed to be called from both the host and device code. This function can seamlessly access memory on both the host and device, making it convenient for sharing code and data between the two execution environments.

Listing 3.5: Combining ___host___ and ___device___ functions in HIP Kernel

```
1  __device__ __host__ void myfunction(int *a){
2    // function implementation here
3  }
```

However, the programmer must exercise caution when using combined qualifiers, as certain GPU-specific data structures cannot be used within functions with host and device qualifiers. For instance, the previously discussed get_global_id in the Listing 3.2 function cannot be assigned the host qualifier. This restriction ensures correct program execution and prevents potential conflicts arising from the distinct programming models of a CPU versus a GPU. Conversely, combining device functions with global functions is not possible. The global qualifier is specifically used to denote kernel functions that execute on the device. Moreover, the device qualifier specifies the function what is meant to execute exclusively on the GPU, but not necessarily in a parallel manner. This means that the function runs individually on each thread of the GPU, without parallel execution. Combining these qualifiers within the same function declaration can lead to confusion regarding the intended behavior and execution target of the function. Similarly, host functions cannot be combined with global functions. Host functions are designed to execute solely on the host and are incompatible with device execution. Therefore, merging host and global functions into a single function is not feasible.

3.2 Using Templates in HIP Kernels

In the previous section, we observed the important role that functions play in reducing code repetition, especially device functions. However, there are scenarios where certain functions still involve repeated code. For instance, implementing a function that compares two integers and returns the larger one is straightforward. However, if we need to compare two single-precision numbers and return the larger one, we would need to duplicate the code with minor differences in the input and output value types. To address this issue, templates are key. Templates provide a powerful mechanism in *HIP* programming that allows us to write generic functions capable of working with various data types, thus they eliminate the need to know the specific data type in advance. The concept of templates is borrowed from the C++ language [67], providing flexibility and increasing code reuse.

Implementing a template in *HIP* involves prefixing the code with the keyword *template*, followed by angled brackets, as shown in Listing 3.6. By defining data types as parameters within the angled brackets, we can easily adapt our code to handle different data types without duplicating or modifying the code.

Listing 3.6: Using Template in HIP Kernel

```
template<typename T>
__global__ void vector_add(T *out, T *a, T *b, int n){
  int tid = blockDim.x * blockIdx.x + threadIdx.x;
  if (tid < N){
    out[tid] = a[tid] + b[tid]
  }
}
```

In Listing 3.6, we present an example of a simple templetized function for vector addition, written in *HIP*. The *vector_add* function is defined as a generic function that can operate on any data type T that supports the addition computation. It accepts four arguments, similar to the *vector_add* kernel we previously used to implement vector addition in *HIP*. This *vector_add* function launches the kernel – it can be called with different types by specifying the T type. For each data type that requires this function's support, the compiler dynamically generates a version of the binary code, allowing any type that supports the plus operator to be executed using this kernel. It is worth noting that templates in HIP can be applied to global, device, and host functions, expanding their versatility and applicability.

Proper template utilization enhances a program's power by supporting multiple data types and reducing code complexity. It provides a streamlined approach to handling generic computations, while maintaining flexibility and increasing reuse.

3.3   Using Structs in HIP

In C and C++, one of the major features is the ability to create customized data types using structs. Structs enable us to combine multiple values and multiple types to describe the properties of a single entity, making it easier to manage related data. This section will explore the basics of structs in HIP, including their syntax, and provide use cases. To facilitate this discussion, we will provide an example and a step-by-step programming example to reinforce the concepts.

In HIP programming, structs are used in a similar way in C [41] or C++ [67] programming. A struct in HIP is a composite data type that groups values of different data types into a single unit, enabling easier management and manipulation of related data. This is particularly beneficial when dealing with a large amount of interconnected data that needs to be organized in a structured manner. By utilizing structs, we can encapsulate data into a cohesive unit, simplifying data passing within the program and reducing the likelihood of errors or inconsistencies. An excellent example of using structs in HIP is their use for complex data structures, such as points in a 2D space. For instance, consider a program that stores information about a set of 2D points. Instead of using separate arrays to store x and y coordinates for each point, we can employ a struct to represent a 2D point. The struct would contain two fields: one for the x coordinate and one for the y coordinate. Utilizing a struct allows us to organize the data into a single object, facilitating easier data management and manipulation. The code snippet in Listing 3.7 defines a struct representing a 2D point in HIP. Once we have defined a struct in HIP, we can declare variables of that specific type and initialize them with data. In this example, we declare a variable *p1* of type Point. By accessing the x and y components of the *p1* variable using the dot notation *p1.x* and *p1.y*, we can assign specific values to represent the x and y coordinates, respectively.

For instance, assigning *p1.x = 1.0f* creates a point with an x-coordinate of 1.0, while *p1.y = 2.0f* assigns a y-coordinate of 2.0 to the same point.

Listing 3.7: Using Struct in HIP Kernel

```
struct Point {
    float x;
    float y;
}
Point p1;
p1.x = 1.0f;
p1.y = 2.0f;
```

To demonstrate how to use structs in HIP, we show an example that calculates the distance to the origin of a list of 2D points. This program calculates the Euclidean distance from a point, represented as (x, y) in 2D space, to the origin (0, 0) using $\sqrt{x^2 + y^2}$.

To begin developing our solution, we must include the necessary header file. In this code, we will use #include <hip/hip_runtime.h>, which provides us with the runtime APIs and data types required for our HIP implementation. To enhance code reuse and increase efficiency, we will use macros. In this code, we define N as a macro representing the number of elements in the array (Listing 3.8).

Listing 3.8: Header files and macros

```
#include <hip/hip_runtime.h>
#define N 1000000000
```

Next, we define a struct called TwoDimensionPoint encompassing three fields: x, y, and distToOrigin (Listing 3.9). We then can use the TwoDimensionPoint struct to create an array of points.

Listing 3.9: Using struct in HIP

```
struct TwoDimensionPoint {
    float x;
    float y;
    float distToOrigin;
};
```

Next, we implement the GPU kernel calculateDistToOrigin, as shown in Listing 3.10. This function, written in HIP, is responsible for calculating the **distToOrigin** field for each element in the array of **TwoDimensionPoint** objects. It takes two arguments: **points**, an array of **TwoDimensionPoint**s, and **n**, the number of elements in the array.

The function uses the expression blockDim.x * blockIdx.x + threadIdx.x to determine the index of the current thread within the GPU grid. The if statement checks that the index is within the bounds of the array. If the index is within the bounds, the function calculates the *distToOrigin* field for the corresponding element using the Euclidean distance formula. This formula computes the distance from the origin (0,0) to the point represented by the **x** and **y** components of the point at the index idx in the *points* array.

Listing 3.10: TwoDimensionPoint GPU kernel

```
__global__ void calculateDistToOrigin(TwodimensionPoint *points, int n) {
    int idx = blockDim.x * blockIdx.x + threadIdx.x;
    if (idx < n) {
  points[idx].distToOrigin = sqrt(points[idx].x * points[idx].x + points[
      idx].y * points[idx].y;
    }
}
```

In the CPU code in Listing 3.11, we declare a pointer h_points that points to an array of TwoDimensionPoint objects with N elements. To allocate memory on the CPU for the host, we use the malloc function, requesting the amount of memory to be allocated equal to the sizeof(TwoDimensionPoint) $\times N$. Note that we utilize the struct in both the CPU and GPU code. In the following for loop, we iterate N times to initialize the x and y values of each TwoDimensionPoint object in the array. We utilize the rand() function to generate a random number between 0 and the maximum value returned by RAND_MAX. The generated random number is divided by RAND_MAX to obtain a float value, which is then stored in the **x** and **y** fields of the TwoDimensionPoint object.

Listing 3.11: Allocation of CPU memory

```
int main() {
    TwoDimensionPoint *h_points;
    h_points = (TwoDimensionPoint*)malloc(TwoDimensionPoint) * N);

    for (int i = 0; i < N; i++) {
     h_points[i].x = rand() / RAND_MAX;
     h_points[i].y = rand() / RAND_MAX;
    }
}
```

Next, we allocate memory on the GPU using the following code snippet in Listing 3.12. In this code we define a pointer pointArray that points to an array of TwoDimensionPoint objects. However, this pointer is used to access device memory. We use the hipMalloc() function to allocate memory on the GPU for the points array. The size of the allocation is determined by sizeof(TwoDimensionPoint) * N.

Listing 3.12: Allocation of GPU memory

```
TwoDimensionPoint *pointArray;
hipMalloc((void*)&pointArray, N * sizeof(TwoDimensionPoint));
```

To ensure that the data from the host memory is accessible for computation on the GPU, we need to copy the data from the host memory to the GPU memory. The following code in Listing 3.13 accomplishes the copying. We use the hipMemcpy API to copy the data from the host memory (h_points) to the GPU memory (points). The size of the data to be copied is determined by sizeof(TwoDimensionPoint) * N. We use the hipMemcpyHostToDevice flag to specify the direction of the memory copy.

Listing 3.13: Memory copy from the CPU memory to the GPU memory

```
hipMemcpy(pointArray, h_points, sizeOf(TwoDimensionPoint) * N,
    hipMemcpyHostToDevice);
```

On the successful transfer of data to the GPU memory, we can launch the calculateDistToOrigin kernel to perform the distance calculations on the GPU. Before launching the kernel, we define the size of each block of threads. We set the blockSize to 256, representing the number of threads per block. We then calculate the gridSize, which determines the number of blocks required to execute the kernel on all the N input points, using the specified block size. Finally, we launch the kernel with the $\langle\langle\langle$ gridSize, blockSize $\rangle\rangle\rangle$ syntax, passing the points array and the number of points N as arguments. After the kernel finishes execution, we use hipDeviceSynchronize() to ensure that the CPU host waits for the GPU device to finish executing the kernel before proceeding with the remaining code.

Listing 3.14: Kernel Launch

```
int blockSize = 256;
int gridSize = (N + blockSize -1) / blockSize;
calculateDistToOrigin<<<gridSize, blockSize>>>(pointArray, N);
hipDeviceSynchronize();
```

Following the kernel execution, we need to copy the results back from the GPU memory to the host memory. The code snippet in Listing 3.15 accomplishes this. Here, we utilize hipMemcpy once again, but this time with the hipMemcpyDeviceToHost flag to copy the results from the GPU memory (points) back to the host memory (h_points). The size of the data to be copied remains the same, sizeof(TwoDimensionPoint) * N. Finally, the next step is to print out the distance to the origin of all the points in the program. While printing, we iterate through the h_points array and print the index, x and y coordinates, and the calculated distToOrigin value for each point.

Listing 3.15: Memory copy from the GPU memory to the CPU memory

```
1  hipMemcpy(h_points, pointArray, sizeof(TwoDimensionPoint) * N,
       hipMemcpyDeviceToHost);
2  for(int i = 0; i < N; i++) {
3      printf("Point %d: (%f. %f), distToOrigin = %f\n", i, h_points[i].x,
           h_points[i].y, h_points[i].distToOrigin);
4  }
```

Before we finish program execution, it is important that we free the allocated CPU and GPU memory. Using hipFree, we free the memory allocated on the GPU, while free is used to free the memory allocated on the CPU (Listing 3.16). By releasing the memory, we ensure efficient resource utilization.

Listing 3.16: Memory deallocation in HIP

```
1  hipFree(pointArray);
2  free(h_points);
```

In this section, we implemented the Distance to Origin application using HIP programming. The application is designed to handle a dataset of 1000 points, each representing coordinates and their distances from the origin. Our implementation successfully generated the output for all 1000 points, computing the distances between the coordinates and the origin. For illustrative purposes, we captured a snapshot of the output containing the data for the first 10 points, which can be seen in Listing 3.17.

Listing 3.17: Output of the "Distance to Origin program" *HIP* example.

```
Point 0: (0.840188, 0.394383), distToOrigin = 0.928145
Point 1: (0.783099, 0.798440), distToOrigin = 1.118370
Point 2: (0.911647, 0.197551), distToOrigin = 0.932806
Point 3: (0.335223, 0.768230), distToOrigin = 0.838183
Point 4: (0.277775, 0.553970), distToOrigin = 0.619711
Point 5: (0.477397, 0.628871), distToOrigin = 0.789548
Point 6: (0.364784, 0.513401), distToOrigin = 0.629800
Point 7: (0.952230, 0.916195), distToOrigin = 1.321422
Point 8: (0.635712, 0.717297), distToOrigin = 0.958459
Point 9: (0.141603, 0.606969), distToOrigin = 0.623268
```

The specific array size we used in the application was chosen to accommodate all 1000 points. The number of points in the output was determined by the array size we used in the application. By specifying the desired array size, we were able to calculate and display the coordinates and distances for each point. Using this example, we have demonstrated the effectiveness of HIP programming in solving real-world problems and obtaining meaningful results. By leveraging the power of GPUs and using techniques, such as a struct abstract datatype, we can efficiently process and analyze large amounts of data efficiently.

3.4 Conclusion

In this chapter, we explored several advanced techniques that can make GPU programming more concise and reusable. We first discussed the function-type qualifiers in HIP, which are crucial for making the most of the GPU's parallel computing capabilities and optimizing your application's performance. We also introduced Templates in HIP kernels, inspired by C++ Templates, eliminating the requirement of repeating code for similar data types. Furthermore, we introduced how to use structs in GPU kernel programs, which allow the bundling of related data entities. Encapsulating data in structs can enhance code organization and simplify complex computations. All these methods effectively can improve your HIP programs in terms of readability, reusability, and manageability.

Chapter 4

HIP Runtime API

In the first three chapters of this book we learned that a HIP program comprises the host component running on the CPU and the device component executing on the GPU. The previous chapter explored methods for crafting GPU kernel programs. In this chapter, we will introduce how to leverage HIP Runtime APIs to improve the host program's control of the GPU.

4.1 HIP Memory Management

In all the examples given in the text thus far, the default style of memory allocation provided by HIP has been used. However, HIP provides more flexibility on how memory is allocated. Flexibility during memory allocation is particularly relevant when working with GPUs, where efficient memory transfers and access are crucial.

4.1.1 Pinned Memory

In this section, we will explore the concept of pinned memory and its significance in optimizing performance of data transfers between the CPU and GPU. By understanding and using pinned memory, we can overcome some of the performance overhead associated with pageable memory.

When memory is allocated using the malloc function, it typically resides in pageable memory, which can be swapped out to disk by the system when physical memory needs to be freed. However, this behavior can result in significant performance overhead, especially in programs that frequently transfer data between the CPU and GPU. To mitigate this issue, we can leverage pinned memory. The HIP

API provides a function called *hipHostMalloc*, which allows us to allocate pinned memory on the host. This function takes three arguments: a pointer that points to the allocated memory, the size of the memory to be allocated, and an optional flag specifying the allocation type, as shown in Listing 4.1. Pinned memory is memory that is kept in a fixed location within physical memory. Unlike conventional pageable memory, pinned memory remains consistently available in its designated physical location, thus eliminating the need for data to be frequently moved around. Both the host and the device can access the allocated memory.

Listing 4.1: Memory allocation in HIP using pinned memory

```
1 float *a;
2 hipHostMalloc(&a, bytes, unsigned int flags);
```

Using pinned memory is particularly advantageous when frequent data transfers between the host and the device are required. Pinned memory can significantly improve data transfer performance by enabling faster memory access. This, in turn, enhances the overall performance of the program. The *hipMemcpy()* and *hipMemcpyAsync()* functions can be used with pinned memory to facilitate data transfer. These functions provide efficient mechanisms for moving data between the host and the device. It is important to note that when freeing pinned memory allocated using *hipHostMalloc()*, the *hipHostFree()* function should be used instead of the standard free function. This ensures the proper release of the pinned memory and frees it from its designated physical location. Attempting to free pinned memory using the *free()* function can lead to complications, as *free()* cannot unpin the memory.

Listing 4.2: Freeing pinned memory

```
1 hipHostFree(d_a);
```

To demonstrate the practical application of pinned memory, let us consider an example of vector addition that uses this memory type. So far in this section, we have discussed the advantages of using pinned memory, and suggested how it can improve GPU performance. To effectively utilize pinned memory for vector addition, we need to modify the memory allocation process. Instead of using the conventional *malloc()* function, as shown in Listing 2.5, we will employ the code snippet provided in Listing 4.3. This updated code snippet ensures that the memory allocation is performed using pinned memory, leveraging its benefits for our vector addition program.

Listing 4.3: Host memory allocation vector addition program

```
// Allocate memory for each vector on host
HIP_ASSERT(hipHostMalloc(&CPUArrayA, bytes));
HIP_ASSERT(hipHostMalloc(&CPUArrayB, bytes));
HIP_ASSERT(hipHostMalloc(&CPUArrayC, bytes));
HIP_ASSERT(hipHostMalloc(&CPUVerifyArrayC, bytes));
```

By using the hipHostMalloc() function, we can allocate the host memory using pinned memory. This ensures that the memory is allocated in physical memory and eliminates the need for frequent data transfers between the CPU and GPU, resulting in improved performance. Additionally, we must make a change in the memory deallocation section. Instead of using the traditional host memory deallocation approach shown in Listing 2.6, we will use the hipHostFree() function, as mentioned in Listing 4.4. However, the device memory deallocation will remain the same.

Listing 4.4: Deallocating host memory for pinned memory

```
// Deallocate host memory
hipHostFree(CPUArrayA);
hipHostFree(CPUArrayB);
hipHostFree(CPUArrayC);
```

By utilizing pinned memory, we can optimize the memory allocation process in our example vector addition program. This allows us to take advantage of the benefits offered by pinned memory, such as improved data transfer performance and reduced overhead. Additionally, proper memory deallocation using the hipHostFree function ensures efficient memory management.

4.1.2 Unified Memory

To further facilitate communication between the host and device, HIP provides unified memory. This abstraction simplifies the process of copying data between host and device memory. Manual data copying between the host and device memory can be time-consuming and error-prone, requiring additional programmer effort. Unified memory provides an efficient solution to this challenge.

Unified memory in HIP offers a unified address space that both the CPU and GPU can access. With unified memory, data can be seamlessly accessed by both the host and the device without the need for explicit data transfers. This eliminates the burden of manual memory copying and simplifies data management. To allocate unified memory, we can utilize the *hipMallocManaged()* function, as shown in Listing 4.5. This function takes a pointer to the memory location where the allocated memory will be stored and the size of the memory to be allocated. Data migration between the CPU and GPU is handled transparently with managed memory. When the GPU accesses the memory, it is automatically migrated to the device, and when the CPU accesses it, it is migrated back to the host. This dynamic migration ensures data availability and optimizes memory utilization. Using unified memory enables developers to write code that seamlessly leverages the power of the GPU without the need for explicit memory management. This significantly reduces program complexity and streamlines the development process.

Listing 4.5: Memory allocation in HIP using unified memory

```
int *a;
hipMallocManaged(&a, bytes);
```

To better understand the use of unified memory, we explore an example that adopts unified memory using our vector addition scenario. In this example, we will utilize unified memory to create a single memory space that can be accessed by both the CPU and GPU. To achieve this, we will employ the *hipMallocManaged* function. In the vector addition example shown previously in Listing 2.5, memory allocation was performed separately for the CPU and GPU using the *malloc* and *hipMalloc* functions, respectively. However, we can simplify this process by utilizing the *hipMallocManaged* function which allocates memory that can be accessed by both CPU and GPU. We can replace the CPU and GPU memory allocation code with the following code snippet, as shown in Listing 4.6. Memory copy is not required as both CPU and GPU can access the unified memory.

Listing 4.6: Memory allocation in HIP using unified memory

```
// Size, in bytes, of each vector
size_t bytes = n*sizeof(double);

// Allocate unified memory for each vector
float *a, *b, *c, *cpuVerifyC;
hipMallocManaged(&a, bytes);
hipMallocManaged(&b, bytes);
hipMallocManaged(&c, bytes);
hipMallocManaged(&cpuVerifyC, bytes);

// Initialize vectors
for(int i = 0; i < n; i++) {
    a[i] = i;
    b[i] = i;
}
```

Similar to our previous example, when deallocating memory, we no longer need to deallocate both the host and device memory separately. Deallocating the memory using the hipFree() function is sufficient.

Listing 4.7: Free unified memory

```
// Release memory
hipFree(a);
hipFree(b);
hipFree(c);
hipFree(cpuVerifyC);
```

By employing unified memory with hipMallocManaged, we can simplify the memory allocation process by creating a unified memory space that can be accessed by both the CPU and GPU. This eliminates the need for separate memory allocations for the CPU and the GPU, as well as explicit memory copies between the CPU and the GPU, streamlining the code. Additionally, by using the hipFree() function, we can efficiently deallocate the unified memory. We discussed how using his approach could be applied to our vector addition example, simplifying memory management and enhancing the overall efficiency of GPU programming.

4.2 HIP Streams

Modern GPUs provide programmers with the flexibility to launch concurrent kernels, as well as overlapping computations and communication. This ability allows incredible performance improvements. Several real-world applications use kernels that work on independent data structures, where the input of one kernel does not necessarily depend on the output of another kernel. Thus, programmers can choose to execute multiple kernels concurrently to maximize GPU utilization. A second kernel can also be launched while data is transferred back to the host by an earlier kernel that has completed processing. This feature utilizes *HIP* streams. In this section, we learn how they work and how GPU programmers can leverage them to improve application performance.

4.2.1 The Basics of Streams

HIP operations, such as data transfers and kernel launches, rely on *HIP* streams. All operations in a stream are executed in order, as specified by the application. Until now, we have used the default stream, which is also known as the NULL stream or stream 0. Recalling the discussion in Chapter 2, we set the stream parameter in the kernel launch argument list to zero. The *HIP* programming model states that, by default, all operations execute in the NULL stream. However, programmers can specify streams for data transfers and memory copies.

HIP streams provide the following features:

- Streams can overlap data communications and kernel launches. For example, the programmer may launch a kernel on Stream 1 and use Stream 2 to copy data from a kernel launched on Stream 2. When using only the default NULL stream, the programmer must wait until the memory copy is complete before launching the next kernel.

- Streams can dispatch multiple kernels concurrently to maximize GPU utilization. This is an important feature, particularly for applications with small kernels that cannot fully saturate the GPU's resources.

Note that, from a programmer's perspective, all program streams execute concurrently. However, the actual execution order is subject to scheduling (by the GPU driver and GPU hardware), as well as the hardware resources available (e.g., the number of memory copy engines).

Before discussing *HIP* streams more deeply, it is important to remember two important points:

- Kernel launches are asynchronous in nature. Thus, after a kernel is executed, program control immediately returns to the host. This is why we place a *hipDeviceSynchronize* call after the kernel launch to provide synchronization between the host and device. This also ensures that the kernel completes execution before executing subsequent code.

- Thus far, the **hipMemcpy** commands have been synchronous. Therefore, the host blocks execution until the memory transfer is complete. However, *HIP* provides APIs that support asynchronous host and device transfers, provided we use multiple streams. We explore this feature in the upcoming sections, as they increase concurrency and improve application performance.

4.2.2   Key Stream-Based APIs

We now examine some of the most commonly used *HIP* APIs and discuss how to utilize them effectively.

Stream Creation and Closing

The programmer is responsible for creating streams and closing them when done. Stream creation is performed using the *hipStreamCreate* API, which takes as an argument a variable type of *hipStream_t*, as shown in Listing 4.8. Similarly, streams are terminated using the *hipStreamDestroy* API, which also takes a *hipStream_t* argument. It is good programming practice to call *hipStreamDestroy* after all stream operations have completed.

Listing 4.8: Stream creation and closing.

```
hipStream_t myStream;
hipStreamCreate(&myStream);

// Use the stream

hipStreamDestroy(&myStream);
```

When working with multiple streams, a developer may want to pause host processing until the kernel in a specific stream is complete. With respect to the host CPU, this serialization is necessary, especially if the CPU requires the stream's output for host-side processing. To support serialization, *HIP* provides the *hipStreamSynchronize* API, which takes the stream object that we wish to synchronize as an argument. In case we do not want to block the host CPU but want to synchronize streams, we can use the *hipStreamWaitEvent* API (which will be introduced in Section 4.3).

Asynchronous Memory Copy

Leveraging the true potential of streams requires understanding of how asynchronous memory copies work. Up to this point, we have used the *hipMemcpy* API to transfer data between the host CPU and GPU. This produces a blocking call in which program control does not return to the host until the data transfer is completed. In contrast, *hipMemcpyAsync* is nonblocking. This API performs a similar task as does the *hipMemcpy* API, except that the *hipMemcpyAsync* API requires the programmer to specify the stream identifier as an argument. The non-blocking nature of this API has another important implication. To issue an asynchronous memory copy, the programmer must ensure that the data being moved is "pinned" in the host memory (see Section 4.1).

4.2.3 Default and Non-Default Streams

When leveraging streams, the implications of using the default versus non-default streams must be understood. Note that all newly created streams are blocking by nature. In the context of streams, the term "blocking" means that any operation issued to the default stream will have to wait until all prior operations in the

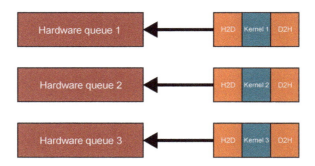

Figure 4.1: Multiple streams performing memory copies and kernel launches concurrently on the GPU.

non-default stream have been completed. Similarly, any operations in non-default streams enqueued after operations in the default stream will also be blocked until the work in the default stream is completed.

This blocking behavior can be disabled using *hipStreamCreateWithFlags*, which takes the user-created stream as its argument, as well as a flag, **hipStreamNon-Blocking**. It is generally recommended that non-blocking streams be used to the fullest extent possible while relying on the synchronization of *HIP* events, rather than relying on implicit runtime synchronization, such as *hipStreamSynchronize*.

4.2.4   Concurrent Kernels

Kernels from two different streams can be executed concurrently, both on the same GPU or each on a different GPU. Listing 4.9 shows a sample host-side code. First, the streams are created, and the host-to-device data transfers are completed. Next, the two kernels are launched across Streams 1 and 2. When complete, the output data is copied back from the device to the host. This illustrates how straightforward it is to use *HIP* streams to enable kernel-level concurrency. The code examples presented in this chapter include both serial (i.e., *serial.cpp*) and concurrent (i.e., *concurrent.cpp*) types. We have also added the code required to measure the performance of these two implementations. Readers are encouraged to use streams to obtain higher performance over serialized kernel execution. In our MI100 GPU system, using stream-based concurrent kernels provides a speedup of up to 2×. This feature is helpful whenever we have kernels that do not saturate the entire GPU.

Listing 4.9: Concurrent kernel host-side code using *HIP* streams.

```
//Declare all arrays here using hipMalloc
hipStream_t stream1, stream2;
hipStreamCreate(&stream1);
hipStreamCreate(&stream2);


HIP_ASSERT(hipMemcpy(&deviceA1,&A1, arraySize,hipMemcpyHostToDevice);
HIP_ASSERT(hipMemcpy(&deviceA2,&A2, arraySize,hipMemcpyHostToDevice);


square<<<gridSize, blockSize, 0, stream1>>>(deviceA1,deviceB1,n );
cube<<<gridSize, blockSize, 0, stream2>>>(deviceA2,deviceB2,n );


HIP_ASSERT(hipMemcpy(&B1,&deviceB1, arraySize,hipMemcpyDeviceToHost);
HIP_ASSERT(hipMemcpy(&B2,&deviceB2, arraySize,hipMemcpyDeviceToHost,
    stream2);
```

Listing 4.10: Kernel code for cube and square kernels.

```
__global__ void square(double *a, double *b, int n)
{
    // Get our global thread ID
    int id = blockIdx.x*blockDim.x+threadIdx.x;

    // Make sure we do not go out of bounds
    if (id < n)
        b[id] = a[id] * a[id];
}

__global__ void cube(double *a, double *b)
{
    // Get our global thread ID
    int id = blockIdx.x*blockDim.x+threadIdx.x;

    // Make sure we do not go out of bounds
    if (id < n)
        b[id] = a[id]*a[id]*a[id];
}
```

4.2.5 Overlapping Computation and Communication

If we can overlapp communication and computation, we can reduce program execution time by utilizing streams for concurrent execution. By assigning compute and communication tasks to different streams, it is possible to mask the latency of data transfers, as these operations do not block each other across streams. This technique is particularly useful for large problems with significant data transfer requirements, allowing for pre-kernel launch transfers.

One particular pattern that allows us to overlap communication and computation involves partitioning the dataset into subsets and pipelining the execution. Streams facilitate this pattern by allowing each stream to handle a subset of the data. Leveraging this pattern can accelerate kernel launches and enable concurrent data transfers. The result will be significantly better performance, produced by optimizing the management of computation and communication tasks.

Here, we revisit the cube kernel provided in Listing 4.10. We first reduce the problem size by partitioning the dataset. Although we have chosen four streams in this example, the reader is encouraged to experiment with other partitioning settings. In our example, we partition 100 million input data elements using four streams, with each stream processing a total of 25 million elements.

A common practice is to launch kernels in multiple streams as a FOR-loop, as shown in Listing 4.9. Let us examine the FOR-loop code. First, we calculate an offset that is used to identify the subset of data associated with each stream. This is followed by a *hipMemcpyAsync* call from the host to the device, where the offset calculated in the previous step is used to mark the chunk of data that must be copied from the CPU to GPU in each stream. This *HIP* call, as we have discussed previously in this chapter, is non-blocking by nature. Thus, the next line in the application (i.e., the kernel launch) is immediately enqueued to the GPU. It is important to note that the completion of the kernel launch command by the host does not guarantee the immediate execution of the kernel by the GPU. Because commands in the same stream are executed in order, the kernel launch waits until the actual memory copy is completed. Similarly, the next *hipMemcpyAsync* is enqueued by the host on the device; however, the data transfer does not begin until the kernel in that stream has finished executing. In the next FOR-loop iteration, the host follows the same steps for the remaining streams. By leveraging streams, the programmer can smartly break down the size of a problem and dispatch it across multiple streams to achieve a good level of concurrency between computation and communication. For example, assume that the kernel in Stream 1 is already finished with its part of the host-to-device memory copy and starts executing. Simultaneously, as the kernel assigned to Stream 1 executes, the data required by the second stream can be concurrently transferred to the GPU. This approach yields benefits, even if the kernel in one stream saturates all the GPU shader resources. The idea here is that if we can overlap computations and communications across streams instead of waiting for all data transfers to finish, we can improve performance.

Listing 4.11: Host-side code used to showcase the benefits of overlapping computations and communications using *HIP* streams.

```
//Declare all arrays here using hipMallocHost

for(int i = 0; i < num_streams; i++)
    {
        int offset = i * elements_per_stream;
        HIP_ASSERT(hipMemcpyAsync(&d_input1[offset],&h_input1[offset],
            bytes_per_stream,hipMemcpyHostToDevice,streams[i]));
        cube<<<gridSizePerStream,blockSize,0,streams[i]>>>(d_input1,
            d_output1,offset);
        HIP_ASSERT(hipMemcpyAsync(&h_output1[offset],&d_output1[offset],
            bytes_per_stream, hipMemcpyDeviceToHost,streams[i]));
    }
```

The code in *compute_comm_overlap.cpp* presents a situation in which the data is partitioned across four streams and launched using a FOR-loop, as shown in Listing 4.11. On an MI100 system, this streaming implementation, which overlaps computations and communications, achieves a speedup of 4× compared with an implementation that only uses the default stream. Thus, depending on the problem, the programmer can break down a large problem into smaller streams and overlap computation and communication to obtain superior performance. This paradigm is also popular in many ML frameworks, such as PyTorch [62] and TensorFlow [1], as they commonly use pipelining to implement neural network training and inference.

4.3 HIP Events

We can examine the process of measuring execution time using timers or clocks in the host code. Although these methods provide a basic understanding of execution time, they may not offer the desired accuracy and reliability when it comes to measuring GPU operations. In this section, we will explore a more advanced approach using HIP events, which provide a precise and dependable way to measure the execution time of GPU operations. By leveraging HIP events, programmers can effectively identify performance bottlenecks and optimize their code for improved efficiency.

HIP events are powerful tools for monitoring the execution of commands on the GPU. They offer fine-grained control and allow for accurate measurement of execution time, making them an essential component in performance analysis. Further, we will look into creating and using HIP events to accurately measure the execution time of vector addition operations, a fundamental task in GPU programming. HIP events play a crucial role in the HIP programming model, offering a powerful mechanism for tracking the status and progress of operations executed on the GPU. By utilizing the *hipEvent_t* type, programmers gain access to a versatile toolset for effectively monitoring the execution of tasks. The *hipEvent_t* type serves as the cornerstone of HIP programming when it comes to representing events as shown in Listing 4.12. Through its usage, programmers can create, record, and synchronize events to gain precise control over the execution flow of GPU tasks. This level of control allows for efficient monitoring and analysis of GPU operations, enabling developers to optimize code and identify performance bottlenecks.

Listing 4.12: Utilizing hipEvent_t type

```
1 hipEvent_t
```

4.3.1   Creating *HIP* Events

In GPU programming, HIP events serve as a powerful tool for recording operations asynchronously on the GPU. By leveraging the *hipEventCreate()* function, developers can effortlessly create events that capture crucial moments in the execution timeline, a shown in Listing 4.13. The creation of HIP events allows the programmer to become a GPU performance engineer.

Listing 4.13: Creating event using hipEventCreate() function

```
1 hipEventCreate(hipEvent_t *event)
```

4.3.2   Recording *HIP* Events

Accurately capturing the start and end times of various operations is crucial for understanding performance and optimizing code. HIP events provide us with an efficient and reliable mechanism to achieve this goal. By utilizing the *hipEventRecord()* function, developers can record the temporal boundaries of different operations, including data transfer and kernel execution. The event parameter of the *hipEventRecord()* function allows programmers to specify the HIP Event that needs to be recorded, and the stream parameter determines the stream in which the event will be recorded (Listing 4.14). By strategically placing these function calls, developers gain insights into the execution timeline of their GPU operations.

Listing 4.14: Recording HIP events using hipEventRecord() function

```
hipEventRecord(hipEvent_t *event, hipStream_t stream))
```

4.3.3 Calculating Elapsed Time using *HIP* Events

Accurate measurement of elapsed time is significant when it comes to analyzing and optimizing performance in software development. In the quest for precise temporal measurement, the HIP programming framework offers a powerful function called *hipEventElapsedTime()*. By employing this function, developers can accurately determine the time interval between two events. The function takes three arguments: *ms*, a pointer to a floating-point variable that receives the calculated elapsed time; *start* representing the initial event; and *stop* denoting the concluding event as shown in Listing 4.15. Executing the API call *hipEventElapsedTime()* returns a floating-point value in milliseconds, allowing developers to capture precise timings between the specified events and store it in the designated variable.

Listing 4.15: Calculating elapsed time using hipEventElapsedTime() function

```
hipEventElapsedTime(float *ms, hipEvent_t start, hipEvent_t stop)
```

4.3.4 Coordinating Operations Using *HIP* Events

Another essential function in the HIP API, *hipEventSynchronize()*, plays a pivotal role in stream synchronization (Listing 4.16). When invoked with a specific event, *hipEventSynchronize()* halts the host thread until the associated event and all previous operations within the corresponding stream have completed their execution. By enforcing synchronization, this function guarantees the desired ordering of events across different streams. *hipEventSynchronize()* serves as a powerful tool for coordinating operations, eliminating race conditions, and ensuring consistency in the execution of GPU tasks. This function provides the means to orchestrate streams effectively, including synchronization of data transfers and kernel executions.

Listing 4.16: Coordinating operations using hipEventSynchronize()

```
hipEventSynchronize(hipEvent_t event)
```

4.3.5   Releasing Memory Using *HIP* Events

Efficient memory management is a crucial programming aspect, ensuring high performance and resource utilization. In HIP programming, memory management plays a vital role. One important function for managing HIP events is *hipEventDestroy()*, as shown in Listing 4.17. This function enables the release of memory associated with a HIP event, freeing up valuable resources and maintaining system efficiency. When using *hipEventDestroy()*, developers pass the event handler as an argument, indicating which event's memory should be released. By properly destroying the event, programmers can ensure that the allocated memory is deallocated and available for other operations.

Listing 4.17: Releasing memory using hipEventDestroy() function

```
1  hipEventDestroy(hipEvent_t event)
```

4.3.6   Creating Event with Specific Flags

The function *hipEventCreateWithFlags()* is used to create an event and allocate memory for it on the device, using the specified flags, as shown in Listing 4.18. This function takes two arguments: a pointer to a *hipEvent_t* variable that will hold the handle to the created event, and an unsigned integer representing the flags. These flags can be used to customize the behavior of the event, such as indicating that the event should be recorded on a specific stream or specifying a particular completion type for the event.

Listing 4.18: Creating event with specific flags using hipEventCreateWithFlags() function

```
1  hipEventCreateWithFlags(hipEvent_t *event, unsigned flags)
```

4.3.7   Ensuring Consistency between the Two Processing Units

The *hipDeviceSynchronize()* function is a valuable tool in GPU programming, as it allows for synchronization between the CPU and GPU (Listing 4.19. This function serves as a blocking call, halting the execution of the host (CPU) code until all the GPU work has been completed. Using *hipDeviceSynchronize()*, programmers can ensure that all preceding GPU operations have completed before proceeding with subsequent CPU operations. This synchronization mechanism is particularly useful for scenarios where the CPU code relies on the results or data generated by the GPU. By employing *hipDeviceSynchronize()*, the CPU can safely wait until the GPU has completed its workload, guaranteeing data integrity and consistency between the two processing units. During the execution of *hipDeviceSynchronize()*, the host thread is temporarily suspended, allowing it to effectively catch up with the progress running on the GPU. This synchronization ensures that all operations across different streams on the GPU have been finalized, eliminating any potential race conditions or data inconsistencies.

Listing 4.19: Ensuring consistency between the two processing units using hipDeviceSynchronize() function

```
hipDeviceSynchronize()
```

4.3.8 Vector Add with *HIP* Events

To explore the use of hip events in a use case, we will revisit the vector addition example. In the vector addition example from Chapter 2, we can incorporate hip events to measure the elapsed time on the GPU. To begin, after the memory allocation in Listing 2.6, we need to introduce a variable to store the GPU elapsed time. Next, two HIP Events of type *hipEvent_t* are created, *start* and *stop* by using the *hipEventCreate()* function, as shown in Listing 4.20. These events are used to measure the time elapsed during the GPU computation. By creating these events, we are preparing to measure the elapsed time on the GPU. Then, we proceed with the memory copy from the CPU to the GPU, similar to the regular vector addition example.

Listing 4.20: Allocation of GPU memory and data copy from CPU to GPU

```
//Declare all GPU arrays here
HIP_ASSERT(hipMalloc(&GPUArrayA, bytes));
HIP_ASSERT(hipMalloc(&GPUArrayB, bytes));
HIP_ASSERT(hipMalloc(&GPUArrayC, bytes));

float gpu_elapsed_time_ms;

hipEvent_t start, stop;
hipEventCreate(&start);
hipEventCreate(&stop);

// Copy host vectors to device
HIP_ASSERT(hipMemcpy(GPUArrayA, CPUArrayA, bytes,
    hipMemcpyHostToDevice));
HIP_ASSERT(hipMemcpy(GPUArrayB, CPUArrayB, bytes,
    hipMemcpyHostToDevice));
```

After the memory copying is complete, the block size and grid size for the kernel launch have been set in Listing 2.4, we can begin recording the hip event using the *hipEventRecord()* function. In this case, we pass the start variable as the parameter, as the *hipEventRecord()* function requires the event to be recorded, as shown in Listing 4.21. After initiating the recording using *hipEventRecord()*, we launch the kernel to perform the vector addition. Once the kernel execution is complete, we stop recording by using the stop variable in the *hipEventRecord()* function. To ensure synchronization and completion of the recorded event, we utilize the *hipEventSynchronize()* function with the stop parameter. Following the synchronization, we finish execution of the kernel by copying the GPU memory back to the CPU memory. Subsequently, we can calculate and print the GPU elapsed time using the *hipEventElapsedTime()* function, as illustrated in Listing 4.21. Finally, we free both the host and device memory using the free and hipFree functions, respectively.

Listing 4.21: Organizing threads and kernel launching

```
1  // Number of threads in each thread block
2  blockSize = 1024;
3  // Number of thread blocks in grid
4  gridSize = (int)ceil((float)n/blockSize);
5
6  hipEventRecord(start, 0);
7
8  // Execute the kernel
9  vecAdd<<<gridSize,blockSize>>>(GPUArrayA,GPUArrayB,GPUArrayC,n);
10
11 hipEventRecord(stop, 0);
12 hipEventSynchronize(stop);
13
14 hipDeviceSynchronize();
15 HIP_ASSERT(hipMemcpy(CPUArrayC, GPUArrayC, bytes,
16     hipMemcpyDeviceToHost));
17
18 hipEventElapsedTime(&gpu_elapsed_time_ms, start, stop);
19 printf("Time elapsed on vector addition on GPU: %f ms.\n\n",
20 gpu_elapsed_time_ms);
```

Through the integration of hip events, we can accurately measure the GPU elapsed time in the vector addition example. By recording the start and stop events, launching the kernel, and synchronizing the events, we ensure precise measurement of the GPU execution time. The utilization of hipEventElapsedTime allows us to calculate and display this time. Furthermore, proper memory deallocation ensures efficient utilization of system resources.

4.4 Conclusion

In this chapter, we introduced more advanced features provided with the HIP runtime API. We started with discussing HIP memory management methods, because adaptability in memory allocation holds particular importance in GPU operations. Efficient memory transfers and access are essential factors in this context. Moving forward, we have learned the concept of HIP streams, powerful tools that can enhance performance. They enable simultaneous computations and communications, improving GPU and network utilization. Using HIP streams in applications, as provided in the APIs, is straightforward and can significantly boost an application's efficiency. Finally, we also discussed HIP events, which play a vital role in GPU synchronization and performance measurement. They provide a robust method to track and monitor operations executed on the GPU. Understanding these HIP APIs allows programmers to better control the GPU in a more flexible and fine-grained manner.

Chapter 5

GPU Programming Patterns

Next, we discuss common GPU programming patterns that are used in a broad range of GPU applications. For each pattern discussed, we cover the layout of the associated data structures, and also review the common operations that are performed upon the data. We will provide programming examples written in HIP, enabling the reader to become proficient in identifying and utilizing these patterns in their GPU programs.

5.1   Two-dimensional Kernels

GPUs provide a massively parallel architecture consisting of thousands of cores. As a result of this architecture, data-parallel computations are well suited to run on the GPU. Two-dimensional kernel patterns are commonly data-parallel, enabling us to leverage a GPU to exploit this inherent form of parallelism. Tasks that involve processing large matrices of data, which are common in image processing and machine learning applications, can be significantly accelerated by distributing computations across these cores.

When we process data in a two-dimensional grid, there are often neighboring elements that depend on each other. Many scientific and engineering simulations involve working with data in a two-dimensional space. Today's GPU architectures are well-suited to solve two-dimensional problems and process two-dimensional data. When developing applications that leverage two-dimensional kernels, code developers are then able to optimize their code for specific tasks and GPU hardware configurations. This level of optimization can lead to substantial speed improvements.

In this section, we will explore a HIP program that uses two-dimensional blocks for matrix multiplication [66]. Before we dive into the HIP code for matrix multiplication, we will review how matrix multiplication is typically computed. Suppose we have two matrices, A and B. Matrix A has m rows and n columns, and matrix B has n rows and k columns. In this particular case, the resulting matrix C will have m rows and w columns.

Listing 5.1: CPU implementation of Matrix Multiplication

```cpp
#include <iostream>
#define N 32
void cpu_matrix_multiplication(
  float *a, float *b, float *result, int n) {
  for (int i = 0; i < n; ++i) {
    for (int j = 0; j < n; ++j) {
      int tmp = 0;
      for (int k = 0; k < n; ++k) {
        tmp += a[i * n + k] * b[k * n + j];
      }
      result[i * n + j] = tmp;
    }
  }
}

int main(){
  float *a, *b, *c;
  a = (float*)malloc(sizeof(float)*N*N);
  b = (float*)malloc(sizeof(float)*N*N);
  c = (float*)malloc(sizeof(float)*N*N);

  // Initialize matrix A
  for (int i = 0; i < N; ++i) {
    for (int j = 0; j < N; ++j) {
      a[i * N + j] = rand() % RAND_MAX;
    }
  }
  // Initialize matrix B
  for (int i = 0; i < N; ++i) {
    for (int j = 0; j < N; ++j) {
      b[i * N + j] = rand() % RAND_MAX;
    }
  }

  cpu_matrix_multiplication(a, b, c, N);
  return 0;
}
```

To compute the product of matrices A and B, we first take the dot product of the first row of matrix A with the first column of matrix B. This gives us the first element in the resulting matrix. We repeat this process for all rows and columns in A and B to obtain the complete resulting matrix. This is a matrix multiplication of two N x N matrices, where N is defined as 32; thus, there will be $32^3 = 32{,}768$ multiplication operations and $32^2 \times (32 - 1) = 31{,}744$ addition operations. Next, we will take a look at a CPU implementation of matrix multiplication to gain a better understanding of the process.

This code (see Listing 5.1) is a program that multiplies two square matrices using the CPU. It includes a function called cpu_matrix_multiplication, which takes three pointers to float variables, with a and b representing the matrices to be multiplied and *result* pointing to the matrix that will store the result of the multiplication. The integer n specifies the size of the matrices. The cpu_matrix_multiplication function uses nested for loops to multiply the two input matrices. The outer two loops iterate over the rows and columns of the resulting matrix, and the innermost loop calculates each element of the result. The multiplication is done by iterating over the row index of matrix a and the column index of matrix b, multiplying corresponding elements and adding the result to a temporary variable. The computation of each output is independent. Once the innermost loop is completed, the temporary variable is stored in the corresponding element of the resulting matrix. The main function initializes two matrices a and b with random values using the *rand()* function. Then, the cpu_matrix_multiplication function is called to perform the matrix multiplication and store the result in matrix c.

To build on this example, we will look at the implementation of matrix multiplication of two square matrices, developed using HIP. The first thing to note is the inclusion of the header that is necessary to use HIP runtime calls. We also added macros for the size of the matrices and the number of blocks per grid, which are set to 16 and 256, respectively (Listing 5.2).

Listing 5.2: Header file and macros

```
#include <hip/hip_runtime.h>
#define BLOCK_SIZE 16
#define N 256
```

Taking a closer look at the HIP kernel (Listing 5.3), we see that the purpose of the kernel is to perform a matrix multiplication on square matrices. The kernel expects four input parameters: pointers to the matrices a, b, and c, along with the size of the square matrices N.

The kernel has been structured such that each individual processing thread is responsible for computing a single element or output value in the result. Each thread within a specific block is identified by *threadIdx.x* and *threadIdx.y*, and each block within a grid is identified by *blockIdx.x* and *blockIdx.y* in the x-direction and the y-direction, respectively.

Next, we initialize the variable *sum* to zero. This variable will be used to add up the elements in the selected row and column. Then, we check if the row and column indices exceed the number of actual rows and columns in the matrices using an *if* statement. We do this to prevent threads from performing operations beyond the scope of the matrices.

The *for* loop inside this kernel performs a dot product using a row in matrix *a* and a column of matrix *b*. After the summation, the result is stored in the corresponding index in matrix *c*.

Listing 5.3: GPU code

```
1  __global__ void gpu_matrix_multiplication(float *a,float *b, float *c,
       int n){
2    int row = blockIdx.y * blockDim.y + threadIdx.y;
3    int col = blockIdx.x * blockDim.x + threadIdx.x;
4    int sum = 0;
5    if( col < n && row < n) {
6      for(int i = 0; i < n; i++) {
7        sum += a[row * n + i] * b[i * n + col];
8      }
9      c[row * n + col] = sum;
10   }
11 }
```

Taking a closer look at the CPU code (Listing 5.4), we declare pointer variables with an integer data type. We also allocate the host memory for the matrices *h_a*, *h_b*, and *h_c*. After this step, we initial matrices *h_a* and *h_b* on the host, filling the matrices with random numbers.

Listing 5.4: CPU memory allocation matrix initialization

```
1  int main(){
2    float *h_a, *h_b, *h_c, *h_cc;
3    h_a = (float*)malloc(sizeof(float)*N*N);
4    h_b = (float*)malloc(sizeof(float)*N*N);
5    h_c = (float*)malloc(sizeof(float)*N*N);
6
7    // Initialize matrix A
8    for (int i = 0; i < N; ++i) {
9      for (int j = 0; j < N; ++j) {
10       h_a[i * N + j] = rand() % RAND_MAX;
11     }
```

```
12    }
13    // Initialize matrix B
14    for (int i = 0; i < N; ++i) {
15      for (int j = 0; j < N; ++j) {
16        h_b[i * N + j] = rand() % RAND_MAX;
17      }
18    }
```

In the next step, we allocate memory on the GPU and copy data from the CPU to the GPU for our input matrices(Listing 5.5). Next, we launch the kernel(Listing 5.6), but we first determine the number of threads per block and blocks per grid. We use a data type called dim3 for this purpose. In our example, we create a grid with dimensions BLOCK_size by BLOCK_size, with BLOCK_size set to 16 initially. As a result, the number of blocks, n_blocks, is calculated by dividing N by BLOCK_size, where N is the matrix size. We use the ceil function to round up to the next integer. This allows us to create more threads than needed and avoids unnecessary work with matrices using an if statement in the kernel. Finally, we use hipDeviceSynchronize to make sure the GPU finishes its work before the CPU continues, preventing data access conflicts.

Listing 5.5: GPU memory allocation and data transfer (Host to Device)

```
1    int *d_a, *d_b, *d_c;
2    hipMalloc((void **) &d_a, sizeof(float)*N*N);
3    hipMalloc((void **) &d_b, sizeof(float)*N*N);
4    hipMalloc((void **) &d_c, sizeof(float)*N*N);
5
6    hipMemcpy(d_a, h_a, sizeof(float)*N*N, hipMemcpyHostToDevice);
7    hipMemcpy(d_b, h_b, sizeof(float)*N*N, hipMemcpyHostToDevice);
```

Listing 5.6: Kernel Launch

```
1    dim3 threadsPerBlock (BLOCK_SIZE, BLOCK_SIZE);
2    int n_blocks = ceil(N/BLOCK_SIZE);
3    dim3 blocksPerGrid (n_blocks, n_blocks);
4
5    gpu_matrix_multiplication<<<blocksPerGrid,threadsPerBlock>>>(d_a, d_b,
         d_c, N);
6    hipDeviceSynchronize();
```

After the kernel execution, we can copy the result from the resulting device matrix *d_c* on the GPU back to the CPU using *hipMemcpy*, just as before. (Listing 5.7). After moving the data back to the CPU, we verify the results. Then we free the memory we allocated in CPU and GPU memory and return 0 to indicate the program has run successfully.

Listing 5.7: Data transfer (Host to Device) and memory deallocation

```
1   hipMemcpy(h_c, d_c, sizeof(float)*N*N, hipMemcpyDeviceToHost);
2
3   hipFree(d_a);
4   hipFree(d_b);
5   hipFree(d_c);
6   free(h_a);
7   free(h_b);
8   free(h_c);
9   return 0;
10 }
```

5.2 Stencils

Stencil operations represent another important class of embarrassingly parallel algorithms. Stencils are a class of algorithms that iteratively update the data in an array based on a data items adjacent to the cell. Stencil algorithms are commonly used in physics simulations and partial differential equations to support convolutional operations for image processing. By applying different image convolution kernels (not to be confused with GPU kernels), the algorithm smooths and sharpens image features and detects edges. As a result, image convolutions are a major building block in convolutional neural networks (CNNs).

Just as discussed with the gamma correction example, image convolutions are also embarrassingly parallel workloads. When mapped to a GPU, each thread calculates the output of a single pixel; hence, there is no need to communicate updates among threads.

However, there are some fundamental differences between image convolutions and gamma corrections. With gamma corrections, all brightness values are treated as independent values, and we do not worry about their location in the image. Therefore, we simply process the entire image as an array, and, as a result, the relative pixel positions matter. We use a two-dimensional grid that maps to the shape of the kernel, significantly simplifying the implementation. Generally, stencil workloads can be one-, two-, or three-dimensional.

Listing 5.8: *HIP* smoothing operation program.

```
1  #include <hip/hip_runtime.h>
2
3  #include <vector>
4
5  #include "image.h"
```

```
6
7   __global__ void conv2d(uint8_t *image, float *mask, int image_width,
8                          int image_height, int mask_width, int mask_height)
                             {
9     int x = blockIdx.x * blockDim.x + threadIdx.x;
10    int y = blockIdx.y * blockDim.y + threadIdx.y;
11
12    if (x >= image_width || y >= image_height) {
13      return;
14    }
15
16    float sum = 0;
17    for (int i = 0; i < mask_width; i++) {
18      for (int j = 0; j < mask_height; j++) {
19        // Calculate the coordinate of the pixel to read.
20        int image_x = x + i - mask_width / 2;
21        int image_y = y + j - mask_height / 2;
22
23        // Do not read outside the image.
24        if (image_x < 0 || image_x >= image_width || image_y < 0 ||
25            image_y >= image_height) {
26          continue;
27        }
28
29        // Accumulate the value of the pixel.
30        int image_index = image_y * image_width + image_x;
31        int mask_index = j * mask_width + i;
32        sum += image[image_index] / 255.0f * mask[mask_index];
33      }
34    }
35
36    int image_index = y * image_width + x;
37    image[image_index] = sum * 255;
38  }
39
40  int main() {
41    int width, height, channels;
42    static const int maskWidth = 200;
43    static const int maskHeight = 200;
44    std::vector<float> mask(maskWidth * maskHeight * channels);
45    for (int i = 0; i < maskWidth * maskHeight; ++i) {
46      mask[i] = 1.0f / maskWidth / maskHeight / channels;
47    }
48
49    // Load an image from disk.
50
51    // Allocate GPU memory and copy data to the GPU.
52    uint8_t *d_image;
53    float *d_mask;
```

```
54    hipMalloc(&d_image, width * height * channels * sizeof(uint8_t));
55    hipMalloc(&d_mask, maskWidth * maskHeight * channels * sizeof(float));
56    hipMemcpy(d_image, image, width * height * channels * sizeof(uint8_t),
57             hipMemcpyHostToDevice);
58    hipMemcpy(d_mask, mask.data(),
59             maskWidth * maskHeight * channels * sizeof(float),
60             hipMemcpyHostToDevice);
61
62    // Calculate grid size and launch the kernel.
63    dim3 block_size = {16, 16, 1};
64    dim3 grid_size = {(width + block_size.x - 1) / block_size.x,
65                     (height + block_size.y - 1) / block_size.y, 1};
66    conv2d<<<grid_size, block_size>>>(d_image, d_mask, width, height, maskWidth,
67                                               maskHeight);
68    hipDeviceSynchronize();
69
70    // Copy the data back to the host.
71    hipMemcpy(image, d_image, width * height * channels * sizeof(uint8_t),
72             hipMemcpyDeviceToHost);
73
74    // Store the image to disk.
75
76    hipFree(d_image);
77    hipFree(d_mask);
78
79    return 0;
80 }
```

In our next code example, we present code that performs image smoothing. The most noteworthy technique leveraged in this kernel is the use of two-dimensional grids. In the host program, rather than using a single integer to represent the size of the grid, we use a **dim3** object containing three values to represent the number of block-based work items per dimension. Given that we want to use a two-dimensional grid, we use a z dimension size of one, and specify the x and y dimensions based on our problem size.

In the kernel, we must obtain the thread IDs in both the x- and y-dimensions. To obtain these values, we use the *threadIdx.x* and *threadIdx.y* operations. The block dimension and ID also have associated variables define in each dimension, as shown in the example.

5.3 Multi-Kernel Example – BFS

In the next example in this chapter, we first examine a *HIP* implementation of the Breadth-First Search (BFS) algorithm. This workload is part of the *Rodinia* benchmark suite [18]. BFS is a graph-search algorithm that is used for several applications for path-finding, peer-to-peer networking, and Global Positioning System (GPS) navigation.

BFS is a layer-wise algorithm in which all nodes of a given graph level or layer are explored before progressing to the next level. For example, to avoid processing the same node twice, BFS uses a queue to mark the node as "visited," as in Figure 5.1(a).

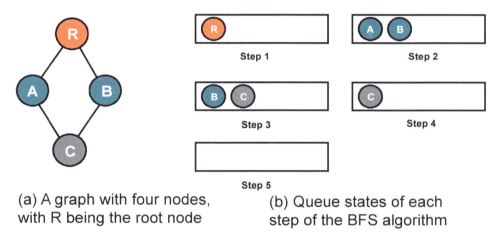

(a) A graph with four nodes, with R being the root node

(b) Queue states of each step of the BFS algorithm

Figure 5.1: Illustration of the BFS algorithm with a graph with four nodes.

The diagram in Figure 5.1(b) shows how the queue is processed. Starting from the root, R, we first mark R and enqueue the node in Step 1. As this is the root node, no other nodes exist at this level. Hence, we "pop" the queue and process the connected nodes, A and B. We push them into the queue and mark them as visited in Step 2. Afterwards, there are no more nodes to be processed at this level. Thus, we pop the head of the queue, which currently contains node A, and process its neighbors. Node A is connected to nodes C and R. Node R has already been visited. Hence, node C is pushed into the queue and marked as visited in Step 3. Following this process, we exhaust the neighbors of node A. Thus, the next item in the queue, B, is dequeued in Step 4, and node C is the only remaining node in the queue. Node B is connected to C and R, and R and C are already marked as visited. Hence, we do not revisit them. Finally, we reach a stage in which node C is the remaining element in the queue, and it is connected to A and B, both of which have already been marked as visited. Thus, node C, the last element, is removed from the queue. At this point, the queue is finally empty, as shown in Step 5. Thus, the algorithm is terminated.

Now that we have covered the basics of BFS, we examine its parallel implementation on a GPU. The implementation demonstrated here is from the *Rodinia* benchmark suite.

The implementation finds the minimum number of edges required to reach all vertices in the graph from a given source vertex. All nodes that are processed at a given level are collectively referred to as the "frontier." The two kernels of the application are executed back-to-back using a DO-WHILE loop, where each instance represents processing of the nodes at a given level. The nodes and edges are stored in variables *g_graph_nodes* and *g_graph_edges*, respectively. *g_graph_mask* is initialized to FALSE for all nodes, though not the root, and is used to determine which nodes to process in the next iteration of the DO-WHILE loop. The cost of visiting one node from a previous node is tracked using the *g_cost* variable. Whenever the neighbors of a given node are visited, *g_cost* is updated accordingly. Additionally, *g_updating_graph_mask* is initialized to FALSE at the beginning. This variable is used to determine which node's information must be updated by the second kernel.

In Kernel 1, in Line 5, we check whether the thread ID is within the bounds of the graph and is part of the current frontier. If both conditions hold, the thread removes itself from the frontier by setting the variable, *g_graph_mask*, to FALSE. Next, we loop through all neighbors of this vertex to check for unvisited neighboring vertices (Lines 11 and 12). For all unvisited neighbors, the thread updates the appropriate entry in the cost array. The processed neighbors are marked by setting *g_updating_graph_mask* to TRUE, such that the second kernel can update it accordingly.

In Kernel 2, we first check whether the thread ID is within the bounds of the graph and update the node based on *g_updating_graph_mask*. If the conditions hold as TRUE, the node is added to the frontier list and marked as visited. Note that *g_graph_mask* is set to TRUE, so that the next iteration of the DO-WHILE loop will process this node in Kernel 1, as the node is part of the next level. The variable, *g_over* is set to TRUE, which signals the CPU to run the DO-WHILE loop again.

A keen reader may wonder why we used two kernels for this implementation. As with several GPU programming languages, *HIP* does not guarantee the order of thread execution. Imagine what would happen if one thread were to set *g_graph_mask* as TRUE inside the IF statement of Line 11 in the first kernel. Another thread from the same kernel could trigger Condition 5 as TRUE and subsequently begin processing the next level's nodes before all nodes on the current level are finished. This would result in a potential error. Recall that the objective of BFS is to search a graph layer-wise or level-wise. Similarly, if we mark a node as visited inside the same IF statement in the first kernel, another thread that shares an edge with the same node would trigger the FALSE condition in Line 11 of the first kernel, even though the cost array must be updated by this thread as well. Hence, this implementation requires two kernels to avoid this behavior, known as a "race condition."

When reaching the termination condition, all graph levels will have been traversed, as there are no more unvisited nodes. Thus, we can guarantee that none of the threads in Kernel 2 will trigger the IF condition in Line 5. Hence, *g_over* will remain FALSE, which eventually terminates the DO-WHILE loop and the search.

Listing 5.9: Kernel 1 from BFS.

```
1  __global__ void
2  Kernel(Node* g_graph_nodes, int* g_graph_edges, bool* g_graph_mask, bool*
        g_updating_graph_mask, bool *g_graph_visited, int* g_cost, int
        no_of_nodes)
3  {
4    int tid = hipBlockIdx_x*MAX_THREADS_PER_BLOCK + hipThreadIdx_x;
5    if( tid<no_of_nodes && g_graph_mask[tid])
6    {
7      g_graph_mask[tid]=false;
8      for(int i=g_graph_nodes[tid].starting; i<(g_graph_nodes[tid].
          no_of_edges + g_graph_nodes[tid].starting); i++)
9        {
10       int id = g_graph_edges[i];
11       if(!g_graph_visited[id])
12         {
13         g_cost[id]=g_cost[tid]+1;
14         g_updating_graph_mask[id]=true;
15         }
16       }
17    }
18  }
19  }
```

Listing 5.10: Kernel 2 from BFS.

```
1  __global__ void
2  Kernel2(bool* g_graph_mask, bool *g_updating_graph_mask, bool*
         g_graph_visited, bool *g_over, int no_of_nodes)
3  {
4    int tid = hipBlockIdx_x*MAX_THREADS_PER_BLOCK + hipThreadIdx_x;
5    if( tid<no_of_nodes && g_updating_graph_mask[tid])
6    {
7
8      g_graph_mask[tid]=true;
9      g_graph_visited[tid]=true;
10     *g_over=true;
11     g_updating_graph_mask[tid]=false;
12   }
13 }
14
15 }
```

5.4   CPU-GPU Computing – KMeans

While GPUs can provide high performance when processing data-parallel work-loads, they may not be a good fit for less well-behaved workloads that cannot be easily parallelized. However, some algorithms incorporate both parallel and serial parts. In this case, a reasonable solution is to let the CPU be responsible for the serial portion and let the GPU be responsible for the parallel portion. We need to move the data back and forth to enable CPU-GPU cooperative computing.

KMeans is a workload that has both a parallel portion and a serial portion. It is a widely used unsupervised machine learning algorithm designed for clustering data. It works by dividing a set of data points (observations) into k groups (clusters), based on the features of the data. Each cluster is characterized by its center, known as the centroid. The algorithm assigns each data point to the nearest centroid, creating clusters with points that are similar to each other. The process involves iteratively updating the centroids and reassigning points to clusters until the clusters are stable and do not change significantly. KMeans is frequently used owing to its simplicity and efficiency, although it assumes clusters are circular in shape and can struggle with complex cluster shapes or varying sizes.

The training process of KMeans begins with the initialization phase, where k initial centroids are selected. This selection can be done randomly or based on a specific heuristic designed to optimize the starting positions. Once these initial centroids are established, the algorithm proceeds to assign each data point in the dataset to the nearest centroid. This assignment typically relies on calculating the Euclidean distance between each data point and every centroid, assigning each point to the closest centroid. As a result, k clusters start to form around these centroids.

Following the assignment phase, KMeans updates the centroids of each cluster. The new position of each centroid is determined by calculating the mean (average) of all points assigned to that cluster. This step essentially moves the centroid to the central location of all points within the cluster, optimizing its position for the next iteration.

The algorithm then checks for convergence, a stage where it assesses whether the centroids have stabilized. This can be detected when the assignment of points to clusters remains unchanged over successive iterations, or if the movement of centroids between iterations falls below a specific threshold. If the centroids have not yet stabilized, the algorithm repeats the assignment and update phases. This iterative process continues until the cluster assignments do not change significantly, indicating that the centroids have found a stable position.

Upon reaching convergence, where the centroids and their respective clusters are stable, the algorithm concludes its training phase. The final centroids define the clusters, and the KMeans algorithm terminates. It is crucial to note that the initial choice of k, the number of clusters, is a significant factor in KMeans and must be determined beforehand.

As described, each KMeans iteration must perform two main operations. First, we find the nearest centroid for each observation. This membership assignment process is highly data-parallel as we can calculate the assignment of each observation independently. Second, we update the centroid location by averaging the location of the observations. This process is not that easily parallelizable as it is an average/sum problem.

We implement this application by using the GPU to calculate the membership of each observation and using the CPU to update the centroid location. The implementation is a modified version of the KMeans code in the Rodinia benchmark suite [18].

Listing 5.11 illustrates the main loop of the KMeans algorithm. Each iteration begins with identifying the membership of each data sample by finding its nearest centroid, a task performed by the **updateMembership** function. If there are no changes in membership, the algorithm is considered to have converged, leading to the cessation of further iterations. Following this, the centroids are updated by calculating the average position of all data samples assigned to each cluster, a process executed within the **updateCentroid** function.

Listing 5.11: KMeans' main loop.

```
1  // length is an integer for the number of entries to be clustered.
2  // dimension is an integer for the number of properties of each entry.
3  // k is an integer that determines the number of clusters.
4
5  std::vector<> centroids = initializeCentroids(length*dimension, k);
6  std::vector<int> memberships(length, 0);
7
8  for (int iteration = 0; iteration < maxIterations; ++iteration) {
9      // Determine the cluster that each entry belongs to. The function
           returns how many entries changed membership.
10     int membershipChanges = updateMembership(data, centroids, memberships
           );
11
12     // Converge checking.
13     if (membershipChanges==0) {
14         break;
15     }
16
17     // Calculate new centroids.
18     std::vector<Point> newCentroids = centroids;
19     updateCentroid(data, newCentroids, memberships);
20     centroids = newCentroids;
21  }
```

Listing 5.12: KMeans' update membership function, which uses GPU to accelerate computing.

```
1  int updateMembership(float* data, float* centroids, int* membership, int
       dataSize, int dimension, int k) {
2      // gpuData is allocated and copied to the GPU earlier.
3
4      float *gpuCentroids, *gpuMembership;
5
6      // Allocate GPU memory
7      hipMalloc(&gpuCentroids, k * dimension * sizeof(float));
8      hipMalloc(&gpuMembership, dataSize * sizeof(int));
9
10     // Copy data from CPU to GPU
11     hipMemcpy(gpuCentroids, centroids, k * dimension * sizeof(float),
           hipMemcpyHostToDevice);
12
13     // Calculate the sizes for the kernel launch
14     int localSize = 256;
15     int globalSize = (dataSize + localSize - 1) / localSize;
16
17     // Launch the kernel
```

```
18    updateMembershipGPU<<<globalSize, localSize>>>(gpuData, gpuCentroids,
          gpuMembership, dataSize, dimension, k);
19    hipDeviceSynchronize()
20
21    // Create CPU Data to hold the results
22    std::vector<int> cpuNewMembership(dataSize);
23
24    // Copy GPU data back to CPU
25    hipMemcpy(cpuNewMembership.data(), gpuMembership, dataSize * sizeof(
          int), hipMemcpyDeviceToHost);
26    hipMemcpy(cpuMembershipUpdate.data(), gpuMembershipUpdate, dataSize *
          sizeof(float), hipMemcpyDeviceToHost);
27
28    // Count membership updates
29    int membershipUpdate = 0;
30    for (int i = 0; i < dataSize; ++i) {
31        if (membership[i] != cpuNewMembership[i]) {
32            membershipUpdate++;
33            membership[i] = cpuNewMembership[i]; // Update the original
                  membership array
34        }
35    }
36
37    // Free GPU memory
38    hipFree(gpuCentroids);
39    hipFree(gpuMembership);
40
41    return membershipUpdate;
42 }
```

Next, we implement the **updateMembership** function. This function serves as the interface between the CPU and GPU. The main goal is to launch the **updateMembershipGPU** kernel. To perform the calculation on the GPU, data must be passed from the CPU to the GPU side. Therefore, at the beginning of the function (Lines 4–11), we allocate new GPU data and copy the data from the host to the device. After the kernel launch, we also need to copy the data back from the GPU to the CPU to examine how many data samples have updated their membership.

CPUs and GPUs are each optimized for distinct types of algorithmic processing. In complex algorithms, such as KMeans, it is common to find sections that are better suited for CPU execution and others that can fully leverage the parallelism available with GPU processing. GPU programmers should strategically use both devices to achieve the best performance. To integrate the CPU and GPU parts of the program, memory transfers are often necessary, unless unified memory is utilized. We will omit the details of the remaining program parts, as they are relatively simple to implement. The complete code is available for interested readers in the specified repository.

5.5   Atomic Operations – Histogram

Across several of the GPU programs we have explored, a key principle has been that the GPU should avoid writing to the same memory address from different threads within a kernel. This is because of the GPU's memory system lacking robust cache coherence and memory consistency mechanisms. Writing to the same address from multiple threads can lead to undefined behavior. This constraint is a trade-off that simplifies GPU hardware and enhances memory access speed. However, it also introduces certain limitations to the programmability of GPUs.

Next, we consider an application that highlights this behavior, a histogram calculation. A histogram is a statistical tool that aggregates data points into specified ranges or "bins", providing a visual representation of the distribution of a dataset. In the context of image processing, for example, a histogram might represent the distribution of pixel intensities. The algorithm for calculating a histogram involves iterating over the dataset, and determining which bin each data point falls into based on its value. Each bin has a count that increases each time a data point is added to the bin. The challenge in a parallel computing context, especially with GPUs, arises when multiple threads attempt to update the same bin concurrently. This situation can lead to a race condition, as traditional GPU architectures do not guarantee memory consistency when multiple threads write to the same memory location simultaneously.

In the histogram calculation on a GPU, the use of atomic operations is crucial for maintaining accuracy in bin counts. Atomic operations guarantee that when a thread updates a bin count, the read-modify-write sequence appears as an indivisible operation. This is essential in a parallel computing environment where multiple threads might attempt to update the same bin concurrently. Without atomic operations, these concurrent updates could lead to race conditions, resulting in incorrect histogram counts.

When a thread performs an atomic operation on a bin, it effectively locks that bin, carries out the update, and then releases the lock. This ensures that even if multiple threads are trying to increment the same bin count at the same time, each update will be processed sequentially, preserving data integrity. This technique is particularly useful in GPU programming owing to the GPU's lack of cache coherence and memory consistency guarantees. Atomic operations allow programmers to harness the parallel processing power of GPUs for tasks such as histogramming, while avoiding the pitfalls of concurrent writes to shared memory locations.

We consider the following histogramming implementation. The application will take in a red-green-blue (RGB) image and use histogramming to report the brightness of the image. The input is a three-channel RGB image, with a memory layout organized as Channel-Height-Weight. We generate the output single-channel histogram that captures the overall brightness of the image. The code is provided below in Listing 5.13.

Listing 5.13: Hitogramming GPU kernel, implemented using atomic operations.

```
__global__ void calculateHistogram(float* imageData, int* histogram, int
    width, int height, int channels, int numBins) {
    int x = hipBlockIdx_x * hipBlockDim_x + hipThreadIdx_x;
    int y = hipBlockIdx_y * hipBlockDim_y + hipThreadIdx_y;

    if (x < width && y < height) {
        // Calculate the index for the pixel
        int idx = (y * width + x) * channels;

        // Calculate brightness by averaging the RGB values
        float brightness = 0.0f;
        for (int c = 0; c < channels; ++c) {
            brightness += imageData[idx + c];
        }
        brightness /= channels;

        // Determine the corresponding bin (assuming brightness range
            [0,1])
        int bin = static_cast<int>(brightness * numBins);

        // Atomic operation to avoid race conditions
        atomicAdd(&histogram[bin], 1);
    }
}
```

In this kernel, each thread in the kernel is responsible for processing a single pixel of the image. The kernel is executed across a two-dimensional grid, where each thread identifies its corresponding pixel using the thread's x and y indices, calculated using the block and thread indices within the grid.

Within the kernel, each thread calculates the index for its pixel in the flattened image data array. It then computes the pixel's brightness by averaging the values of the three color channels (assuming RGB format). This averaging approach converts the RGB values into a single brightness value, simplifying the histogram computation to a single dimension. The brightness value is then used to determine the appropriate bin in the histogram. An atomic operation, atomicAdd, is used to increment the count in this bin. Atomic operations are crucial to avoid race conditions, as multiple threads might simultaneously attempt to update the same bin. By ensuring that these updates are atomic, the kernel guarantees the correctness of the histogram, even when executed in parallel across thousands of threads on the GPU. This approach efficiently leverages the parallel processing capabilities of the GPU, making it well-suited for processing large images where each pixel can be handled independently.

In addition to **atomicAdd**, HIP supports various atomic operations that can provide data integrity in multi-threaded programming. These include atomicSub (subtraction), atomicMax (maximum), atomicMin (minimum), atomicInc (increment), atomicDec (decrement), atomicCAS (compare and swap), and atomicExch (exchange). Each operation ensures the read-modify-write sequence is executed indivisibly, preventing race conditions in parallel environments. For example, atomicMax and atomicMin update a shared variable to the maximum or minimum value of two given values, and atomicCAS allows conditional updates of a variable. These functions are important in GPU programming when manipulating shared data safely and efficiently. For a comprehensive list of supported atomic operations and their detailed descriptions, the reader should refer to the ROCm HIP Programming documentation.

The previous implementation purely relies on atomic operations to avoid race conditions. However, relying heavily on atomic operations in GPU programming can lead to performance bottlenecks, particularly in applications where several threads frequently access and modify the same memory locations. Atomic operations are used to ensure data integrity in concurrent environments by serializing access to memory. When multiple threads concurrently access the same memory address, one thread must wait for other threads to complete their updates, effectively reducing the parallel power available on the GPU. This serialization can significantly impact the execution, especially in algorithms where such concurrent updates are common.

5.6 Conclusion

Building on the HIP programming techniques introduced in previous chapters, this chapter presented several code examples, demonstrating different programming patterns. We covered a number of two-dimensional kernels and examined how to use multiple kernels to implement an algorithm. Additionally, the chapter explores the use of atomic operations to overcome concurrent memory access that occur in GPU programming models, thereby broadening the range of tasks that can leverage a GPU. This chapter is designed to function as a guide or *cookbook* for readers embarking on implementing a wider range of GPU programs.

Chapter 6

AMD GPU Internals

Although Chapter 2 introduced the basics of writing a *HIP* GPU program, it did not reveal how to tune its performance. The motivation for using a GPU accelerator is to achieve the best possible performance. Thus, a GPU software programmer should not be satisfied with an implementation that merely produces a correct answer. Instead, an attempt should be made to improve the implementation with the goal of optimizing the kernel's runtime performance. In this chapter and the next, we discuss several optimization techniques. This chapter covers important concepts associated with the organization of GPU hardware and lays the foundation for understanding high-performance GPU programming techniques that exploit amazing hardware features.

A GPU's architecture has a profound impact on program performance, and optimization usually involves leveraging hardware-specific mechanisms (e.g., memory coalescing). This chapter begins with a brief introduction to AMD GPUs, which are supported by *ROCm* and *HIP*. Unless otherwise specified, features specific to the MI100 GPU [10] are discussed.

6.1 AMD GPUs

Before digging into the architectural details, we will examine the evolution of the AMD GPU to deepen our understanding. A list of notable AMD GPU products is presented in Table 6.1.

Modern AMD GPU architectures date back to the first Graphics Core Next (GCN) architecture design. GCN is the name of the family of AMD GPU archi-

tectures that was first released in 2011 and used until 2018. The first GCN GPU
was the AMD Radeon HD 7970. Afterward, AMD enhanced the architecture,
creating several new and improved versions (i.e., GCN2 and GCN3). The first
three GCN models were manufactured using 28-nm technology. However, GCN4
and GCN5 were manufactured using 12-nm and 14-nm technologies (i.e., Polaris
and Vega, respectively). The Radeon VII was the first 7-nm GPU and is part of
the GCN5 family.

AMD uses a "gfx" versioning nomenclature, and all chip versions begin with
the "gfx" prefix. Each version's name comprises three numbers (i.e., major version, minor version, and revision). For example, the MI100 GPU uses a gfx908
chip, where "9" is the major version number, "0" is the minor version number, and
"8" is the revision number. For example, the Radeon RX 5700XT is the 10th generation AMD GPU; thus, its major version number is 10. A new version number
generally indicates a new, non-backward compatible, instruction set architecture
(ISA), whereas minor versions and revisions involve instruction extensions and
configuration changes.

The versatility of a single-chip AMD GPU design lies in its ability to be
adapted for various GPU products through minor modifications and parameter
adjustments. An example of this design approach is the gfx803 chip, which is the
foundation for at least five distinct GPUs. It is used in AMD's high-end gaming
and computing GPUs (e.g., R9 Fury X, R9 Fury Nano), their mid-tier gaming
GPUs (e.g., Radeon RX 480, Radeon RX 580), and in specialized compute-only
GPUs (e.g., MI8).

More recently, as transistor sizes became smaller and smaller, AMD started
to specialize its GPU architecture design by splitting its single GPU architecture
into two architectures, targeting different use cases.

For high-performance general-purpose computing, AMD developed a Compute
DNA (CDNA) architecture. Although the CDNA architecture maintains the same
architectural principles of the GCN architecture, evident in its continued use of
the gfx9 series chips, it introduces significant innovations to enhance compute performance and adapt to modern workloads. A notable feature of CDNA GPUs is
the inclusion of matrix cores, designed to execute matrix multiplication operations
with substantially higher throughput. Following the introduction of the CDNA
architecture, AMD has launched two new iterations: CDNA2 and CDNA3. The
CDNA2 architecture, exemplified by the MI210 and MI250 GPUs, leverages multi-
chip module technologies. This advancement significantly increases the number
of transistors and computing resources available on each GPU, offering enhanced
performance capabilities. Furthermore, the CDNA3 architecture advances this
concept by employing 3D integration technologies. This approach involves stack-

ing multiple chips vertically, which effectively boosts transistor density and overall performance.

For the gaming market, AMD developed the RDNA architecture. The RDNA architecture redesign is a major overhaul of the GCN architecture, mainly to reduce latency for a better gaming experience. Meanwhile, the RDNA GPUs can still be used for general-purpose computing. We will introduce the RDNA architecture by comparing it with the GCN and CDNA architectures in Section 6.10.

Table 6.1: Summary of recent AMD GPU products.

Release Date	Product Name	Chip	Architecture	Transistor Size
Dec. 2011	Radeon HD 7970	gfx600	GCN	28 nm
Nov. 2013	Radeon R9 290	gfx701	GCN2	28 nm
Jun. 2015	R9 Fury X	gfx803	GCN3	28 nm
Aug. 2015	R9 Fury Nano	gfx803	GCN3	28 nm
Dec. 2016	Radeon Instinct MI8	gfx803	GCN3	28 nm
Jun. 2016	Radeon RX 480	gfx803	Polaris (GCN4)	14 nm
Apr. 2017	Radeon RX 580	gfx803	Polaris (GCN4)	14 nm
Aug. 2017	Radeon RX Vega 56	gfx900	Vega (GCN5)	14 nm
Aug. 2017	Radeon RX Vega 64	gfx900	Vega (GCN5)	14 nm
Jun. 2017	Radeon Instinct MI25	gfx900	Vega (GCN5)	14 nm
Feb. 2019	Radeon VII	gfx906	Vega (GCN5)	7 nm
Jul. 2019	Radeon RX 5700XT	gfx1010	RDNA	7 nm
Oct. 2020	Radeon RX 6900XT	gfx1030	RDNA2	7 nm
Nov. 2020	Instinct MI100	gfx908	CDNA	7 nm
Nov. 2021	Instinct MI210/MI250	gfx90a	CDNA2	6 nm
Nov. 2022	Radeon RX 7900 XTX	gfx1100	RDNA3	5/6 nm
Jan. 2023	Instinct MI300	gfx940	CDNA3	5 nm

6.2 Overall Architecture

A GPU comprises several interconnected blocks (not to be confused with thread blocks) of relatively independent digital circuits that can complete predefined tasks. Some are programmable, but others perform fixed operations. Working together, they enable the GPU to execute complex programs and massively parallel computing tasks. Here, we introduce the GPU blocks that are essential to general-purpose computing and discuss their organization (see Figure 6.1). We cover each block in more detail later in this chapter.

There are three main groups of AMD GPU blocks (i.e., controlling, user-programmable shader, and memory). The controlling group, which includes the command processor, asynchronous compute engine (ACE), and direct memory access (DMA), has the primary responsibility of interacting with the CPU and controlling the shader and memory blocks.

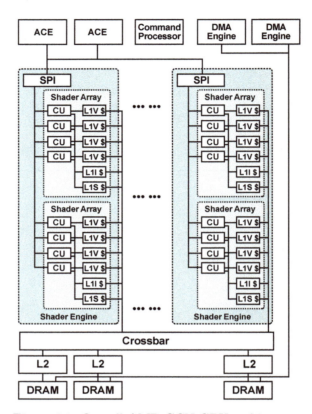

Figure 6.1: Overall AMD GCN GPU architecture.

The shader blocks are organized in a three-level hierarchy of shader engines, shader arrays, and compute units (CUs). This organization allows blocks at each level to share different resources. For example, CUs in a shader array share an instruction cache; those in a shader engine share a shader pipe input (SPI) block. This organization enables a modular hardware design in which the GPU's configuration can be easily changed. For example, although both the R9 Fury X and Radeon RX 480 GPUs use the gfx803 design, they are configured differently. The R9 Fury X contains 16 shader arrays with four CUs each, whereas the RX 480 GPU contains 12 shader arrays with only three CUs in each Shader Array.

Finally, the memory group includes L2 caches, and the memory controllers are connected using a data fabric design to support coherency. They jointly store the data needed for GPU computations. These GPUs typically contain multiple banks of L2 caches and memory controllers that provide access to segments of the address space. GPU memory banks can work in parallel to supply CUs with massive amounts of data.

6.3 Command Processor and the DMA Engine

From the previous chapter, we know that the GPU must work under the CPU's close supervision to perform computational tasks. The command processor is the GPU block that receives commands from the CPU (e.g., memory-copying and kernel-launching). Generally, the command processor delegates its received commands to other GPU blocks according to type. For example, memory-copying commands are forwarded to the DMA engine, whereas kernel-launching commands are forwarded to ACEs.

If data are to be copied from the CPU to the GPU, the DMA engine fetches small chunks from the CPU's system memory and directly stores them in its local dynamic random-access memory (DRAM). A GPU-to-CPU memory copy follows a similar pattern in the opposite direction. A DMA engine oversees the memory transfer but cannot handle two memory copying commands simultaneously. The CPU is not directly involved in the memory copying process, but it is responsible for initializing the DMA engine.

Most GPUs are equipped with two DMA engines, such that two memory copies can be processed concurrently in the same or opposite directions. Having two DMA engines better utilizes the bidirectional Peripheral Component Interconnect Express (PCIe) connection bus.

6.4 Workgroup Dispatching

Kernel launch commands are handled by the Asynchronous Compute Engines (ACEs), that break down kernels into workgroups for distribution to SPI blocks, where they are further broken down into wavefronts.

As the expanded name suggests, an ACE processes commands from different command queues or streams concurrently and asynchronously. See Chapter 4 for more details. AMD GPUs are equipped with multiple ACEs that process multiple commands in parallel. ACEs also enable concurrent kernel execution. Although each ACE can dispatch one kernel at a time, a GPU with multiple ACEs can execute multiple kernels simultaneously. We discuss the tradeoffs of concurrent kernel executions in Section 4.2.4.

The SPIs are responsible for dispatching wavefronts to the CUs, as well as initializing registers so that wavefront instructions can be executed with the necessary parameters. They guarantee that all wavefronts in a workgroup are dispatched to the same CU so that they can be synchronized.

Executing a wavefront in a CU consumes resources that can run out. When this happens, the wavefronts are queued to wait for the active wavefronts to finish. CUs consume four resource types: wavefront slots, scalar general-purpose registers (SGPRs), vector general-purpose registers (VGPRs), and local data share (LDS). We discuss these when we discuss structure later in this chapter.

It is common for a kernel to have more workgroups than the GPU can execute simultaneously. Hence, the ACE unit dispatches new workgroups when active ones finish execution. As not all workgroups can be executed simultaneously, the GPU cannot synchronize all work items in a single kernel. Considering the example in Listing 6.1, each thread in the kernel performs Step 1 of the task and increments the counter by one. Then, each kernel waits for the counter to match its total number of threads, which indicates that Step 1 is complete. Then, all threads move to Step 2. Whether the kernel can finish executing depends on the relationship between its number of workgroups and how many GPUs can execute simultaneously. If a GPU can run 64 workgroups on all CUs at one time, and if the number of launched workgroups is smaller than 64, the kernel will execute them as designed. However, if the number of workgroups is greater than 64, the kernel will deadlock in a loop because only the first 64 workgroups can execute on the CUs; the rest will not be scheduled. Hence, the counter will never achieve a suitable **num_thread_in_kernel** level, resulting in a non-recoverable deadlock.

Listing 6.1: Sample deadlock code. The counter is defined as a volatile pointer and is initialized with the value of zero.

```
1   // Do step 1.
2
3   atomicInc(counter);
4   while(true) {
5       if (*counter >= num_thread_in_kernel) {
6           break;
7       }
8   }
9
10  // Do step 2.
```

Workgroup-to-CU mapping is non-deterministic. ACEs and SPIs assign workgroups to CUs according to the resources available per CU. Even launching a kernel twice with the same parameter may not result in the workgroups being launched to the same CUs. Therefore, programmers must not assume a certain workgroup-to-CU mapping and should not attempt to improve performance based on the location of the workgroup execution.

6.5 Sequencer

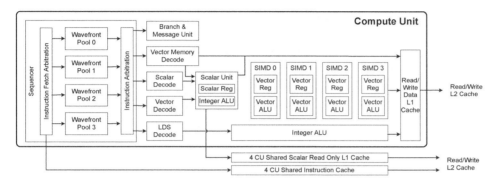

Figure 6.2: CU architecture (courtesy of AMD).

A GPU CU can be further divided into sub-blocks (see Figure 6.2). In this section, we describe CU organization by tracing how instructions flow through the sub-blocks.

Central to the CU is its instruction sequencer block (SQ), which is responsible for issuing instructions to the execution units. The SQ holds a list of wavefronts and their instructions. This list is organized into four pools, each containing 10 wavefront slots. A slot includes the hardware resources needed to host a wavefront, including wavefront-level registers (e.g., a program counter) and an instruction buffer. Therefore, in theory, a CU can execute at most 40 wavefronts simultaneously.

Instruction-fetching. To execute an instruction, it must first be fetched from memory. To determine which wavefront can fetch an instruction, the SQ is equipped with a fetch arbiter. During each cycle, the fetch arbiter selects the earliest dispatched wavefront from those waiting. Thus, a CU can fetch 32 bytes of instructions (four-to-eight total) per cycle, as each is 4 to 8 bytes in size.

Instruction-issuing. Fetched instructions must be issued to the executing unit. Therefore, the SQ is equipped with an issue arbiter that determines which instructions can be issued per cycle.

Note that instructions are always issued at the wavefront level. The execution units run the instructions for all work items in the wavefront. Thus, the work items effectively execute in lockstep so that they always execute the same instructions at a given time.

Each CU has different execution units per instruction class (e.g., scalar, branching, vector, vector memory, and LDS). This is advantageous in that different instruction types can be executed in parallel. The type is encoded in the instruction's binary code so that the arbiter can identify where to dispatch it.

During each cycle, the issue arbiter selects wavefronts from one of the four pools. Hence, the issue arbiter has, at most, 10 wavefronts from which to choose. Multiple wavefronts can issue instructions in a single cycle as long as they meet the following two conditions. First, the wavefront must not issue instructions that occupy the same execution unit. This is straightforward, as the execution units can handle only one instruction at a time. Second, if the wavefront is already executing an instruction, it should not issue another instruction. This simplifies the sequencer design, as it does not need to consider complex register ordering dependencies. The issue arbiter switches wavefront pools after each cycle, following a round-robin pattern.

A GPU's instruction pipeline design differs dramatically from that of a typical CPU. In a CPU, the instructions executed in a pipeline generally come from the same thread. However, because they rely on thread-level parallelism, GPU instructions executed at different stages of the pipeline originate from different wavefronts.

An often overlooked aspect of GPU execution is that it incurs context-switching when it moves to another work item or wavefront, that occurs every cycle; hence, there is no overhead involved with context-switching on the GPU.

6.6   SIMD Unit

SIMD units are the blocks that deliver most of the GPU's computing capabilities. They are responsible for executing the vector instructions dispatched by the SQ, and each includes a set of arithmetic logic units (ALUs) that can perform computing operations on specific data types. Typically, a SIMD unit has 16 single-precision ALUs. During each cycle, one instruction from the 16 work items is executed by a SIMD unit. Considering that each wavefront contains 64 work items, it takes a SIMD unit four cycles to execute one instruction.

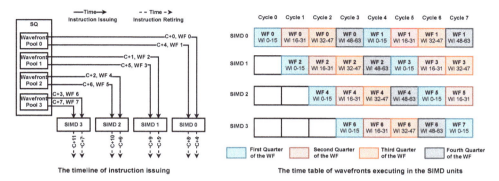

Figure 6.3: Timing for issuing instructions to SIMD units.

As shown in Figure 6.3, the wavefront pools and SIMD units have a one-to-one mapping. Wavefronts from one pool can only be issued to their corresponding SIMD units. It is no coincidence that the number of SIMD units matches the number of cycles required to execute a wavefront instruction. If one vector instruction is issued in cycle C+0, the SIMD unit executes it during C+1 and C+4. As there are four wavefront pools, it takes four cycles for the issue arbiter to have an opportunity to issue another instruction from the same pool. Thus, in cycle C+4, another instruction can be issued to begin execution in cycle C+5. This design guarantees that the SIMD unit can be fully utilized if there are a sufficient number of SIMD instructions awaiting execution.

We can estimate the SIMD unit's theoretical computing throughput based on the number of units. Because each MI100 GPU has 120 CUs, each contains four SIMD units, and each of those contains 16 single-precision ALU units. Thus, each GPU can execute $120 \times 4 \times 16 = 7,680$ single-precision instructions per cycle (IPC). If we multiply this number by 1,502 MHz, which is the clock frequency of MI100 CUs, we find that this GPU can execute $7,680 \times 1 \times 1,502^6 \approx 11.5 \times 10^{12}$ single-precision instructions per second. Finally, as each instruction can encode two operations in the fused multiply–add register, the theoretical computing capability rises as high as $11.5 \times 10^{12} \times 2 \approx 23$ single-precision tera-floating-point units (TFLOPS) per second.

6.7   Thread Divergence

Ideally, the wavefront instruction execution will produce results for all 64 work items comprising the wavefront. In reality, thread divergence is inevitable, and a simple example is shown in the following kernel code, where 32 work items must run Line 2, and another 32 must run Line 4:

Listing 6.2: Sample Diverging Code.

```
1  if (thread_id < 32) {
2      a = a + 1;
3  } else {
4      a = a + 2;
5  }
```

Because GPU instructions are issued at the wavefront granularity, it is impossible to issue the instruction in Line 2 of our example for some work items, while issuing that of Line 4 for others. The instructions executing at Line 2 must be executed for all 64 work items in the wavefront. To avoid producing incorrect results, each wavefront is associated with a 64-bit execution mask register. Each bit in the mask indicates how the result of each work item will be updated. For example, at Line 1, the execution mask is set to a hex value of **0x0000,0000,ffff,ffff**, indicating that only the results associated with the lower 32 work items will be updated (i.e., committed) when executing Line 2. The ELSE statement flips the execution mask, changing it to **0xffff,ffff,0000,0000** while allowing the upper 32 work items to take effect when executing Line 4. Finally, the execution mask is reset to **0xffff,ffff,ffff,ffff** so that all work items will execute the remainder of the kernel. Predication is the process of using a mask to determine which instruction can take effect. Notably, the predicated execution of GPUs causes thread divergence, meaning that the threads in a wavefront follow different branches of a conditional statement.

Note that IPC is a common CPU performance evaluation metric. However, to analyze GPU performance, it is necessary to clarify the level of instruction being reported. Predication slightly complicates performance analysis. Generally, programmers use both wavefront- and work item-level instructions. The wavefront-level instruction count does not consider the state of the execution mask, whereas the work item-level instruction count only adds the work items marked as valid by the execution mask. Assuming the execution mask is **0xffff,ffff,ffff,ffff**, and all instructions are vector ALU types, which are handled by SIMD units, then a CU should yield a wavefront-level IPC of one and a work item-level IPC of 64.

According to our analysis of the snippet shown in Listing 6.2, Lines 2 and 4 cannot be executed in parallel. Moreover, although only half of the work items will generate results in Lines 2 and 4, executing all of their vector instructions still takes four SIMD unit cycles. That is, with no branching, it will take four cycles for a SIMD to execute 64 work item-level instructions. In the example of Listing 6.2, executing 64 work item-level instructions takes at least eight cycles. In this case, although the wavefront-level IPC of the CU is still one, the work item-level IPC is reduced to 32. The worst case occurs when each thread executes a different branch. In this case, it would take $64 \times 4 = 256$ cycles to execute 64 work item-level instructions, causing the work item-level IPC to be reduced to one. Therefore, thread divergence must be avoided whenever possible.

6.8 Memory Coalescing

GPUs are well-designed to process data. However, before processing can commence, the data must be fetched from the GPU memory and delivered to each CU. Later, the results are written back to the GPU memory. AMD CUs rely on special load and store instructions to read from and write to the GPU memory, respectively. The memory transactions created by these instructions are handled by the texture-addressing (TA) block.

A GPU's load and store instructions are vectorized in memory. For one wavefront-level instruction, each work item will have its own address and data. However, it is common for two work items to read from and write to the same memory address. More often, the work items may access adjacent data items or those in close proximity. In such cases, both data items can be accessed by a single memory transaction (typically 64 B). Thus, the TA block can combine some of the work item memory access, resulting in fewer memory transactions. This important mechanism is called "memory coalescing."

The example code in Figure 6.4 loads matrix data into CU registers, illustrating memory coalescing. If we have a $1,024 \times 1,024$ single-precision matrix stored in the GPU memory organized in a column-major layout (i.e., sequential addresses are located in adjacent columns), and the starting address is zero, we can assume two options: we can load the data vertically, accessing the data row-by-row, or we can load them horizontally, accessing them column-by-column. When loading vertically, the first work item accesses Address 0, the second accesses Address 4,096, the third accesses Address 8,192, and so on. As such, the TA block cannot combine memory access and must issue 64 memory transactions for a single wavefront. We refer to this memory access pattern as "non-coalescable," and it significantly impacts performance.

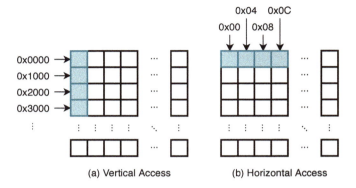

Figure 6.4: Comparing vertical matrix and horizontal memory access.

In contrast, we can access the data horizontally across columns. The first work item accesses Address 0, the second accesses Address 4, the third accesses Address 8, and so on. In this case, the memory to be accessed by the 64 work items in the wavefront is a 256-B chunk of consecutive addresses. Thus, if the memory access granularity is 64 B, the TA block can reduce the transaction to only four fetches: only 6% of the memory transactions compared to the vertical layout. We refer to this type of access pattern as "coalescable."

Memory coalescing offers major performance advantages over non-coalesced access, as the latter can waste valuable memory bandwidth. Therefore, whenever possible, coalesced access should be used. Later, in Section 8.5, we examine more software solutions that convert non-coalesced access to coalesced types.

6.9   Memory Hierarchy

Before a kernel can begin execution, the data are stored in the GPU memory. A GPU typically hosts DRAM memory units, such as graphics double-data rate (GDDR) or high-bandwidth memory (HBM) DRAM types. Typically, GDDR has lower access latency, whereas HBM provides a higher bandwidth. As big-data processing applications are highly memory-intensive and sensitive to bandwidth, HBM is more suitable for general-purpose computing. HBM is used on the MI100 GPU.

CUs must transfer data from GPU memory to local registers before computation. Generally, it does not matter whether GDDR or HBM is used as the latency

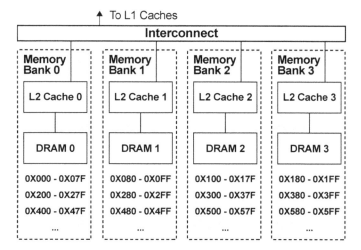

Figure 6.5: GPU memory bank organization.

and bandwidth cannot fulfill requirements to ensure SIMD units are working at the full rate. To reduce latency and boost bandwidth, two levels of caching are provided between CUs and DRAMs using static random-access memory technology, which responds much faster than DRAMs and can provide higher bandwidth.

As an L1 cache, one texture cache-per-pipe (TCP) block is dedicated to each CU. The L1 cache is a write-through cache, meaning that all data written to the L1 cache are also directly written to the L2.

AMD GPU L2 caches (i.e., texture cache channel (TCC) block) are memory-side caches. As shown in Figure 6.5, each L2 cache is attached to a DRAM controller, and an L2 group and memory controller form a memory bank, not to be confused with DRAM banks, which work at a finer granularity. A memory bank covers a fixed range of memory addresses, typically interleaved at 128-B granularity. Interleaving allows memory banks to read and write simultaneously, thereby increasing the effective memory bandwidth.

Cache coherency support is a major design factor for multi-core CPUs. If cache coherency is not maintained, multithreaded executions may produce incorrect results. For example, as seen in Figure 6.6, a data item, which is identified by the data address, can reside in three caches simultaneously. If Core 1 writes the data, it will only be updated in the local L1 cache, and the data in the other L1 and L2 caches will become stale. Future reads from Core 2 will then be unable to fetch

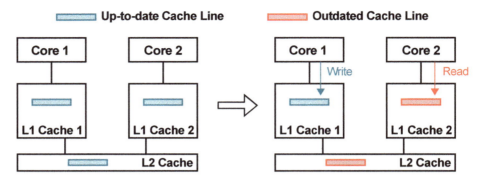

Figure 6.6: Example of the cache coherency problem in a multi-core CPU.

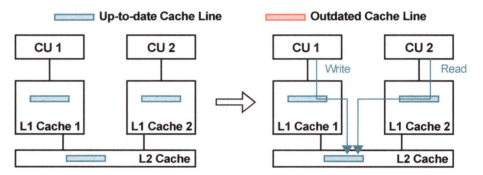

Figure 6.7: GPU coherency support with write-through L1 caches.

updated data. For CPUs, a common solution is to introduce a cache coherency protocol to remove the cache line from the other L1 caches before writing.

The cache coherency support on GPUs is simpler. As every store instruction writes to both L1 and L2 caches, the L2 cache always maintains an updated version. Using a write-through L1 cache removes the need to add a complex and performance-limiting coherency protocol.

Inquisitive readers may ask what happens if a cache line exists in two L1 caches such that one CU writes it before another CU can read it (see Figure 6.6). Although the GPU's write-through L1 cache can update data in L2, the cache lines in the other L1 caches are not invalidated or updated. Generally, writing a piece of data from one thread and reading the updated version from another is not a supported operation in GPU programming. If this kind of synchronization is required, programmers must either use global memory fences or atomic operations. Another option is to separate the reads and writes using two kernels.

AMD GPUs execute atomic operations in the L2 cache. When a CU executes an atomic instruction, the instruction is sent to the L2, where it is processed in local storage. Although GPUs do not require coherency protocols, we must still consider the occasion when two CUs write to different parts of the same cache line ("false sharing"). Without a careful design, the second write will overwrite the first in the L2. To avoid this, AMD GPUs use a write-mask-based design in which, with each memory write request, the CUs and the L1 caches send a write ("dirty mask") using bits to represent which set of bytes should be updated in the L2 cache. Note that a bit is provided for every 4 B per cache line. Using this method, two writes can be easily merged in the L2 cache, allowing CUs to write in parallel while maintaining correctness and improving overall memory throughput.

6.10 AMD RDNA GPUs

The AMD RDNA architecture, which was a natural evolution based on the GCN architecture, is primarily tailored for next-generation, high-performance gaming. It introduces significant core and memory architecture design modifications to enhance scalability and efficiency. Although primarily aimed for gaming workloads, RDNA-equipped GPUs, with their highly efficient computing cores, are also suitable for general-purpose computing. As of ROCm 6.0, five RDNA GPU products are supported: Radeon RX 7900 XTX, Radeon RX 7900 XT, Radeon Pro W7900, Radeon Pro W6800, and Radeon Pro V620.

A key distinction between GCN and RDNA architectures is their respective wavefront sizes. GCN operates with a wavefront size of 64 work-items, whereas RDNA reduces this to 32 work-items. This change aims to improve the CUs' handling of thread divergence in modern workloads. The smaller wavefront size is also designed to lower the number of memory transactions generated by load/store instructions, with a goal of decreasing memory access latencies and increasing ALU utilization. However, for backward compatibility, RDNA GPUs support 64-work-item wavefronts in a compatibility mode. The decision to compile a kernel to use 32 or 64 work-item mode is made by the compiler.

RDNA GPUs introduce a notable change with the introduction of Dual Compute Units (DCUs), replacing the CDNA CUs. Each DCU contains four schedulers, responsible for fetching and issuing instructions, a significant increase from the single scheduler in CDNA CUs. This enhancement improves the instruction issue rate. In contrast to the GCN architecture, where one scheduler dispatches instructions to four SIMD (Single Instruction, Multiple Data) units, an RDNA scheduler handles just one SIMD unit. With each SIMD unit comprising 32 single-precision ALUs and operating with narrower 32-work-item wavefronts, a DCU's SIMD unit can execute one instruction per cycle, a marked improvement over the four cycles required per instruction in a GCN CU. Furthermore, each DCU has double the computing resources of a single CU and includes a unified local data share unit.

The RDNA architecture revamps the cache hierarchy by implementing a three-level cache structure comprising L0, L1, and L2 caches. The L0 caches in the RDNA correspond to the L1 caches in the GCN architecture, as they are directly connected to the DCUs and are dedicated to each DCU. In addition, RDNA introduces an intermediate L1 cache situated between the L0 and L2 caches. This L1 cache serves a cluster of DCUs (typically, five in most hardware configurations). Its role is to reduce the frequency of requests to the L2 cache, thereby reducing data traffic across the chip. This optimization boosts performance and reduces power consumption.

Another significant change in the RDNA's cache design is the doubling of the cache line size across the L0 vector caches, L1 caches, and L2 caches from 64 bytes to 128 bytes. This increase is strategic, facilitating the delivery of a unique set of single-precision numbers for all 32 work-items in a wavefront, given that 4 bytes multiplied by 32 work-items equals 128 bytes. This enhancement aligns with the architecture's emphasis on efficiency and performance optimization.

These modifications in the RDNA architecture are primarily aimed at optimizing gaming and graphics workloads by minimizing latency, rather than maximizing throughput. For instance, the ability to process one wavefront instruction per cycle reduces processing latency, ensuring faster delivery of results. However, this alteration does not necessarily enhance the overall computational capacity. Consequently, the CDNA architecture, which targets different application areas, does not adopt these RDNA-specific changes. Instead, the CDNA architecture retains design features more aligned with the traditional GCN-style, focusing on aspects relevant to its intended use-cases.

6.11   Conclusion

In this chapter, we learned about the hardware architecture of a GPU. It is key for GPU programmers to have a general understanding of how GPU hardware works, especially if they want to get the best performance on these devices. This knowledge will allow them to optimize their code, taking full advantage of the parallel hardware of the GPU. Additionally, learning about the basic features present in the hardware can help the programmer develop error-free parallel programs.

Chapter 7

HIP Tools

As we have seen thus far, the *HIP* support provided by the *ROCm* OS greatly simplifies the creation of parallel GPU programs. However, to achieve the best performance, a deeper understanding of the most suitable approaches is required. Some people may learn performance tuning via trial and error; however, leveraging performance analysis tools benefits everyone by offering a systematic approach that saves time and effort, while minimizing confusion. In addition, developing and porting applications while targeting different GPU architectures can be challenging, especially when it comes to migrating applications written in CUDA to new architectures. Therefore, in this chapter, we examine tools provided by ROCm that can be used for analyzing performance and porting applications to different GPU architectures.

ROCm provides programmers with *ROCmInfo*, a command-line utility that provides detailed information about the ROCm software stack and the hardware configuration of the system. Developers can quickly and easily access important information about their system's configuration and use it to optimize performance. Another helpful tool is the *ROCm* System Management Interface (*SMI*), which helps the GPU programmer visualize GPU utilization, frequency, temperature and several other parameters. Based on OS privilege levels, programmers can use *ROCm SMI* to change GPU core and memory frequencies (as permitted by the device specifications). To locate and debug kernel errors, *ROCm* provides *rocgdb*, a GNU debugger (*GDB*) that allows GPU programmers to step through lines of their kernel source code. It also enables the inspection of wavefront register states. *ROCm* also provides programmers with *rocProf*, an easy-to-use GPU hardware profiler that provides application developers with insight into how their program is behaving on a GPU and helps to identify potential performance bottlenecks. *ROCm* provides tools for converting an entire codebase written in CUDA to HIP. There are several situations in which a programmer or researcher will need to run an application developed in CUDA for NVIDIA systems on an AMD GPU, including to compare performance differences. Prior to HIP, the only porting method involved the manual conversion of the CUDA source to OpenCL, which is a cumbersome and error-prone path. Chapter 13 also provides guidance on various third-party tools that are used to analyze *ROCm*-supported GPU performance.

7.1   *ROCmInfo*

When it comes to optimizing code for maximum performance, developers often rely on their own understanding of the system they are working on. This is where *ROCmInfo*, a powerful command-line utility that can be used to obtain information about the system hardware and software, can help. *ROCmInfo* provides detailed information about the ROCm software stack and the hardware configuration of the system.

With *RocmInfo*, developers can easily access crucial information about their system's configuration, enabling them to optimize their code effectively. This utility proves particularly advantageous when developing GPU-accelerated applications, as it provides developers insight into the capabilities and limitations of the hardware. Typically, rocminfo can be found in the /opt/rocm/bin directory if a standard ROCm installation is present on the computer. Assuming this directory is included in the system's PATH variable, developers can open a terminal and simply enter *rocminfo* to easily retrieve information about their ROCm stack and hardware configuration. ROCm itself is built upon the Heterogeneous System Architecture (HSA), which defines a standardized hardware architecture and software interface for heterogeneous computing systems. Rocminfo acts as a gateway to accessing vital information about the system's attributes and agents, providing developers with a comprehensive understanding of their HSA-compliant hardware configuration.

Within the ROCm environment, the HSA system attributes offer valuable metadata that sheds light on the characteristics of a GPU and its associated system resources. By using the "rocminfo" utility, developers can investigate this information, gaining deep insights into their hardware and be empowered to fine-tune their code for optimal performance. HSA agents (an HSA agent is a device that can execute ROCm kernels) serve as the backbone of a system, delivering essential compute resources such as CPUs and GPUs. In the context of ROCm, these HSA agents can be broadly classified into two categories: CPU agents and GPU agents. GPU agents specifically refer to the AMD GPUs supported by ROCm, opening up a world of possibilities for GPU-accelerated computing. By leveraging rocminfo and the knowledge it provides about HSA agents, developers can harness the full potential of their system's resources. This allows them to design and optimize their code to fully utilize CPU and GPU capabilities, leading to impressive performance gains in their applications.

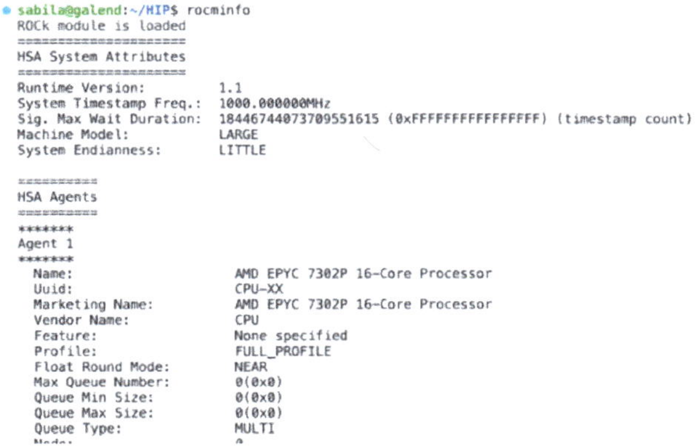

```
● sabila@galend:~/HIP$ rocminfo
ROCk module is loaded
=====================
HSA System Attributes
=====================
Runtime Version:         1.1
System Timestamp Freq.:  1000.000000MHz
Sig. Max Wait Duration:  18446744073709551615 (0xFFFFFFFFFFFFFFFF) (timestamp count)
Machine Model:           LARGE
System Endianness:       LITTLE


==========
HSA Agents
==========
*******
Agent 1
*******
  Name:                    AMD EPYC 7302P 16-Core Processor
  Uuid:                    CPU-XX
  Marketing Name:          AMD EPYC 7302P 16-Core Processor
  Vendor Name:             CPU
  Feature:                 None specified
  Profile:                 FULL_PROFILE
  Float Round Mode:        NEAR
  Max Queue Number:        0(0x0)
  Queue Min Size:          0(0x0)
  Queue Max Size:          0(0x0)
  Queue Type:              MULTI
  Node:                    0
```

Figure 7.1: A screenshot of the execution of **rocminfo**.

As we have discussed earlier, rocminfo is a powerful utility that enables developers to gain valuable insight into the capabilities and configuration of their GPUs. Figure 7.1 showcases some of the valuable information available through rocminfo. This wealth of information provides developers with comprehensive details about their GPUs, allowing them to make informed decisions and optimize the code and fine-tune their applications to leverage the specific features and capabilities of their GPUs.

In the ROCm ecosystem, each HSA agent is assigned a unique identifier that facilitates communication and resource allocation for compute tasks. This identifier, known as the Universally Unique Identifier, distinguishes each agent from each other in the system. We can take a closer look at the example screenshot provided in Figure 7.2. In this example, we observe that Agent 1 is identified as a 16-core CPU device. This information allows developers to tailor their code to effectively utilize the CPU resources offered by Agent 1, optimizing performance and efficiently executing compute tasks. It enables them to make informed decisions regarding task allocation, resource utilization and communication strategies

```
==========
HSA Agents
==========
*******
Agent 1
*******
  Name:                       AMD EPYC 7302P 16-Core Processor
  Uuid:                       CPU-XX
  Marketing Name:             AMD EPYC 7302P 16-Core Processor
  Vendor Name:                CPU
  Feature:                    None specified
  Profile:                    FULL_PROFILE
  Float Round Mode:           NEAR
  Max Queue Number:           0(0x0)
  Queue Min Size:             0(0x0)
  Queue Max Size:             0(0x0)
  Queue Type:                 MULTI
  Node:                       0
  Device Type:                CPU
  Cache Info:
    L1:                            32768(0x8000) KB
  Chip ID:                    0(0x0)
  Cacheline Size:             64(0x40)
  Max Clock Freq. (MHz):      3000
  BDFID:                      0
  Internal Node ID:           0
  Compute Unit:               32
  SIMDs per CU:               0
  Shader Engines:             0
  Shader Arrs. per Eng.:      0
  WatchPts on Addr. Ranges:1
  Features:                   None
```

Figure 7.2: HSA agent 1—the CPU in the system.

within their GPU-accelerated applications.

In addition to Agent 1, we also have valuable information associated with Agent 2, as shown in Figure 7.3. Agent 2 is identified as a Radeon Pro W6800 GPU device. This GPU device offers powerful capabilities that can significantly enhance compute performance. Upon examining the information provided by rocminfo, we discover that the Radeon Pro W6800 GPU incorporates three levels of cache, namely an L1 cache with a size of 16KB, a L2 cache with a size of 4MB, and a L3 cache with a size of 128MB. These caches play a critical role in reducing memory access latency and improving overall performance, owing to their ability to store frequently accessed data closer to the CUs. Furthermore, the Radeon Pro W6800 GPU boasts 60 CUs, making it a formidable computational powerhouse. Each compute unit within the GPU consists of 60 SIMD units. This architectural design allows the GPU to concurrently execute up to 60 operations on individual pieces of data using the same instruction within each compute unit. This parallelization capability significantly enhances the GPU's ability to handle computationally intensive tasks efficiently. The wavefront size of the Radeon Pro W6800 GPU is 32, indicating that 32 threads can be executed in parallel on each CU. This parallel execution of threads enables the GPU to process multiple threads simultaneously, leading to improved throughput and faster execution of parallelizable workloads.

Understanding these technical details of the Radeon Pro W6800 GPU provides

```
*******
Agent 2
*******
  Name:                    gfx1030
  Uuid:                    GPU-bfb96ea7c351b9b3
  Marketing Name:          AMD Radeon PRO W6800
  Vendor Name:             AMD
  Feature:                 KERNEL_DISPATCH
  Profile:                 BASE_PROFILE
  Float Round Mode:        NEAR
  Max Queue Number:        128(0x80)
  Queue Min Size:          64(0x40)
  Queue Max Size:          131072(0x20000)
  Queue Type:              MULTI
  Node:                    1
  Device Type:             GPU
  Cache Info:
    L1:                        16(0x10) KB
    L2:                      4096(0x1000) KB
    L3:                    131072(0x20000) KB
  Chip ID:                 29603(0x73a3)
  Cacheline Size:          64(0x40)
  Max Clock Freq. (MHz):   2555
  BDFID:                   768
  Internal Node ID:        1
  Compute Unit:            60
  SIMDs per CU:            2
  Shader Engines:          8
  Shader Arrs. per Eng.:   2
  WatchPts on Addr. Ranges:4
  Features:                KERNEL_DISPATCH
  Fast F16 Operation:      TRUE
  Wavefront Size:          32(0x20)
  Workgroup Max Size:      1024(0x400)
  Workgroup Max Size per Dimension:
    x                          1024(0x400)
    y                          1024(0x400)
```

Figure 7.3: HSA agent 2 — The GPU in the system.

developers with insights into the underlying architecture and capabilities of this high-performance device. By leveraging this knowledge, developers can optimize their GPU-accelerated applications, ensuring effective utilization of the GPU's resources and achieving maximum performance.

7.2 *ROCm SMI*

ROCm SMI enables system administrators to track a variety of system level metrics, such as power, frequency, and temperature. Typically, *ROCm SMI* can be found in the /opt/rocm/bin directory if a standard ROCm installed on the computer. Assuming this directory is included in the system's PATH variable, developers can open a terminal and simply enter *rocm-smi* to access and monitor a wide range of system-level parameters related to the PCIe, power management, clocking, performance, errors, and events. The *ROCm SMI* also provides a simple method of checking the *ROCm* kernel driver to determine whether it is loaded correctly and make sure all system GPUs are initialized properly.

A list of all available functions from *ROCm SMI* version can be viewed by executing **rocm-smi -h**, where **-h** stands for "help." In this section, we examine the functionality provided by this tool, keeping in mind that monitoring GPU information does not require administrator privileges. However, changing clock frequencies and power states requires **sudo** access. Moreover, the GPU ID can be obtained by executing **rocm-smi –showid**, where –**showid** allows users to easily identify the GPU device that they are working with, which can be especially useful in multi-GPU systems where it may be difficult to distinguish between different devices.

In addition to providing information about the GPU devices, *ROCm SMI* also allows the user to monitor changes in the hardware in real time. By using the command **watch -n0 rocm-smi**, real-time updates of the temperature and average power consumption of the GPU device can be retrieved. Here, **watch** is a standard Linux command, and n0 represents the smallest possible interval to execute the **rocm-smi** command. This feature can be particularly useful for monitoring performance and identifying any issues or anomalies that may arise during operation.

ROCm SMI is typically used to view dynamic information on the system, as shown in Figure 7.4. The output shown is from the system used during the development of this book. There are eight GPUs (0–7), the GPU clock is set to 800 MHz for all devices, and the memory clock is set to 1,600 Mhz. Because the system is idle, both the GPU's video random-access memory (VRAM) and utilization percentage are at 0%. The "perf" column shows "auto," meaning that the dynamic power management (DPM) feature is active. The DPM module automatically scales the voltage and frequency based on the workload requirements and power constraints of the system. Furthermore, the GPU configuration can be changed with **rocm-smi**. We have noticed in Figure 7.4 that the performance level is set to auto by default. To change this, we can use the **rocm-smi –setperflevel low** command to set the performance level to low. This adjustment allows us to better optimize GPU performance for specific needs, which can significantly enhance the efficiency of the workloads.

A list of supported GPU clock frequencies can be queried using **rocm-smi –showsclkrange**, and the list of memory clock frequencies can be queried using **rocm-smi –showmclkrange**. Programmers with superuser privileges have the option of changing clock parameters. For example, –**setclk** is used to change the graphics clock, and –**setmclk** is used to change the memory clock. Note that different GPU systems provide different levels of flexibility with regard to changing clock behaviors. Thus, if a certain configuration is not supported by your system, the *ROCm SMI* will return **NOT_SUPPORTED**.

Another useful *ROCm SMI* command is –**showtopo**, which presents the node topology. The programmer can leverage this information on a multi-GPU system to see how the different GPUs are interconnected (e.g., PCIe or AMD's Interchip Global Memory Interconnect). The command also provides the distance between

GPUs in terms of number of hops from a GPU to another in the system. This can be useful to optimize the communication patterns in multi-GPU systems.

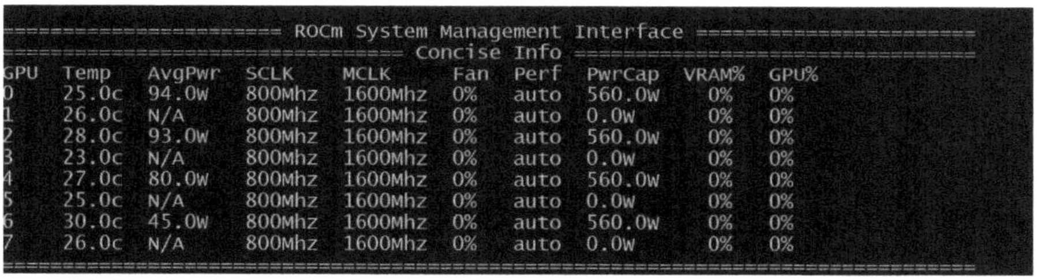

Figure 7.4: Output of the *ROCm SMI* tool.

If a programmer wants to use the *ROCM SMI* command directly in their application instead through using CLI, they may use *ROCm-SMI-Lib*, which provides a direct *C/C++* graphical user interface (GUI). This open-source library is available on *Github* [12]. The set of APIs currently supported is documented in the *rocm_smi.h* header file.

Listing 7.1 presents a code example that accesses the *ROCm SMI* library. The code loops through all AMD GPUs in the user's system and prints the unique PCI **domain:bus:device:function** identifier for each GPU. The routine initializes *ROCm-SMI-Lib* and determines the number of *ROCm* devices in the system. Then, using a loop, the code retrieves the PCI connection **domain:bus:device** for each device. After displaying this information, the program calls *rsmi_shut_down* to perform any necessary cleanup before terminating the program. For more details on the functionality of code in this example, please refer to the library header file, *rocm_smi.h*, which is part of the open-source repository [12].

Both the command line utilities and the API-level calls have their own use cases. The API-level call is useful if you want to have to have code related to locking frequencies, measuring power over time self-contained in the application itself. This is typically used in extensive benchmarking experiments as it avoids the need to manually look at the output from *ROCm SMI* command line utility for doing measurements.

Listing 7.1: *ROCm-SMI-Lib* example.

```
1  #include <stdio.h>
2  #include <stdint.h>
3  #include "rocm_smi/rocm_smi.h"
4
5  int main() {
6    rsmi_status_t ret;
7    uint32_t num_devices;
8    uint64_t bdf;
9
10   // Return code checks are skipped for clarity.
11   ret = rsmi_init(0);
12   ret = rsmi_num_monitor_devices(&num_devices);
13
14   for (int i=0; i < num_devices; ++i) {
15     ret = rsmi_dev_pci_id_get(i, &bdf);
16     printf("Device[%d] : PCI:%04lX:%02lX:%02lX:%02lX\n", i,
17                     (bdf >> 32) & 0xffffffff, (bdf >> 8) & 0xff,
18                     (bdf >> 3) & 0x1f, bdf & 0x7);
19   }
20   ret = rsmi_shut_down();
21   return 0;
22 }
```

7.3   *The ROCm* Debugger

The availability of a well-designed debugger is critical to support GPU programmers. If your application produces unexpected results or crashes during runtime, stepping through the kernel line-by-line will help identify the source of the problem. A debugger is a key tool for examining the contents of each thread's registers or for inspecting parameter values. For these purposes, *ROCm* provides the *rocgdb* debugger, which is built on top of *GDB*, a utility commonly provided for debugging CPU applications.

In this section, we learn how to effectively debug and print wavefront information using the *rocgdb* debugger. Each thread in our example kernel reads an element from the input array, multiplies it by its thread ID, and stores the result in an output array. The value of the input array is initialized such that the ith element contains the value i. Adopting this simple convention, Index 0 contains a zero, Index 1 contains a one, and so forth. At the beginning of kernel execution, we calculate the thread ID and use the value to step into the input and output arrays. On line 18 of the Listing 7.2 kernel, we read the **a** array and the thread ID. We then multiply them together and store the result in the **c** array. In our example, we launch 256 threads, each with a workgroup size of 64. Thus, there are a total of four workgroups of 64 threads each.

Our example is compiled and executed on an AMD GPU with 64 threads per wavefront. It is important to recall that we have four wavefronts in total. Pay attention to the difference between the thread concept we have demonstrated thus far and the "*GDB* threads." A *GDB* thread can refer to a host-side thread spawned by the OS during execution, or it may be specific to a wavefront mapped to a specific *GDB* thread. Therefore, if we focus only on device-side *GDB* threads of which we only have four, given that our sample execution has four total wavefronts. In the following example, when we mention "threads" and "thread IDs," we are referring to threads that are actually running on the GPU. We explicitly refer to "debugger" threads as "*GDB*" threads.

To inspect the register values of wavefront 0, we follow the following steps:

1. Before debugging any GPU kernel, we must compile the program using the **-g** flag so that the debug information will be included in the output binary. As an example, we run **hipcc -g scale_hip.cpp -o scale_hip**, which generates the binary, *scale_hip*.

2. Now, we are ready to debug with *rocgdb*. To launch the debugging session, we enter **rocgdb ./scale_hip**. Once inside the debug environment, we run the program from the *GDB* environment's CLI.

3. We set a breakpoint inside our kernel at Line 19, which is the point at which the output result is computed. To set the breakpoint using the *GDB* CLI, we enter **break scale_hip.cpp:19**. Then, we continue execution using the *GDB* command, **c** (i.e., issuing the continue command). Each wavefront will hit this breakpoint as all wavefronts will follow the same control flow.

4. Setting up multiple breakpoints, we can analyze the program's state at each breakpoint and gain insight into its logic. Once the breakpoints are in place, we can use the **info b** command in GDB's Command Line Interface to show the status and details of the breakpoints that we have set up in our program. The details include the information about how many breakpoints are set up, providing the source line against where each breakpoint has been set, and the breakpoint ID, which is a number.

5. To begin debugging, we can use the **r** (run) command. This command will start the program with the designated breakpoints and pause execution at the first one encountered.

6. After reaching a breakpoint, the **c** (continue) command enables us to resume the program's execution from the current breakpoint. Upon using this command, the debugger executes the program until it hits the next breakpoint, where it halts the execution once more. This feature is helpful for analyzing the program's behavior at different stages by stepping through the code in larger steps.

7. We then use **info threads** to view the list of currently active threads. The output is shown in Listing 7.3.] Recall that we are discussing *GDB* threads here, which must not be confused with the threads running on the GPU. *GDB* threads with IDs of 1, 2, and 3 are host-side threads spawned by the operating system. Thread IDs 5, 6, 7, and 8 refer to the four wavefronts launched by this kernel. The asterisk next to *GDB* Thread 5 denotes that the wavefront has hit the breakpoint.

8. Next, we need to check what code is currently executing around the breakpoint. If we were debugging on a CPU, we probably would use the 'l' or the 'list' command to check the source code. The same applies to GPU programs. However, because the GPU binary is optimized, it may not be easy to identify where you are executing in the assembly code or how variables are mapped to registers. Therefore, GPU debugging is usually done at the assembly level. If the reader is not familiar with the AMD GPU assembly, please refer to Chapter 6 for a detailed introduction. To check assembly code, we can use the **disassemble** command. The output of the command gives a series of assembly code. The assembly code consists of a list of instructions, each identified by a memory address.

9. To inspect the register values of this wavefront, we issue the *GDB* command, **info registers**, which prints all registers associated with the currently active thread: thread ID 5 in wavefront 0. Listing 7.4 shows the partial output of this command. Provided with this information, the programmer can verify the specific register at which the output value is stored by viewing the assembly-level kernel code. Inside our *GDB* session, this is easily achieved using the **disassemble scaleKernel** command.

Continuing with our example, we observe that register v3 stores the final result prior to writing the value back to the main memory. Thus, by examining Line 4 in Listing 7.4, we can see the values of register v3 for all 64 threads in wavefront 0. For example, the third value is 0x4, which corresponds to thread ID 2 of this wavefront. For reference, thread ID 2 loads a value of two from the input array, **a**, multiplies it by a thread ID value of two and outputs 0x4.

10. After continuing, the breakpoint will be hit again by a different wavefront. We can then inspect additional register values in the wavefront.

Listing 7.2: Scalar multiply kernel

```
1  #include "hip/hip_runtime.h"
2  #include <stdio.h>
3  #include <stdlib.h>
4  #include <math.h>
5  #define HIP_ASSERT(x) (assert((x)==hipSuccess))
6
7  // HIP kernel. Each thread takes care of one element of c
8  __global__ void scaleKernel(int *a,int *c, int n)
9  {
10     // Get our global thread ID
11     int id = blockIdx.x*blockDim.x+threadIdx.x;
12     // Make sure we do not go out of bounds
13     if (id < n)
14     {
15
16        c[id] = id*a[id];
17     }
18 }
```

Listing 7.3: Output of info threads command

```
   Id   Target Id     Frame
   1     Thread 0x7ffff7fdc880 (LWP 58984) "a.out" 0x00007ffff5fc9ef7 in
         sched_yield () from /lib/x86_64-linux-gnu/libc.so.6
   2     Thread 0x7ffff4f9e700 (LWP 58990) "a.out" 0x00007ffff5fdc317 in
         ioctl () from /lib/x86_64-linux-gnu/libc.so.6
   4     Thread 0x7ffff4573700 (LWP 58992) "a.out" 0x00007ffff5fdc317 in
         ioctl () from /lib/x86_64-linux-gnu/libc.so.6
 * 5     AMDGPU Thread 2:1:1:1 (0,0,0)/0 "a.out"   scaleKernel (a=<
       optimized out>, c=<optimized out>, n=<optimized out>) at vadd_hip.cpp
       :20
   6     AMDGPU Thread 2:1:1:2 (1,0,0)/0 "a.out"   scaleKernel (a=<
       optimized out>, c=<optimized out>, n=<optimized out>) at vadd_hip.
       cpp:20
   7     AMDGPU Thread 2:1:1:3 (2,0,0)/0 "a.out"   scaleKernel (a=<
       optimized out>, c=<optimized out>, n=<optimized out>) at vadd_hip.
       cpp:20
   8     AMDGPU Thread 2:1:1:4 (3,0,0)/0 "a.out"   scaleKernel (a=<
       optimized out>, c=<optimized out>, n=<optimized out>) at vadd_hip.
       cpp:20
```

Listing 7.4: Partial output of info registers command

```
v0              {0xe8202000, 0xe8202004, 0xe8202008, 0xe820200c, 0
    xe8202010, 0xe8202014, 0xe8202018, 0xe820201c, 0xe8202020, 0xe8202024
    , 0xe8202028, 0xe820202c, 0xe8202030, 0xe8202034, 0xe8202038, 0
    xe820203c, 0xe8202040, 0xe8202044, 0xe8202048, 0xe820204c, 0xe8202050
    , 0xe8202054, 0xe8202058, 0xe820205c, 0xe8202060, 0xe8202064, 0
    xe8202068, 0xe820206c, 0xe8202070, 0xe8202074, 0xe8202078, 0xe820207c
    , 0xe8202080, 0xe8202084, 0xe8202088, 0xe820208c, 0xe8202090, 0
    xe8202094, 0xe8202098, 0xe820209c, 0xe82020a0, 0xe82020a4, 0xe82020a8
    , 0xe82020ac, 0xe82020b0, 0xe82020b4, 0xe82020b8, 0xe82020bc, 0
    xe82020c0, 0xe82020c4, 0xe82020c8, 0xe82020cc, 0xe82020d0, 0xe82020d4
    , 0xe82020d8, 0xe82020dc, 0xe82020e0, 0xe82020e4, 0xe82020e8, 0
    xe82020ec, 0xe82020f0, 0xe82020f4, 0xe82020f8, 0xe82020fc}
v1              {0x7fff <repeats 64 times>}
v2              {0x0 <repeats 64 times>}
v3              {0x0, 0x1, 0x4, 0x9, 0x10, 0x19, 0x24, 0x31, 0x40, 0x51, 0
    x64, 0x79, 0x90, 0xa9, 0xc4, 0xe1, 0x100, 0x121, 0x144, 0x169, 0x190,
    0x1b9, 0x1e4, 0x211, 0x240, 0x271, 0x2a4, 0x2d9, 0x310, 0x349, 0x384
    , 0x3c1, 0x400, 0x441, 0x484, 0x4c9, 0x510, 0x559, 0x5a4, 0x5f1, 0
    x640, 0x691, 0x6e4, 0x739, 0x790, 0x7e9, 0x844, 0x8a1, 0x900, 0x961,
    0x9c4, 0xa29, 0xa90, 0xaf9, 0xb64, 0xbd1, 0xc40, 0xcb1, 0xd24, 0xd99,
    0xe10, 0xe89, 0xf04, 0xf81}
v4              {0x7fff <repeats 64 times>}
v5              {0x7fff <repeats 64 times>}
```

As we have seen, *rocgdb* enables us to debug GPU kernels by setting breakpoints and jump through them breakpoint-by-breakpoint. We can also retrieve detailed runtime information at each breakpoint, including the details of each register in a wavefront.

7.4   *ROCm* Profiler

When it comes to optimizing GPU performance, profiling and tracing are two essential tools that can help developers gain insight into how their application is utilizing the GPU device. ROCm provides two powerful tools for profiling and tracing: *ROCTracer* and *rocprofiler*.

7.4.1   ROCTracer

ROCTracer is used for measuring the performance of an application, and GPU profiling mode can provide us with more detailed measurements collected from the GPU hardware performance counters. *ROCTracer* measures the performance of the application by tracing its execution and measuring the time taken by each function or block of the code. *ROCTracer* is designed to help developers identify the portions of the code that consume the most time. Then, the programmer can focus on optimizing these time-consuming portions of their code. To perform application tracing, there are a number of options available for us. The system structure comprises hardware at the bottom, an operating system, such as AMD KFD driver in the middle, and interfaces such as HSA and the HIP runtime at the top. We can perform application tracing at different levels. For instance, if we use the **–hip-trace** option, we will trace at the user-level where the HIP runtime is located. Using the **–hsa-trace** option will enable tracing at the HSA-level. Using the **–kfd-trace** option will enable tracing at the AMD KFD driver-level. In general, tracing at a higher level allows users to easily associate the tracing results with the source code and identify the source of the problem issue. By tracing at a lower level, we can obtain more detailed information about performance issues.

To perform application tracing with *ROCTracer*, we can use the **rocprof –hip-trace <your_application>** command, followed by the application binary we want to trace. Using this command, the programmer will generate four output files containing information about the application's execution. The *results.copy_stats.csv* file (Listing 7.5) records time measurements for each hip runtime call, with data presented in a CSV format. This includes the portion of the execution time spent performing memory copy operations between the device and host, with data presented in nanoseconds.

Listing 7.5: *results.copy_stats.csv* output in application tracing mode.

```
"Name","Calls","TotalDurationNs","AverageNs","Percentage"
"CopyDeviceToHost",2,9654400,4827200,81.6235566612597
"CopyHostToDevice",2,2173558,1086779,18.376443338740298
```

The *results.hip_stats.csv* (Listing 7.6) file summarizes the execution time, broken down by API. In addition to the APIs that we discussed earlier, this file also includes the execution time of three new APIs, which are *hipLaunchKernel*, *___hipPushCallConfiguration*, and *___hipPopCallConfiguration*. These three functions are the actual API calls that are associated with the triple angled bracket syntax used with each kernel launch. When we initiate a kernel launch, HIP will send the call configuration, which includes the kernel dimensions, stream, local memory size, and kernel arguments, to the GPU using the *___hipPushCallConfiguration* API. Following this, the *hipLaunchKernel* command triggers the execution of the kernel. Finally, the *___hipPopCallConfiguration* is responsible for removing kernel-related information so that the next kernel can start with a clean profile.

Listing 7.6: *results.hip_stats.csv* output in application tracing mode.

```
"Name","Calls","TotalDurationNs","AverageNs","Percentage"
"hipMemcpy",4,537814533,134453633,99.25629643299268
"hipDeviceSynchronize",1,2834079,2834079,0.5230431088750803
"hipLaunchKernel",1,766035,766035,0.141375497262822228
"hipMalloc",3,246963,82321,0.04557822675271806
"hipFree",3,125437,41812,0.02315001044359153
"hipEventRecord",2,34503,17251,0.00636769701392124
"hipEventElapsedTime",1,6146,6146,0.0011342742905706734
"__hipPushCallConfiguration",1,5727,5727,0.00105694579959808406
"hipEventCreate",2,5238,2619,0.0009666984598127542
"hipEventSynchronize",1,2794,2794,0.0005156463338520113
"__hipPopCallConfiguration",1,2793,2793,0.0005154617789723219
```

There is another output file named *results.stats.csv* (Listing 7.7). This file aggregates the kernel execution time. Finally, besides the aggregated data, we want a version of the data that is broken down in more detail. In this case, we have the *results.json* file. Although this file is readable (with effort) by a human, it is easier to visualize the trace to understand the breakdown of the execution. The *results.json* file follows a standard tracing format to enable us to use the chrome tracing tool to visualize the execution trace. We start by issuing to the chrome browser *chrome://tracing*, and then uploading our json file there. We can then visualize the trace contents.

Listing 7.7: *results.stats.csv* output in application tracing mode.

```
"Name","Calls","TotalDurationNs","AverageNs","Percentage"
"vector_add(float*, float*, float*, int)",1,2850719,2850719,100.0
```

7.4.2   rocprofiler

As discussed earlier, *rocprof* allows programmers to retrieve profile information from the hardware counters during kernel execution. These counter values can help the programmer better understand how the various software-based optimizations can improve hardware utilization. *rocprof* produces statistics on cache hits and misses, the frequency of the different types of instructions executed, cycles spent waiting for memory instructions to complete, and other key performance-related information. The profiler can also present selective profiling rules for kernels in a group, or even a specific kernel invocation.

Note that the number of GPU hardware counters differs on different GPU architectures. One of the first steps of attempting to optimize application performance is to extract hardware counter details for the GPU using **rocprof –list-basic**.

The output will contain a list of all of the basic hardware counters. Additionally, **rocProf –list-derived** shows metrics produced by the profiler, which are collected using the basic hardware counters. The programmer can then choose to extract a specific set to quantify the profiling overhead. This is important because every GPU has a limited number of counters that can be collected on a single pass. When the programmer specifies a large number of performance counters to profile, the hardware will replay the GPU kernels to collect the data, which ultimately increases the profiling time. *rocProf* supports two profiling modes: i) performance measurements, which measures the kernel execution times, and ii) performance counters, which collects specific hardware counter data.

Next, we look at a profiling example using the *vector_add* kernel developed in Chapter 2. We compile our application using *hipcc* to produce an output binary, *vadd*. We begin by using performance measurement mode, because we want to collect the kernel execution time. This is done by running **rocprof – stats <your_application>**, which outputs the file, *results.stats.csv*, as shown in Listing 7.8. The information contained in this comma-separated value (CSV) file includes statistics, such as the number of the times the kernel was called (once in our example), the total and average kernel execution duration in nanoseconds (5,920 ns for *vadd*), and the percentage of the total GPU application consumed by the kernel (100% in our example, as it is the only kernel). These performance measurements are helpful in identifying the active kernels in an application and in providing a breakdown of the total runtime per kernel. This information will aid the programmer, enabling them to narrow down the set of kernels consuming a majority of the execution time.

Listing 7.8: *rocProf* output in performance measurement mode.

```
"Name","Calls","TotalDurationNs","AverageNs","Percentage"
"vecAdd(double*, double*, double*, int) [clone.kd]",1,5920,5920,100.0
```

Next, we show an example using performance counter mode, which demonstrate how to collect hardware performance counters. Listing 7.9 shows the sample input file, *input.txt*. The first line contains "pmc, which specifies the counters we wish to collect during our profiling run. In this example, we collect **TCC_EA_RDREQ_sum** and **TCC_EA_WRRREQ_sum**. These counters count the numbers of read and write transactions taking place between the cache and main memory, respectively. The second line specifies the invocation range we wish to profile. In this case, we have only a single invocation; thus, we specify 0:1. If we had launched this kernel multiple times in an application, though are only interested in profiling a specific invocations, we could specify that detail accordingly. For example, if we wanted to profile the 55th invocation out of 100, we would just specify "55". To profile all invocations, beginning with the 55th onwards, we would set the range to "55:". The third line, "gpu," specifies the ID of the GPU that we wish to profile. In a multi-GPU system, this number is set accordingly, depending on the GPU in question. The final line is the "kernel" line, which specifies the kernel name. To profile multiple kernels, we use a comma separator. In this example, we only deal with a single kernel, *vecAdd*. When we have our input file, we are then ready to profile the *vector_add* kernel. To profile its execution, we pass the input text file to the profiler with **rocprof -i input.txt -o vadd_profile.csv ./vadd**, which triggers *rocProf*, which profiles the desired metrics. The final output is stored in *vadd_profile.csv*, as shown in Listing 7.10. Recall that this is the name we passed to *rocprof* using the **-o** flag. The output file will include many different values, such as the kernel name, process ID, and register usage. Toward the end of the file, we will find the results of the two profiled metrics: **TCC_EA_RDREQ_sum** and **TCC_EA_WRREQ_sum**. Their outputs are "2610" and "1280," respectively, as this kernel reads twice as many times as it writes (i.e., *vadd* reads both **a** and **b** and writes to **c**).

Listing 7.9: *rocProf* input file for the vectorAdd kernel.

```
pmc: TCC_EA_RDREQ_sum,  TCC_EA_WRREQ_sum
range: 0:1
gpu: 0
kernel: vecAdd
```

Listing 7.10: *rocProf* output file for the vectorAdd kernel.

```
Index,KernelName,gpu-id,queue-id,queue-index,pid,tid,grd,wgr,lds,scr,vgpr
    ,sgpr,fbar,sig,obj,TCC_EA_RDREQ_sum,TCC_EA_WRREQ_sum
0,"vecAdd(double*, double*, double*, int) [clone .kd]"
    ,0,0,0,15239,15242,10240,256,0,0,12,24,0,0x0,0x7f9ba4c45800,2610,1280
```

Now that we have learned how to leverage the *rocprof* profiler, in the next chapter, we will profile and optimize full GPU applications. Recall that the goal of the profiler is to provide programmers with useful information that enables focused optimization.

7.5 ROCm Profiler V2

The second version of the ROCm profiler, introduced with ROCm 6.0, is a non-backward-compatible update of **rocprof**. Owing to its incompatibility with the earlier version, both versions coexist in a standard ROCm installation: **rocprof** v1 and its successor. Similar to rocprof v1, rocprof v2 also supports application tracing and kernel profiling models.

7.5.1 Application Tracing

To use rocprofv2 with various trace options for tracing HIP/HSA API, asynchronous activity, and kernel dispatches. These trace options are shown below. Note that these commands do not generate output yet, we need output plugins (to be introduced soon) to generate output.

Listing 7.11: Commands to be used for using the application trace feature of rocprofv2.

```
# HIP API & asynchronous activity tracing
rocprofv2 -hip-api <app_relative_path>
rocprofv2 -hip-activity <app_relative_path>

# HSA API & asynchronous activity tracing
rocprofv2 -hsa-api <app_relative_path>
rocprofv2 -hsa-activity <app_relative_path>

# Kernel dispatches tracing
rocprofv2 -kernel-trace <app_relative_path>

# HIP & HSA API and asynchronous activity and kernel dispatches tracing
rocprofv2 -sys-trace <app_relative_path>
```

The rocprofv2 CLI supports tracing APIs at both the HIP and the HSA levels. In general, HIP APIs directly interact with the user program. It is easier to analyze HIP traces as users can directly map the traces to the program. HSA API tracing is more suitable for advanced users who want to understand the hardware behavior at a lower level.

Both HIP and HSA APIs support asynchronous behavior (e.g., asynchronous memory copy). If a –hip-api or –hsa-api trace is collected, the trace will only record the API execution time, but not the time that the associated action (e.g., memory copy) is performed. To also record the actual action time, the –hip-activity and –hsa-activity options can be used. Additionally, to record kernel executions, rocprofv2 CLI provides a dedicated –kernel-trace option.

Multiple trace options can be used together in one profiler run. To simplify the command, users can use the –sys-trace command, which includes all the traces mentioned above.

The rocprofv2 CLI uses a modular plugin system to allow users to select the profiler output format. Plugins that are shipped with ROCProfilerV2, and the output format description, are listed in Table 7.1.

Table 7.1: The plugins supported by rocprofv2.

Plugin	Output Format
File	Text files (.txt)
Perfetto	Protobuf, in the format of the Chromium Project's trace-event format
Advanced Thread Tracer	Binary, for the Analysis View tool
CTF	Binary, formatted in the CTF format that can be consumed by public tools such as Babeltrace
OTF2	Binary, formatted in the Open Trace Format Version 2 (OTF2). The trace can be consumed by tools such as Score-P, TAU, and Vampire.

To generate output, the OUTPUT_PATH variable must be set to the desired directory. Otherwise, no output will be generated. The only exception is the file plugin, which dumps the trace to standard output, in case the OUTPUT_PATH is absent.

Given that the rocprofv2 CLI supports the Perfetto output format, users can easily visualize the execution trace with Perfetto. To use Perfetto, open https://ui.perfetto.dev, select "Open trace file" from the left navigation, and select the trace to visualize.

The figure below is a screenshot from the Perfetto interface. The tasks are organized in a Gantt chart style, with the x-axis representing time and each rectangle representing the start and the end time of a task. The tasks are organized in rows. Here, we have HIP API, HSA API, a queue, and a stream.

7.5.2 Kernel Profiling

The application tracing functionality allows users to evaluate how long a kernel executes but provides little information about why the kernel takes this long time. To investigate, users would need to use the kernel profiling functionality to investigate into the kernel execution. The kernel profiling functionality allows users to collect performance metrics collected by the hardware.

To check supported performance counters and metrics, the rocprofv2 CLI provides the –list-counters option. The output will include a list of metrics like the example shown below.

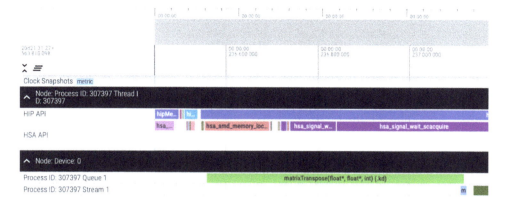

Figure 7.5: Using Perfetto to visualize rocprofv2 captured application trace.

Listing 7.12: Example of a rocprofv2 counter.

```
gfx1030:0 : SQ_WAVES
: Count number of waves sent to SQs. {emulated, global, C1}
     block SQ can only handle 8 counters at a time
```

These entries can be understood as listed below.

1. Gfx1030: The GPU architecture

2. 0: the GPU ID. There may be multiple GPUs in the current machine.

3. SQ_WAVES: The counter name. Typically, the first token before the first underscore is the GPU block name. Here, SQ is the block that is responsible for managing wavefronts and issuing instructions.

4. Count number ...: The description of the counter

5. Block SQ ...: Hardware limitations on using performance counters. Each SQ has eight counters. Therefore we cannot collect too many metrics in one run.

To use rocprofv2 to collect hardware counters and derived metrics, users can provide an input file using the -i option.

Listing 7.13: Command used to profile kernels with rocprofv2.

```
rocprofv2 -i samples/input.txt <app_relative_path>
input.txt
```

An input file is a text file that can be supplied to rocprofv2 for counter and metric collection. It typically consists of four parts, namely, the performance counter to use, the GPUs to profile, name of the kernels to be profiled, and the range of kernels to profile. All fields other than the pmc are optional.

Listing 7.14: Input file for kernel profiling feature of rocprofv2.

```
pmc: SQ_WAVES TA_UTIL
range: 0:1
gpu: 0
kernel: matrixTranspose
```

The fields in the input file are described here:

- PMC: The rows in the text file beginning with "pmc" are the group of metrics the user is interested in collecting. The performance counters can be selected from the output generated by –list-counters option.

  The number of metrics that can be collected in one run of profiling is limited by the GPU hardware resources. If too many metrics are selected, the kernels need to be executed multiple times to collect the metrics. For multi-pass execution, include multiple rows of pmc in the input file. Metrics in each pmc row can be collected in each run of the kernel.

- GPU: The row beginning with the keyword gpu specifies the GPU(s) on which the hardware counters are to be collected. This enables the support for profiling multiple GPUs. You can specify multiple GPUs separated by commas, for example, gpu: 1,3.

- Kernel: The row beginning with the keyword kernel specifies the name(s) of the kernel(s) that need to be profiled.

- Range: The row beginning with the keyword range specifies the range of kernel dispatches. Specifying range is helpful in cases where the application causes multiple kernel dispatches and users want to filter some kernel dispatches. In the above example, the range 0:1 depicts that one kernel is profiled.

The rocprofv2 CLI reports one value per metric per kernel in the output. In terms of the output format, users can still use the plugins to control the output format. Here, let's focus on the file output and the Perfetto output.

The file plugin generates a data entry per kernel innovation (see the example below). For each kernel, basic information (e.g., gpu_id, sgpr count, etc.) is listed before the user-specified performance counters. Each value is listed in the format of "value_name(value)."

Listing 7.15: Output of kernel profiling feature of rocprofv2.

```
dispatch[1], gpu_id(0), queue_id(1), queue_index(0), pid(320661), tid
    (320661), grd(1048576), wgr(16), lds(0), scr(0), arch_vgpr(8),
    accum_vgpr(0), sgpr(128), wave_size(32), sig(140670227584384), obj(1)
    , kernel-name("matrixTranspose"), start_time(1811083228321204),
    end_time(1811083228892614)
, SQ_WAVES (65536.000000)
, GRBM_COUNT (288690.000000)
, GRBM_GUI_ACTIVE (288690.000000)
, SQ_INSTS_VALU (1048512.000000)
dispatch[2], gpu_id(0), queue_id(1), queue_index(2), pid(320661), tid
    (320661), grd(1048576), wgr(16), lds(0), scr(0), arch_vgpr(8),
    accum_vgpr(0), sgpr(128), wave_size(32), sig(140670227584384), obj(2)
    , kernel-name("matrixTranspose"), start_time(1811083230510950),
    end_time(1811083231072480)
, SQ_WAVES (65552.000000)
, GRBM_COUNT (286162.000000)
, GRBM_GUI_ACTIVE (286162.000000)
, SQ_INSTS_VALU (1048704.000000)
```

Users can also use the Perfetto plugin to generate visualizable output. Below is a screenshot of the Perfetto UI when visualizing the kernel profile output. There are several rows. The last row is the kernel execution timeline, which is the same as the –kernel-trace used in the application tracing mode. Other rows above represent the performance counters selected by the user.

The visualization provides a good overview of both kernel execution times and how performance metrics value changed across the kernels. Additionally, users can also get detailed values by hovering on or clicking a bar to show the exact value of the performance metric.

7.5.3 ROCSys

As part of rocprofv2, ROCSys is a command line utility tool that can control a profiling session (launch/start/stop/exit) within the application to be traced or profiled. When running long-running workloads (DNN training), users may want to control the application and profile part of it as the application is running. ROCSys allows starting/stopping a profiling session while it is running, analyzing

Figure 7.6: Using Perfetto to visualize rocprofv2 captured kernel profiling results.

the results, and exiting the session. Users can launch the session from one terminal and control the application (start/stop/exit) using ROCSys from another terminal.

Next, we demonstrate the full flow of using the ROCSys.

We first create a session by calling both ROCSys and rocprofv2. The application will be halted until the session is started by ROCSys in the second step.

Listing 7.16: Creating a session using ROCSys and rocprofv2.

```
/opt/rocm/bin/rocsys  --session session1 launch rocprofv2 -i ../samples/
    input.txt <long_running_app>
ROCSYS:: Session ID: 2109
ROCSYS Session Created!
ROCProfilerV2: Collecting the following counters:
- SQ_WAVES
- GRBM_COUNT
- GRBM_GUI_ACTIVE
- SQ_INSTS_VALU
- FETCH_SIZE
Enabling Counter Collection
```

Second, in another terminal window, users can start the tool session. Starting the session will trigger the application to run.

Listing 7.17: Starting the profiling session.

```
/opt/rocm/bin/rocsys  --session session1 start
ROCSYS:: Starting Tools Session...
Dispatch_ID(1), GPU_ID(1), ... // All the metrics of a kernel
Dispatch_ID(2), GPU_ID(1), ... // All the metrics of a kernel
Dispatch_ID(3), GPU_ID(1), ... // All the metrics of a kernel
```

Third, we can also stop the tool session. After stopping the profiling session, the application keeps running. As we run any rocsys command, kernel profiling information will be dumped to the terminal. These kernels are executed between the current and previous commands.

Listing 7.18: Stopping the profiling session.

```
/opt/rocm/bin/rocsys  --session session1 stop

ROCSYS:: Stopping Tools Session...
Dispatch_ID(22397), GPU_ID(1), ... // All the metrics of a kernel
Dispatch_ID(22398), GPU_ID(1), ... // All the metrics of a kernel
Dispatch_ID(22399), GPU_ID(1), ... // All the metrics of a kernel
```

Fourth, after stopping the profiling session, we can restart the profiling session again, analyzing the results and starting the tool session again

Listing 7.19: Restarting the profiling session.

```
/opt/rocm/bin/rocsys  --session session1 start

ROCSYS:: Starting Tools Session...
Dispatch_ID(22400), GPU_ID(1), ... // All the metrics of a kernel
Dispatch_ID(22401), GPU_ID(1), ... // All the metrics of a kernel
```

Finally, we exit the tools session. Once the session is exited, it cannot be restarted.

Listing 7.20: Exiting the profiling session.

```
/opt/rocm/bin/rocsys  --session session1 exit
Dispatch_ID(16828), GPU_ID(1), ... // All the metrics of a kernel
Dispatch_ID(16829), GPU_ID(1), ... // All the metrics of a kernel
ROCSYS:: Exiting Tools Session...Application might still be finishng up..
```

Note that exiting the session only stops profiling. The application might still be running/finishing up in the background. If you no longer want to wait for the application, use CTRL+C to exit the application OR wait for the application to finish.

7.6   Porting *CUDA* Programs to *HIP* Using Hipify

One of the most valuable tools provided by the *HIP* language is an automated method of converting an entire codebase written in *CUDA* to *HIP*. There are many situations in which a programmer or researcher will need to run an application developed in *CUDA*, targeting an NVIDIA system, on an AMD GPU. It may be to compare the performance obtained on the two platforms (one of the major motivations for learning *HIP* is to avoid being locked into a single hardware vendor). Prior to *HIP*, the only porting method available entailed manually converting the *CUDA* source to *OpenCL*: a cumbersome and error-prone path. With *ROCm*, programmers can now leverage easy-to-use source-to-source translators. Further, and perhaps most importantly, the use of *HIP* enables programmers/developers to leverage their existing code, skillsets and coding experience, continuing to leverage those same investments for future development. In this chapter, we examine this process in detail and present an example. We also cover some common post-translation challenges and the Hipifying tools used to overcome them.

7.6.1   *Hipify* Tools

ROCm provides two tools for converting *CUDA* to *HIP*, *Hipify-clang* and *Hipify-perl* [9]. Both run on Linux and Windows systems. Each has their own pros and cons, as discussed later in this chapter. These tools take *CUDA* source files as input and generate *HIP* files as output, including host-side APIs (e.g., *CUDA Driver*, *Runtime*, *Device*, and *Runtime Compilation*). *Hipify* tools also translate *cuComplex*, *cuBLAS*, *cuDNN*, *cuFFT*, *cuRAND*, and *cuSPARSE* libraries [8].

Hipify-clang

Hipify-clang, as the name suggests, is a *clang*-based tool used to convert *CUDA* code to *HIP*. It works by converting the *CUDA* source into an abstract syntax tree [47] and traversing it using transformation matchers. After running through this process the *HIP* output is produced. The main advantage of this approach is that it leverages the *clang* frontend. *Hipify-clang* can automatically support any new *CUDA* version, enabling future interoperability with new platforms. Furthermore, *Hipify-clang* can parse and convert complicated constructs into *HIP* source code quite easily. The conversion includes macro expansions, redefinitions of the *CUDA* entities declared in user namespaces, complex templates, and function argument lists. *Hipify-clang* distinguishes device and host function calls and includes the required header files. However, care must be taken to ensure that the input *CUDA* code is correct; all the "includes" and "defines" must be accounted for. Incorrect code will not be translated, and errors will be reported.

To process a file, *Hipify-clang* requires access to the same headers required to compile *CUDA* code with *clang*. Thus, *CUDA* should be installed and specified in case of multiple installations using the '**--cuda-path**' option. An example is shown below:

```
./hipify-clang square.cu --cuda-path=/usr/local/cuda-11.6
```

Hipify-clang's arguments are specified first, followed by the separator, '**--**'. Arguments are then passed to *clang* if the input file is to be compiled. For example:

```
./hipify-clang square.cu -- -std=c++17
```

The option of include-based file searching is the same as in *clang* and other *C/C++* compilers: '**-I**=<**directory**>'. Using the '**-D**=<**macro**>=<**value**>' option, macros can be defined (the value is an optional parameter). The '=' symbol may be omitted in both options, or the space symbol may be used instead. The command-line syntax is as follows:

```
./hipify-clang square.cu -I../../include -D USE_GPU -D=GFX=1033
```

For more information on compiling *CUDA*, please refer to the "Compiling *CUDA* with *clang*" manual [48].

Hipify-clang supports the compilation of multiple source files in which all specified options are applied.

To provide compilation options for the Hipification of complex multi-source *CUDA* projects, it is worth using a JavaScript Object Notation (*JSON*) compilation database that can be generated by *clang* using *cmake*. This database can be provided as a *compile_commands.json* file using '**-p**=<**folder** with **compile_commands.json**>' commands. More information on the creation of a *JSON* compilation database can be found in the clang *JSON* database documentation [19].

Some *CUDA* APIs are experimentally supported and are not translated by default. To translate them, the option, '**--experimental**', can be set. To see all supported and experimental *CUDA* APIs, including information about "appeared," "deprecated," and "approved" versions, one can generate documentation in markdown or CSV format using '**./hipify-clang --md**' or '**./hipify-clang ---csv**' commands, respectively. The files will be placed in the working folder.

CUDA2HIP documentation can be generated in full, strict, or compact format using the '**--doc-format=<format>**' option. An example of the documentation in its full format is listed in Table 7.2, where the corresponding *CUDA* and *HIP* API versions are presented in Columns "A," "D," "R," and "E." "A" indicates the version in which the API was added, "D" means "deprecated," "R" means "removed," and "E" indicates the *HIP* release version in which the API became experimental (usually the version of the most recent *HIP* release). The absence of a *HIP* API indicates that the corresponding *CUDA* API is not yet supported by *HIP*.

Table 7.2: *CUDA2HIP* documentation example in full format.

CUDA	A	D	R	HIP	A	D	R	E
cudaDeviceSetGraphMemAttribute	11.4							
cudaGraphAddChildGraphNode	10.0							
cudaGraphAddDependencies	10.0			hipGraphAddDependencies	4.5.0			4.5.0
cudaGraphAddEmptyNode	10.0			hipGraphAddEmptyNode	4.5.0			4.5.0

Hipify-clang has an important difference from regular *clang* and other *C/C++* compilers regarding its preprocessor behavior. The difference is related to parsing conditional preprocessor blocks **#if**, **#else**, and **#endif**. Most compilers calculate the compile-time conditions and skip false conditional blocks. *Hipify-clang* does not skip false conditional blocks by default when transforming them to *HIP*. This behavior may lead to compilation errors, as with any platform-dependent code. To switch *Hipify-clang* to a default preprocessor behavior, the option, '**--skip-excluded-preprocessor-conditional-blocks**', should be specified.

HIP currently supports *CUDA* kernel launch syntax with its kernel execution configuration [57]. However, for compatibility, this syntax is being transformed by *Hipify-clang* to a regular function call. Below is an example of the *CUDA* kernel launch syntax and the transformed *hipLaunchKernelGGL*.

```
matrixTranspose<<<dimGrid, dimBlock>>>(
    gpuTransposeMatrix, gpuMatrix, WIDTH);

hipLaunchKernelGGL(
    matrixTranspose, dim3(dimGrid), dim3(dimBlock),
    0, 0, gpuTransposeMatrix, gpuMatrix, WIDTH);
```

To retain the *CUDA* kernel launch syntax in the Hipified code, use the '**--cuda-kernel-execution-syntax**' option. In future *Hipify* releases, this option will be set by default and the kernel call will look similar to CUDA syntax.

The '**--inplace**' option allows *Hipify-clang* to modify the input file in-place, replacing the input *CUDA* file with a *HIP* file. This is a useful option when porting large multi-source projects, as it is best to copy the entire codebase and Hipify it. A folder comparison can then be made as desired by the user.

Hipify-clang gathers statistics on the converted and unconverted APIs from different perspectives. To print these statistics to standard output, '**--print-stats**' should be added as an option. To print to a CSV file, the '**--print-stats-csv**' option should be used. Sample statistics are shown later in this chapter, as we work through an example. In the case of multiple source files, statistics are provided per file and overall, which is helpful when analyzing large *CUDA* projects that have been Hipified. For instance, all unconverted APIs are presented in a single location, with each instance counted.

Another useful option is '**--examine**', which provides statistics like those produced by the '**--print-stats**' command; however, it does not generate a Hipified file and allows for quicker portability estimation.

The option, '**--o-dir**', allows programmers to specify an output directory for the Hipified source and statistics.

To see all available options and their descriptions, we use the '**--help**' option.

Below is a list of the most commonly generated warnings and errors that appear during Hipification by *Hipify-clang*.

- Unsupported API. This warning means that *HIP* does not support the API yet. Thus, the source code should be rewritten without the unsupported API if possible. If the programmer believes that the API is essential, and there is no way to execute their application without it, the issue can be raised here [6]. An example of such a warning is shown below:

```
intro.cu.hip:77:3: warning: CUDA identifier is unsupported in HIP.
  CUmemLocation memLoc.
    ^
```

- Experimental API. This warning means that the API is supported only experimentally, and full correctness is not guaranteed. To force Hipification using experimental APIs, one uses the '**--experimental**' option. Below, we see an example of such a warning:

```
Simplemechs.cu.hip:35:1: warning: CUDA identifier is experimental
in HIP. To Hipify it, use the '--experimental' option.
```

- Deprecated API. This warning means that the API is deprecated in *CUDA*, but is supported and enabled in *HIP*:

```
intro.cu.hip:46:3: warning: 'cudaThreadSynchronize' is deprecated
[-Wdeprecated-declarations]
  cudaThreadSynchronize().
    ^
```

- Removed API. This error message means that the API was removed from *CUDA*. In this case, the source code must be rewritten without the removed API; otherwise, the Hipification should be run against the *CUDA* version in which the API persists:

```
intro.cu.hip:78:12: error: use of undeclared identifier
'CU_COMPUTEMODE_EXCLUSIVE'
  if (cm == CU_COMPUTEMODE_EXCLUSIVE).
          ^
```

If compilation errors occur, the Hipified output will either not be generated, or be generated incorrectly. Hence, the generated statistics will also be incorrect:

```
ERROR: Statistics is invalid due to failed hipification.
```

Hipify-perl

Hipify-perl is an autogenerated *Perl*-based script that heavily uses regular expressions. To generate *Hipify-perl*, run '**./hipify-clang --perl**'. The *Hipify-perl* script will then be generated and placed in the working directory by default. An output directory for the generated *Hipify-perl* file can be specified using the '**--o-hipify-perl-dir**' option.

Unlike *Hipify-clang*, *Hipify-perl* does not require *CUDA* to be installed, and it does not depend on third-party tools. Only *Perl* is needed, and the source file does not have to be syntactically correct. However, when relying on regular expressions, some *CUDA* code may not convert to *HIP* automatically. Currently, the tool cannot correctly expand all possible macros, distinguish redefinitions of *CUDA* entities declared in user namespaces, apply the user namespace, add directives to APIs or data types, distinguish device/host function calls, inject header files, or parse complicated function argument lists.

Generally, *Hipify-perl* works efficiently but is slower than *Hipify-clang*. In most cases, the programmer can improve upon the conversion-related issues by manually intervening with error and warning corrections.

The objective of the script-based translator is to provide a quick tool for ad hoc Hipification of any *CUDA* source and to estimate the amount of work required for porting. For porting complicated projects, involving a large number of source files, *Hipify-clang* is the recommended tool.

Hipify-perl also supports multiple input source files and the following options that have parallel *Hipify-clang* meanings:

```
-examine, -experimental, -inplace, -o=, -print-stats
```

Unlike *Hipify-clang*, *Hipify-perl* supports a few specific options that provide the scripting requirements of *Hipify-perl*.

The option, '**-whitelist=<list>**', allows the specification of comma-separated identifiers, which must not be hipified; otherwise, certain APIs may be erroneously Hipified.

The option, '**-quiet-warnings**', suppresses all warnings. Options '**-exclude-dirs=**' and '**-exclude-files=**' exclude the specified directories or files, respectively, in case of multiple source-file Hipification.

7.6.2 General Hipify Guidelines

Programmers are encouraged to follow the basic guidelines outlined below when Hipifying *CUDA*:

- Run Hipify in a separate source code folder so that separate source code trees are produced. This makes it easy to perform a source-code comparison between the two folders. This approach allows end users to easily separate versions and use the version that they want to on their target platform.

- After successful Hipification, compiling the resulting *HIP* code, run it and verify that the results compare favorably to the original *CUDA* or CPU version. However, this may not always be possible. For example, an application that relies on random number generators or stochastic applications (e.g., machine learning) may not always give the same result, even across multiple runs on the same platform. As with any execution comparison, correctness is the first thing to check, followed by precision and performance.

- Programmers are encouraged to have a basic understanding of the application and source code prior to Hipification so that they can identify and may fix compiler errors, as well as debug runtime problems.

- Programmers should consult the latest *HIP* manual [8] to ensure that the API calls used in *CUDA* are supported.

7.6.3   Hipification of Matrix-Transpose

In this section, we examine the Hipification process using a simple *CUDA* example, *MatrixTranspose.cu*, as shown in Listing 7.21, which is converted to *HIP* using the *Hipify-clang* tool.

Listing 7.21: *CUDA* matrix-transpose example snippet.

```
 1  cudaDeviceProp devProp;
 2  CHECK(cudaGetDeviceProperties(&devProp, 0));
 3  // Memory allocation on GPU
 4  CHECK(cudaMalloc((void**)&gpuMatrix, NUM * sizeof(float)));
 5  CHECK(cudaMalloc((void**)&gpuTransposeMatrix, NUM * sizeof(float)));
 6  // Memory transfer from CPU to GPU
 7  CHECK(cudaMemcpy(gpuMatrix, Matrix, NUM * sizeof(float),
        cudaMemcpyHostToDevice));
 8  const uint32_t THREADS_PER_BLOCK_X = 4;
 9  const uint32_t THREADS_PER_BLOCK_Y = 4;
10  const uint32_t THREADS_PER_BLOCK_Z = 1;
11  const uint32_t GRID_X = uint32_t(WIDTH / THREADS_PER_BLOCK_X);
12  const uint32_t GRID_Y = uint32_t(WIDTH / THREADS_PER_BLOCK_Y);
13  dim3 dimGrid(GRID_X, GRID_Y);
14  dim3 dimBlock(THREADS_PER_BLOCK_X, THREADS_PER_BLOCK_Y,
        THREADS_PER_BLOCK_Z);
15  // Kernel launching
16  matrixTranspose<<<dimGrid, dimBlock>>>(gpuTransposeMatrix, gpuMatrix,
        WIDTH);
```

```
17  // Memory transfer from device to host
18  CHECK(cudaMemcpy(TransposeMatrix, gpuTransposeMatrix, NUM * sizeof(float)
        , cudaMemcpyDeviceToHost));
19  for (uint32_t i = 0; i < NUM; ++i) {
20    printf("Matrix[%d]: %.2f  | cpuTransposeMatrix[%d]: %.2f\n", i, Matrix[
        i], i, cpuTransposeMatrix[i]);
21  }
```

To demonstrate the utility of hipifying CUDA code, the *matrixTransposeGPU* function is used in the example. We Hipify the CUDA code, which is based on *CUDA* version 11.6, and generate the corresponding statistics. The full application code is provided in the source code that accompanies this text. To Hipify *MatrixTranspose.cu*, we use the following command:

```
./hipify-clang MatrixTranspose.cu --print-stats --print-stats-csv
--cuda-kernel-execution-syntax
--cuda-path=/usr/local/cuda-11.6
```

Running this command generates a *HIP* version of the matrix transpose operation, producing the *MatrixTranspose.cu.hip* file, as shown in Listing 7.22.

Listing 7.22: Hipified matrix-transpose example snippet.

```
1   hipDeviceProp_t devProp;
2   CHECK(hipGetDeviceProperties(&devProp, 0));
3   // Memory allocation on GPU
4   CHECK(hipMalloc((void**)&gpuMatrix, NUM * sizeof(float)));
5   CHECK(hipMalloc((void**)&gpuTransposeMatrix, NUM * sizeof(float)));
6   // Memory transfer from CPU to GPU
7   CHECK(hipMemcpy(gpuMatrix, Matrix, NUM * sizeof(float),
        hipMemcpyHostToDevice));
8   const uint32_t THREADS_PER_BLOCK_X = 4;
9   const uint32_t THREADS_PER_BLOCK_Y = 4;
10  const uint32_t THREADS_PER_BLOCK_Z = 1;
11  const uint32_t GRID_X = uint32_t(WIDTH / THREADS_PER_BLOCK_X);
12  const uint32_t GRID_Y = uint32_t(WIDTH / THREADS_PER_BLOCK_Y);
13  dim3 dimGrid(GRID_X, GRID_Y);
14  dim3 dimBlock(THREADS_PER_BLOCK_X, THREADS_PER_BLOCK_Y,
        THREADS_PER_BLOCK_Z);
15  // Kernel launching
16  matrixTranspose<<<dimGrid, dimBlock>>>(gpuTransposeMatrix, gpuMatrix,
        WIDTH);
17  // Memory transfer from GPU to CPU
18  CHECK(hipMemcpy(TransposeMatrix, gpuTransposeMatrix, NUM * sizeof(float),
        hipMemcpyDeviceToHost));
```

Listing 7.23 shows the conversion statistics, printed to *stdout* for inspection, as the percentage of the source code successfully ported is reported. The listing also

contains information about which API calls were converted from *CUDA* to *HIP*.
We can see that all of the APIs were converted, as confirmed by the 100% value
under *CONVERSION*. In total, 13 *CUDA* APIs were converted to *HIP*. We can
also see that three types of converted APIs (i.e., error, device, and memory) were
ported from the *CUDA Runtime* API only. The last part of Listing 7.23 reports
the number of *CUDA* API types successfully converted.

Listing 7.23: Matrix-transpose *HIP* conversion statistics.

```
[HIPIFY] info: file 'MatrixTranspose.cu' statistics:
  CONVERTED refs count: 13
  UNCONVERTED refs count: 0
  CONVERSION %: 100.0
  REPLACED bytes: 182
  TOTAL bytes: 3383
  CHANGED lines of code: 11
  TOTAL lines of code: 78
  CODE CHANGED (in bytes) %: 5.4
  CODE CHANGED (in lines) %: 14.1
  TIME ELAPSED s: 0.75
[HIPIFY] info: CONVERTED refs by type:
  error: 1
  device: 1
  memory: 6
  include_cuda_main_header: 1
  type: 1
  numeric_literal: 3
[HIPIFY] info: CONVERTED refs by API:
  CUDA RT API: 13
[HIPIFY] info: CONVERTED refs by names:
  cudaDeviceProp: 1
  cudaFree: 2
  cudaGetDeviceProperties: 1
  cudaGetErrorString: 1
  cudaMalloc: 2
  cudaMemcpy: 2
  cudaMemcpyDeviceToHost: 1
  cudaMemcpyHostToDevice: 1
  cudaSuccess: 1
  cuda_runtime.h: 1
```

We are now ready to compile the application using the *HIP* compiler and
execute it on an AMD GPU. To run the code, use the following commands:

```
hipcc MatrixTranspose.cu.hip -o MatrixTranspose -v
```

Option '**-v**' specifies a verbose compiler output.

We now demonstrate *HIP*'s portability by compiling and running our Hipified code on an AMD GPU platform. Note that the environment variable, *HIP_PLATFORM*, should be set to **nvidia**:

```
export HIP_PLATFORM=nvidia
```

For compilation, the '**-x cu**' option is added:

```
hipcc MatrixTranspose.cu.hip -o MatrixTranspose -x cu -v
```

If your configuration has two GPUs, such as an NVIDIA-enabled GPU and a *ROCm*-enabled GPU, both compiled executables should run successfully.

7.6.4 Common Pitfalls and Solutions

It is important to be pay attention to specific items when Hipifying *CUDA* source code:

- Hipify tools successfully translate supported *CUDA* API function calls and data types. However, at the time of writing this book, *HIP* did not support all *CUDA* functions. Some APIs are supported only experimentally, and some are not supported at all. To see the list, please refer to [8].

- In terms of kernel-side functionality, warp-level shuffle sync functions, which were recently introduced in *CUDA* are not currently supported in *HIP*. Programmers must carefully examine these functions and replace them with *HIP*-supported warp shuffle versions.

- Many *CUDA* codebases rely on calculating offsets and operations using *warp_id*. The wavefront size is 32 on *CUDA* devices. However, on AMD GPUs (non-RDNA), the wavefront size is 64. Thus, any code relying on a wavefront size of 32 for correct execution must be manually updated. In the *CUDA* kernel code, the *warpSize* variable is used, versus keepng the *warpSize* a constant value of 32. When converted to *HIP*, the *warpSize* variable is automatically translated to the correct specific wavefront value.

- Some NVIDIA GPU-specific APIs do not map to AMD GPU hardware, and they probably never will. The positive aspect is that there are few examples to be concerned about.

7.7   Conclusion

In this chapter, we examined important tools provided by *ROCm*. First, we discussed *ROCmInfo*, which is used to obtain detailed information about the ROCm stack and the hardware configuration of the system. The second tool was the *ROCm SMI*, which provides a simple command-line utility for controlling the GPU cores, memory clocks, power management, temperature, and utilization. The programmer can embed this *SMI* function directly into their application. *ROCm* also provides the easy-to-use *ROCm-SMI-Lib* function. We also introduced the *ROCm* debugger, *rocgdb*, which allows programmers to step through a GPU kernel line-by-line for debugging purposes. We also covered *rocTracer*, which can provide performance measurements of the application, and the use of *rocProf* for obtaining detailed profiles using the GPU's hardware performance counters was shown. This information is vital for tuning GPU performance. Later in this book, we use this tool for additional performance analyses. Finally, we looked at converting CUDA code to HIP using the Hipify tools provided with ROCm. We also discussed common pitfalls and solutions when porting CUDA code to HIP. Programmers should always check the latest ROCm documentation to know which APIs and features are supported and to make the porting process less error-prone. AMD's continued collaboration with research institutions has resulted in a rich ecosystem of new open-source performance analysis and debugging tools, such as the Performane API (*PAPI*, the Tuning and Analyses Utility (*TAU*), and the Lawrence Livermore National Laboratory (LLNL) high-performance computing (HPC) toolkit (*HPCToolkit*), just to name a few. These tools are discussed later later chapters.

Chapter 8

HIP Performance Optimization

In this chapter, we cover a few strategies that can improve the performance of GPU programs. We will use a couple of concrete GPU applications (e.g., image gamma, matrix multiplication) as examples and provide an implementation for each application. We then compare the performance of the implementations, demonstrating the potential improvements of various performance optimization methods.

Before elaborating on the specific methods, it is crucial to address the issue of performance portability in GPUs. Generally, GPUs exhibit limited performance portability. This means a method that performs well on one GPU might not yield similar results on another, owing to architectural differences. Consequently, programmers should not rely solely on a single method. It is advisable to conduct experiments and profiling on the targeted GPU, to select the most effective optimization strategy.

8.1 Highly Parallel Workload – Image Gamma Correction

A GPU typically has thousands of computing cores that run in parallel. These cores are best utilized when each calculates one partition of the output results so that they do not need to communicate with other cores. Such algorithms are often classified as "embarrassingly parallel," as the required programming effort is minimal. In our earlier *vector_add* example (see Chapter 2), we found identified an embarrassingly parallel workload example. In this chapter, we discuss another one: image gamma correction.

| Original | Gamma = 0.4 | Gamma = 0.8 | Gamma = 2.0 | Gamma = 4.0 |

Figure 8.1: Image gamma correction algorithm. A gamma value smaller than one renders the image more brightly, whereas a value greater than one renders a darker image.

Image gamma correction is a common image processing algorithm that adjusts the brightness of an image without changing the content. As shown in Figure 8.1, when we apply a gamma value less than one, the image becomes brighter, whereas a value greater than one darkens it.

Pictures stored on a computer are typically organized using pixels (see Figure 8.2), which are square regions of an image that are each rendered with a single color. For example, the images used in Figure 8.1 and Figure 8.2 have 267 (width) × 267 (height) pixels total. If the image were colored, three values representing red, green and blue (RGB) would be required for each pixel, which represents the brightness. Brightness is coded using an 8-bit integer [0–255], where zero represents the darkest, and 255 represents the brightest. The other key method uses a floating-point number between zero and one. The red brightness values of all pixels comprise the "red channel," and a colored image typically has three channels (RGB).

$$V_{out} = V_{in}^{\gamma}. \tag{8.1}$$

Image gamma correction is an element-wise operation that applies simple floating-point manipulation to all pixels and their channels. As shown in Equation 8.1, the gamma value is applied as a power to the brightness value. A greater-than-one gamma decreases the brightness value. As suggested by the equation, the number of output values matches the number of input values, and the calculation of each output value is independent of the calculation of neighboring values. The

Figure 8.2: Computerized image organized using pixels. A color image usually requires RGB brightness values to represent the final pixel color.

image gamma correction algorithm is embarrassingly parallel; thus, it is suitable for GPUs. Here, we present a simple implementation in Listing 8.1.

Listing 8.1: Image gamma correction application as an embarrassingly parallel algorithm. Each thread is responsible for processing a value in the array of image pixels. The grid size reflects their number.

```
1  #include <hip/hip_runtime.h>
2  __global__ void image_gamma(uint8_t *d_image, float gamma, int num_values
      ) {
3    int idx = threadIdx.x + blockIdx.x * blockDim.x;
4    if (idx < num_values) {
5      d_image[idx] = pow(d_image[idx] / 255.0, gamma) * 255.0;
6    }
7  }
8
9  int main() {
10   int width, height, channels, num_values;
11   uint8_t *data;
12
13   // Load an image from file.
14
15   int blockSize = 256;
```

```
16   int gridSize = (num_values + blockSize - 1) / blockSize;
17
18   float gamma = 4.0;
19   image_gamma<<<gridSize, blockSize>>>(
20     d_image, gamma, num_values);
21
22   hipMemcpy(data, d_image, num_values * sizeof(uint8_t),
23     hipMemcpyDeviceToHost);
24
25   // Save the image to an output file.
26
27   hipFree(d_image);
28   return 0;
29 }
```

To address this GPU programming problem, a programmer must first consider how to map the threads to the input and output elements. For embarrassingly parallel algorithms, the mapping is straightforward, as each thread is responsible for a part of the output channel (a pixel). Therefore, the total number of threads will equal the height × width × number of channels = *num_values*. To calculate the grid size, we divide *num_values* by the block size. If the block size is not a multiple of *num_values*, we can round up to the next integer, as shown in Line 17 of Listing 8.1.

The block size can be between 1 and 1,024, depending on the device limitation. Note that selecting a suitable block size will improve the overall performance. According to Figure 8.3, the performance is best when the block size is a multiple of 64, because AMD GPUs organize groups of 64 threads in a wavefront, which is the smallest resource allocation unit. Otherwise, the CUs will be forced to allocate more resources for each block, resulting in performance degradation. The selection of the block size as a multiple of 64 is likely to optimize embarrassingly parallel applications with AMD GPUs.

8.2   Fixed-Sized Kernels—Image Gamma Correction

In most of the examples presented thus far, each thread calculates a single output element. Upon closer observation, we can see that the overhead is high because for each output element, a thread must be dispatched to the CU to calculate the global ID and check the boundary conditions. To reduce this overhead, we assign more tasks to each thread to amortize the cost of launching threads on the GPU.

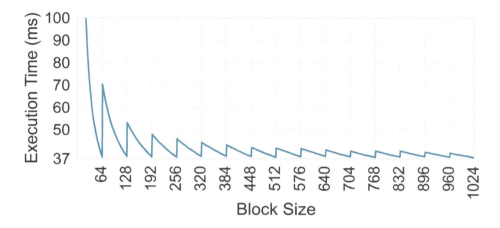

Figure 8.3: Impact of block size on program performance. The image gamma correction execution time reflects an 16,384 × 16,384 RGB image on an MI100 GPU.

Rather than changing the grid size to grow with the input and output image, we can fix the number of workgroups in the kernel and change the amount of work per thread according to the image size. Here, we reimplement the image gamma correction example using a fixed-sized kernel (see Listing 8.2).

This new implementation approximates the previous one but with two minor modifications. First, we move the boundary checking IF statements in the kernel into a FOR loop. This allows each thread to process multiple values and increment the index by the number of threads in each iteration. For example, if we have 640 threads, Thread 0 will process values with Indices 0, 640, 1,280, etc., and Thread 1 will use Indices 1, 641, 1,281, etc. From this change, we can set the number of threads, regardless of the problem size.

Listing 8.2: GPU implementation of the image gamma correction using fixed-sized kernel patterns. The kernel is launched with a predefined size, and each thread is responsible for multiple pixels in the image.

```
#include <hip/hip_runtime.h>

__global__ void image_gamma(uint8_t *d_image, float gamma, int num_values
    ) {
  int global_size = blockDim.x * gridDim.x;
```

```
5   int idx = threadIdx.x + blockIdx.x * blockDim.x;
6   for (; idx < num_values; idx += global_size) {
7     float value = d_image[idx] / 255.0f;
8     value = pow(value, gamma);
9     d_image[idx] = (uint8_t)(value * 255.0f);
10  }
11  }
12
13  int main(int argc, char *argv[]) {
14    int width, height, channels;
15    uint8_t *data;
16
17    // Load an image from file.
18
19    int blockSize = 256;
20    int gridSize = [Grid Size];
21
22    float gamma = 4.0;
23    image_gamma<<<gridSize, blockSize>>>(d_image, gamma, num_values);
24
25    hipMemcpy(data, d_image, num_values * sizeof(uint8_t),
              hipMemcpyDeviceToHost);
26
27    // Save the image to disk.
28
29    return 0;
30  }
```

Next, we must identify the best grid size to use. We did this by conducting a quick experiment that measures the kernel execution times based on its size. The results are shown in Figure 8.4. At a high level, we observe four major trends. First, the performance improves as the number of workgroups increases because when there is a small number of workgroups, only a fraction of the CUs are used. Second, the performance saturates with 1,200 workgroups (4,800 wavefronts), which is the maximum number that an MI100 can handle in parallel (120 CUs × 40 wavefronts = 4, 800). Third, the fastest execution possible with a fixed-sized kernel is 15 ms. Compared with the results shown in here, where the execution time is no less than 37 ms, the fixed-sized kernel implementation improves performance by 2.5×. This is because a fixed-size kernel can reduce the overhead of wavefront dispatching. Finally, a clear zig-zag pattern of execution times appears in Figure 8.4. The sudden increases occur after multiples of 120 CUs. Given 120 workgroups, each CU executes one workgroup in parallel; hence, whey will likely finish at the same time. A few extra workgroups would not fully overlap with the first 120, but they would significantly increase the kernel execution time. This happens because although the last set of remaining workgroups may not be able to entirely utilize the GPU, they still have to do the same amount of work as the first set of workgroups. This effect, which is known as the tail-effect, is more pronounced when we have small grid sizes and should be avoided, if possible. In summary, our experiment suggests that a fixed-sized kernel can be used to optimize an embarrassingly parallel implementation. The best workgroup size should be the smallest that can fill all the CUs of the GPU and should always be a multiple of the CU number.

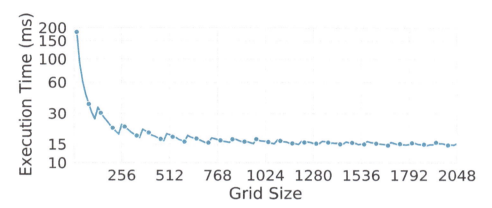

Figure 8.4: Impact of grid size on image gamma program performance. The execution time is measured based on a $16,384 \times 16,384$ RGB image on an MI100 GPU.

8.3   Reduce—Array Sum

Unfortunately, not all GPU applications are embarrassingly parallel. As a simple example, if we need to sum the numbers in an array, we cannot simply allow each thread to process an element. With a typical CPU, a sum is used to accumulate the elements into a list, and the algorithm is highly serial, which is unsuitable for GPU execution. Hence, we must find a parallel solution.

A "reduction" operation can solve this and similar problems by calculating the sum of an array. The idea is to maximize the level of parallelism available while carefully considering device utilization.

The reduction operation is illustrated in Figure 8.5. We divide the program into several rounds, and in the first, we use each thread to sum the pairs of adjacent

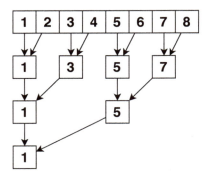

Figure 8.5: Reduction programming pattern.

elements, thus reducing the remaining number of elements by half. In the second round, half of the threads are again reduced. This continues until we have a single sum.

A practical issue with such a reduction pattern is that the threads must communicate with each other. For the example in Figure 8.5, the results calculated by Thread 3 in the second round must be read by Thread 1 in the third round. If we store the data back to the main memory in Thread 3 and load it back to Thread 1 later, the overhead becomes extremely high. Ideally, we want to keep the data in the CU to reduce the data travel distance.

To allow communication among threads, the easiest solution applies the LDS memory, which is a part of the addressable memory located in CUs and is built similar to the L1 cache. Hence, it has extremely low latency and high bandwidth. The data in the LDS memory can be shared by the threads within a block. Therefore, LDS accelerates reduction operations.

We next use the *sum* kernel (see Listing 8.3) to demonstrate how to program using LDS memory.

Listing 8.3: *HIP* program that sums the numbers in an array.

```
1  #include <hip/hip_runtime.h>
2
3  #include <iostream>
4  #include <vector>
5
6  const static int BLOCKSIZE = 256;
7
8  __global__ void reduction_sum(const float* input, float* output, int size
       ) {
```

```
 9    int grid_size = blockDim.x * gridDim.x;
10
11    // Parallel sum phase.
12    int idx = blockIdx.x * blockDim.x + threadIdx.x;
13    float sum = 0;
14    for (int i = idx; i < size; i += grid_size) {
15      sum += input[i];
16    }
17
18    // Store local sum in shared memory.
19    __shared__ float local_sum[BLOCKSIZE];
20    local_sum[threadIdx.x] = sum;
21    __syncthreads();
22
23    // Reduction phase.
24    for (int s = BLOCKSIZE / 2; s > 0; s /= 2) {
25      if (threadIdx.x < s) {
26        local_sum[threadIdx.x] += local_sum[threadIdx.x + s];
27      }
28      __syncthreads();
29    }
30
31    if (threadIdx.x == 0) {
32      output[blockIdx.x] = local_sum[0];
33    }
34  }
35
36  int main() {
37    const static int N = 10485760;
38    const static int num_blocks = 1200;
39
40    std::vector<float> a(N);
41    std::vector<float> b(num_blocks);
42
43    // Randomize a.
44
45    // Allocate device memory.
46    float* d_a;
47    float* d_b;
48    hipMalloc(&d_a, N * sizeof(float));
49    hipMalloc(&d_b, num_blocks * sizeof(float));
50
51    // Copy a to device memory.
52    hipMemcpy(d_a, a.data(), N * sizeof(float), hipMemcpyHostToDevice);
53
54    // Compute the sum of a.
55    reduction_sum<<<num_blocks, BLOCKSIZE>>>(d_a, d_b, N);
56
57    // Copy the result back to host memory.
```

```
58   hipMemcpy(b.data(), d_b, num_blocks * sizeof(float),
         hipMemcpyDeviceToHost);
59
60   // Finalize the sum
61   hipDeviceSynchronize();
62   float sum = 0;
63   for (int i = 0; i < num_blocks; ++i) {
64     sum += b[i];
65   }
66
67   // Verify the result.
68   double expected_sum = 0;
69   for (int i = 0; i < N; ++i) {
70     expected_sum += a[i];
71   }
72   if (abs(sum - expected_sum) > 1e-5 * expected_sum) {
73     printf("Error: sum = %f, expected_sum = %f\n", sum, expected_sum);
74   }
75 }
```

In this example, we use a fixed-sized kernel to implement *sum* kernel. We set the block size to 256 and launch 1,200 blocks (as suggested in Section 8.2). Note that we do not change the number of blocks with the array length.

The *sum* kernel function is divided into two phases: parallel summation and reduction. Each thread sums the specific elements in the list during the parallel summation phase. For example, the first kernel calculates the sum of elements with Indices 0, 307,200, 614,400, etc., because we have $256 \times 1,200 = 307,200$ threads in the kernel according to the code in Listing 8.3. Following parallel summation, we reduce the number of elements to 307,200.

Next, we use the reduction algorithm to sum the remaining elements. The reduction phase requires LDS memory to allow the threads in a block to communicate. In Line 19, we first allocate a buffer in shared memory using the ___**shared**___ prefix. We allocate shared memory buffers for each block. In the example, because we have 256 threads per block, and each thread uses 4-B single precision data, each block requires $256 \times 4 = 1,024B$ of LDS memory. The threads in the block then access the data in the buffer owned by the block.

Reading and writing to LDS is the same as reading and writing global memory, as shown in Line 20. Here, we store the sum calculated by the parallel summation phase into shared memory.

After writing the data into the LDS memory, we must call the ___*syncthreads* function, which is also known as a "barrier." A barrier is used to ensure that all threads in a block finish executing a particular line of code before any thread runs additional operations. Without this function, different wavefronts in a block would fall out of sync. If some threads are still working on Line 20, when others begin using the data of Line 26, the results will become inconsistent. Therefore, LDS memory operations are often used with barriers to ensure proper synchronization.

A common barrier mistake is placing one inside a conditional statement because CUs wait for all wavefronts to arrive at a barrier, but not any specific one. Based on the code in Listing 8.4, one wavefront executes the first IF statement, and the other executes the second. The first wavefront waits at Line 4, and the second waits at Line 9. However, this is not the desired behavior, as synchronization should be enforced at a single line of code. To avoid this, the straightforward solution is to never place a barrier inside a conditional statement.

Listing 8.4: Example of mismatched barrier.

```
1  __global__ void kernel() {
2    if (global_id < 64) {
3      // Do something.
4      __syncthreads();
5    }
6
7    if (64 <= global_id && global_id < 128) {
8      // Do something.
9      __syncthreads();
10   }
11 }
```

Next, in Lines 23–29, we perform the reduction operation until all 256 elements are summed into a single result. Finally, we write the data from shared memory back to global memory using a single thread per block. Then, the 307,200 numbers in the array are summed to produce 1,200 partial sums. Because interblock communication is challenging to implement, we rely on the CPU to sum the last 1,200 numbers, as shown in Lines 62–64 in Listing 8.3.

8.4 Tiling & Reuse – Matrix Multiplication

Matrix multiplication is one of the most important GPU workloads as it supports many computational problems. Recently, with the increased popularity of deep neural networks (DNNs), matrix multiplication has become vital, and it is found in the most computationally-intensive layers (i.e., fully connected and convolutional) of neural networks. In several cases, we want to convert a problem to use matrix multiplications because GPUs are optimized to execute matrix multiplication efficiently. Matrix multiplications are likely to outperform an iterative implementation of the original problem [78].

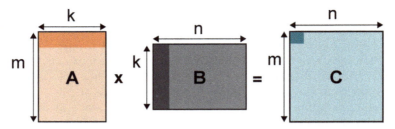

Figure 8.6: Matrix multiplication operation.

As shown in Figure 8.6, a matrix multiplication operation involves three matrices, **A**, **B**, and **C**. Matrices **A** and **B** are input matrices, and matrix **C** is the output matrix. We denote matrix **A** as having m rows and k columns and matrix **B** as having k rows and n columns. Matrix multiplication operations require the number of columns in **A** to equal the number of rows in **B**. Output matrix **C** then inherits m rows and n columns. Each element in **C** is the sum of the k multiplications of each element in the corresponding row of **A** and column of **B**, as formally represented in the equation below:

$$c_{ij} = a_{i1}b_{1j} + a_{i2}b_{2j} + ... + a_{ik}b_{kj} = \sum_{l=1}^{k} a_{il}b_{lj}$$

for $i = 1, ..., n$ and $j = 1, .., m$.

An iterative CPU implementation will apply three nested loops that traverse through m, n, and k. Each iteration will perform single multiplication and accumulation operations. Therefore, theoretically, a total of $2mnk$ operations are required.

A GPU implementation by comparison is embarrassingly parallel. The GPU kernel parallelizes the m and n loops by calculating each element in the output matrix using a thread. Thus, we need a total of $m \times n$ threads, with each traversing a loop of k iterations.

Although the naive implementation produces the correct result, the resulting performance is not ideal. Profiling the kernel execution shows that it reads from the GPU's DRAM several times more often than the combined size of the input matrices. To further explore this issue, we must examine how the threads read the input matrices.

Listing 8.5: Naive *HIP* kernel for matrix multiplication.

```
__global__ void matrix_multiply(float* a, float* b, float* out, size_t m,
                                size_t n, size_t k) {
  int gidx = blockDim.x * blockIdx.x + threadIdx.x;
  int gidy = blockDim.y * blockIdx.y + threadIdx.y;

  if (gidx >= n && gidy >= m) {
    return;
  }

  float sum = 0;
  for (int i = 0; i < k; i++) {
    sum+= a[gidy * k + i] * b[i * n + gidx];
  }

  out[gidy * n + gid_x] = sum;
}
```

As shown in Figure 8.7, each thread in the kernel reads an entire row in matrix **A** and a column in matrix **B**. The same data item must be accessed by multiple threads from different wavefronts. In our naive implementation, all memory reads are handled by the main memory system, and although there are repeated memory references made to the same location, these memory accesses should instead be serviced by the cache. However, given the limited cache space and the large number of threads involved, this places inordinate memory pressure on the caches. Then, as we increase the matrix size, the caches will become incapable of accommodating the data and memory reads, which will quickly push the data to the main memory, causing huge delays.

Ideally, GPU programmers will want to have more control over caches. When data are loaded into the cache, it should be reused by as many threads as possible before being released. In CPU programming, caches are fully transparent to the programmer and are typically not under their control. In contrast, GPUs provide LDS memory, which is effectively a programmable L1 cache.

To use LDS to improve matrix multiplication performance, we apply a common GPU programming technique called "tiling." Tiling methods use all threads from a workgroup to collectively process parts of the data before moving to the next portion of the problem. As shown in Figure 8.8, the first workgroup loads the data of matrices **A** and **B** in the blue tile to the LDS. Then, matrix multiplication is applied to the loaded tile. Next, the wavefronts move to the orange tile, continuing to accumulate multiplication results.

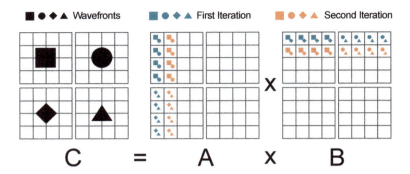

Figure 8.7: Memory access pattern for a naive implementation of a matrix multiplication GPU kernel. The pattern suggests that all data items are loaded multiple times.

Listing 8.6: Tile-based *HIP* kernel for matrix multiplication.

```
1  __global__ void matrix_multiply_tile(float *A, float *B, float *Out,
2                    int m, int n, int k) {
3    __shared__ float subTileA[TileSize][TileSize];
4    __shared__ float subTileB[TileSize][TileSize];
5
6    int bx = blockIdx.x;
7    int by = blockIdx.y;
8    int tx = threadIdx.x;
9    int ty = threadIdx.y;
10
11   int row = by * TileSize + ty;
12   int col = bx * TileSize + tx;
13
14   float sum = 0;
15   for (int i = 0; i < ((k - 1) / TileSize + 1); i++) {
16     int a_index = row * k + i * TileSize + tx;
17     int b_index = (i * TileSize + ty) * n + col;
18
19     if (i * TileSize + tx < k && row < m) {
20       subTileA[ty][tx] = A[a_index];
21     } else {
22       subTileA[ty][tx] = 0.0;
23     }
24
25     if (i * TileSize + ty < k && col < n) {
26       subTileB[ty][tx] = B[b_index];
27     } else {
```

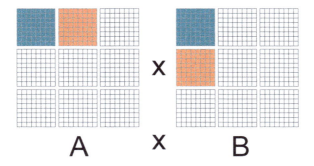

Figure 8.8: Using tiling to accelerate a matrix multiplication GPU kernel.

```
28      subTileB[ty][tx] = 0.0;
29    }
30
31    __syncthreads();
32
33    for (int j = 0; j < TileSize; j++) {
34      if (j + TileSize * i < k) {
35        sum += subTileA[ty][j] * subTileB[j][tx];
36      }
37    }
38
39    __syncthreads();
40  }
41
42  if (row < m && col < n) {
43    Out[row * n + col] = sum;
44  }
45 }
```

The tiling-based kernel implementation is shown in Listing 8.6. The kernel's interface is identical to the native implementation. The only special requirement is that the macro, *TileSize*, must be defined so that it may determine the number of elements in each of the two dimensions to group into a single tile. The workgroup size must match the tile size to help ensure the correctness of the output.

The kernel implementation must also be modified to use two FOR loops, rather than just one. The outer loop addresses memory across the tile, and the inner loop accumulates multiplications. Before the loop starts, we allocate two buffers for the tiles for matrices **A** and **B**: one on Line 3 and the other on Line 4 of Listing 8.6. In each iteration of the outer loop, we load the data from the main memory to the LDS, as shown in Lines 20–26. Here, the complexity of the implementation mainly comes from the index calculation and boundary checking. Next, we use the inner loop in a way similar to the naive implementation to perform multiplication and accumulation. Note that we need barriers before and after the inner loop to guarantee that all data are loaded and used, respectively. Finally, on Line 43, we store the final result in the output matrix.

Tiling is an effective way to reduce DRAM access and improve performance. In our example, when running matrix multiplication on an MI50 GPU with $m = n = k = 8,192$, the naive implementation takes 1.60s. With tiling, the kernel completes the job in 0.76s, achieving a 2.1× speedup.

8.5   Tiling & Coalescing: Matrix Transpose

The matrix transpose is a fundamental linear algebra operation that serves as a building block for many tasks. At a high level, it does not involve calculations; it involves only memory movement. Because GPUs typically have significantly higher memory bandwidth than CPUs, they have a unique advantage when performing matrix transpose operations.

Like the previous examples, the matrix transpose is an embarrassingly parallel implementation (see Listing 8.7), in which each thread is responsible for moving a matrix element.

Listing 8.7: Kernel example of the simple matrix transpose.

```
1  __global__ void matrix_transpose_simple(float *in, float *out,
2                                           int width, int height)
3  int x_index = blockIdx.x * tile_dim + threadIdx.x;
4  int y_index = blockIdx.y * tile_dim + threadIdx.y;
5
6  int in_index = y_index * width + x_index;
7  int out_index = x_index * height + y_index;
8
9  out[out_index] = in[in_index];
```

We profile the kernel performance of a matrix transpose of a 16,384 × 16,384 matrix on an MI50 GPU. Then, using profiler metrics, $TCC\_EA\_WRREQ\_sum$ and $TCC\_EA\_RDREQ\_sum$, we can check the total number of reads and writes to DRAM, respectively. Theoretically, the numbers of reads and writes for the matrix transpose approximate each other as we write all the data that are read from the input matrix. However, the profiling results suggest that the kernel writes significantly more data than those that are read (1,551,894 writes vs. 524,288 reads).

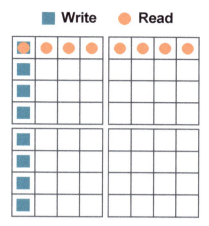

Figure 8.9: Memory access pattern of the naive memory transpose kernel implementation.

To understand why the kernel writes more data, we need to deeply examine the memory access pattern. The matrix transpose kernel is unlikely to be the cause of the repeated memory access problem, as in the matrix multiplication kernel, because each element is only accessed once. Instead, the issue must lie in the address pattern of the associated read and write operations.

In Figure 8.9, we show the data that are accessed by the threads in a kernel. In our implementation, adjacent threads read data horizontally and write them vertically. Because we use row-major matrices, adjacent threads read data from adjacent addresses, but write data using a large address stride (i.e., the difference between two consecutive addresses). As we explained in Section 6.8, if the addresses fall into the same cache line, the GPU can coalesce the memory access to reduce the total transactions. In the matrix transpose kernel, the read transactions are coalescable, whereas the writes are not. Therefore, we naturally observe more DRAM writes than reads.

It is possible to convert non-coalescable memory access to coalescable ones using the LDS. As shown in Figure 8.10, we split the matrix transpose process into two steps. First, we move the data from the input matrix to LDS memory. For this, we read the data horizontally, ensuring that the memory access is coalesced. When the LDS buffer is filled, we then move the data from the LDS to the main memory. In this step, we read the data vertically and write them horizontally. As LDS memory has a significantly higher bandwidth than global memory, reading

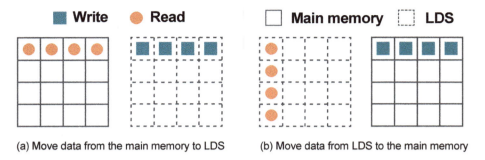

Figure 8.10: Avoiding non-coalescable memory access with LDS.

them horizontally and vertically does not impact overall performance. However, we write the data horizontally so that the writes to the main memory can also be coalesced. Thus, we use the LDS as an intermediate data transfer buffer between the input and output matrices, allowing us to make both read and write operations coalescable.

Listing 8.8: Kernel example for the LDS matrix transpose.

```
1  __global__ void matrix_transpose_lds(float *in, float *out,
2                                        int width, int height) {
3    __shared__ float tile[tile_dim][tile_dim];
4
5    int x_tile_index = blockIdx.x * tile_dim;
6    int y_tile_index = blockIdx.y * tile_dim;
7
8    int in_index = (y_tile_index + threadIdx.y) * width +
9                   (x_tile_index + threadIdx.x);
10   int out_index = (x_tile_index + threadIdx.y) * height +
11                   (y_tile_index + threadIdx.x);
12
13   tile[threadIdx.y][threadIdx.x] = in[in_index];
14
15   __syncthreads();
16
17   out[out_index] = tile[threadIdx.x][threadIdx.y];
18 }
```

8.6　Conclusion

In this chapter, we used a variety of applications to demonstrate important kernel design considerations that optimize GPU program performance. Starting with simple workloads (e.g., image gamma correction), we discussed how to organize embarrassingly parallel GPU workloads using both fixed per-thread workloads and fixed kernel-size solutions. These are great examples of the performance impact of selecting the best block size for kernel implementation.

Second, we focused on optimizing the kernels to better fit the nature of GPU memory systems, especially LDS memory. By creatively using the LDS memory, we can improve ALU utilization (e.g., array summation), reduce memory access (e.g., matrix multiplication), and enable memory coalescing (e.g., matrix transpose operation).

Chapter 9

ROCm Libraries

Chapters 2, 6, 5, and 4 focused on creating functional and high-performing programs for AMD GPUs using the *HIP* programming language. In this chapter, we introduce commonly used first-party libraries provided by the *ROCm* platform. Integrating these libraries can save precious development time, while helping non-experts leverage a GPU's power more quickly.

A small number of algorithms/applications dominate GPU execution cycles. Matrix multiplication operations are the most common, followed by linear algebra operations. Rewriting these operations for each application leads to unnecessary repetition and wastes programmer time. Thus, the *HIP* libraries provide configuration-managed code reuse that saves time and reduces the amount of debugging required.

Generally, GPU programming is more challenging than CPU programming. The large number of GPU kernel threads, for example, requires programmers to consider collective thread behaviors rather than serial ones. The high degree of concurrency of GPU programs also makes debugging more challenging. Thus, improving GPU program performance requires a deep understanding of GPU hardware. Non-expert GPU programmers often struggle when writing and tuning GPU programs. Even experienced programmers have difficulty "squeezing every drop" of performance from a GPU. *HIP* provides highly optimized libraries for frequently used algorithms to improve programmer productivity. These libraries can also be called within programs without being concerned about implementation details.

This chapter introduces a few widely used *HIP* libraries, including *rocBLAS*, *rocSPARSE*, *rocFFT*, and *rocRAND*. Generally, there is a corresponding *HIP* library prefixed with "hip" for every *ROCm* library prefixed with "roc"). The *ROCm* libraries provide high-performance implementations for the *ROCm* platform. In contrast, the *HIP* libraries serve as a thin compatibility layer that invokes corresponding *ROCm* or *CUDA* libraries on AMD or NVIDIA GPU platforms, respectively. In this chapter, we explain how to use the *ROCm* libraries. Readers can use *HIP* libraries with minor modifications to the code by referring to `https://docs.amd.com/category/libraries`. Additionally, readers can find additional library documentation using the link above.

9.1   *rocBLAS*

Linear algebra algorithms benefit greatly from parallel GPU computing. *HIP* provides the *rocBLAS* library that implements the most commonly used linear algebra algorithms. This library follows the principles used in legacy basic linear algebra subprogram (*BLAS*) libraries (these libraries were first released as a Fortran library in 1979.) Thus, programmers can easily find one-to-one mappings between *BLAS* and *rocBLAS* APIs. A major advantage of the *HIP* compatibility for GPU programmers is that they can leverage their existing programming skillsets to create hardware-agnostic software products.

9.1.1   Using *rocBLAS*

The code in Listing 9.1 demonstrates the use of one of the simplest *rocBLAS* functions, *rocblas_sswap*. This function simply swaps the contents of two vectors stored in buffers **dx** and **dy**.

Listing 9.1: *rocBLAS* library example. For simplicity, error handling code is omitted.

```
1  #include <hip/hip_runtime.h>
2  #include <rocblas.h>
3  #include <vector>
4
5  int main() {
6      rocblas_int n = [vec_size]; // Replace [vec_size] with an integer.
7      float *dx, *dy;
8      std::vector<float> hx(n);
9      std::vector<float> hy(n);
10
11     // Initialize host memory. Omitted.
12
13     // Allocate device memory.
```

```
14    hipMalloc(&dx, n * sizeof(float));
15    hipMalloc(&dy, n * sizeof(float));
16
17    // Copy host memory to device.
18    rocblas_set_vector(n, sizeof(float),
19        hx.data(), 1, dx, 1);
20    rocblas_set_vector(n, sizeof(float),
21        hy.data(), 1, dy, 1);
22
23    // Create rocBLAS handle.
24    rocblas_handle handle;
25    rocblas_create_handle(&handle);
26
27    // Call the swap function. The "s" before "swap"
28    // indicates the function being called works with
29    // single-precision data.
30    rocblas_sswap(handle, n, dx, 1, dy, 1);
31
32    // Copy the data back from the GPU memory.
33    rocblas_get_vector(n, sizeof(float),
34        dx, 1, hx.data(), 1);
35    rocblas_get_vector(n, sizeof(float),
36        dy, 1, hy.data(), 1);
37
38    // Release resources.
39    hipFree(dx);
40    hipFree(dy);
41    rocblas_destroy_handle(handle);
42
43    return 0;
44 }
```

Although the example is straightforward, there are a few points worth noting.

First, programs using the *rocBLAS* library must include the **rocblas.h** header. On a system with a standard *ROCm* installation, the header file can be found in the */opt/rocm/include* or */opt/rocm/rocblas/include* directory/folder. Additionally, programs that use *rocBLAS* must also include the **hip/hip_runtime.h** header, because the program still requires regular *HIP* APIs to function properly.

Second, *rocBLAS* works on regular *HIP*-allocated GPU buffers. For memory management, we continue to rely on the basic *HIP* APIs, such as *hipMalloc* and *hipFree*.

Third, *rocBLAS* has a set of helper functions, including *rocblas_set_vector*, *rocblas_get_vector*, *rocblas_set_matrix*, and *rocblas_get_matrix*, for data transfers between CPU and GPU. Furthermore, the *rocblas_set_vector* and *rocblas_get_vector* functions require two additional integer arguments. In the example shown in Listing 9.1, we always assign a value of one to these arguments as they are used to describe the layout of the memory that stores the data. Specifically, the arguments in the two functions represent the stride of the data structure that we need to copy. If Lines 18 and 19 are rewritten, as in Listing 9.2, the helper function will copy every other value from the **hx** vector and densely place the values in the **dx** vector.

Listing 9.2: Example of using a different value.

```
1  // This line is equivalent to the following.
2  //      dx[0] = hx[0];
3  //      dx[1] = hx[2];
4  //      dx[2] = hx[4];
5  //      ...
6  rocblas_set_vector(n, sizeof(float),
7                     hx.data(), 2, dx, 1);
```

Fourth, although we omitted the error-handling code in Listing 9.1, product-ready code that uses *rocBLAS* should handle errors properly. Most *rocBLAS* functions return a **rocblas_status** code. Thus, the program will check whether the returned value states **rocblas_status_success**. Other return values indicate improper execution; hence, the error code should be carefully checked. A simple example of handling *rocBLAS* is shown in Listing 9.3.

Listing 9.3: Example of handling *rocBLAS* API errors.

```
1  rocblas_status status;
2  status = rocblas_set_vector(n, sizeof(float),
3                     hx.data(), 1, dx, 1);
4  if  (status != rocblas_status_success) {
5      printf("Failed to set vector.\n");
6      exit(-1);
7  }
```

Fifth, a handle is required when calling most *rocBLAS* functions, as it stores contextual information shared by multiple *rocBLAS* function calls. Apart from simple helper functions, a handle must be created before the function is called. This activity is shown in Line 25 of Listing 9.1. The handle must be freed after using the *rocBLAS* functions to release the occupied resources.

Finally, as seen in Line 30 of Listing 9.1, we must invoke *rocBLAS* functions to perform linear algebra operations. Its library provides a wide range of linear algebra functions, which we introduce in Section 9.1.2.

9.1.2 *rocBLAS* functions

rocBLAS functions are organized into three levels. The first contains functions that perform vector–vector operations. The second and third provide matrix–vector and matrix–matrix operations, respectively.

The different *rocBLAS* functions include variations designed to operate on different types of data, which can be inferred from the function name. Generally, a *rocBLAS* function is named using the format, **rocblas_[type][operation]**. For example, in **rocblas_sswap**, **s** denotes the data type, and **swap** denotes the operation name. The full list of supported data types is provided in Table 9.1.

Table 9.1: Data types supported by *rocBLAS*.

Letter	Data Type
s	Single-Precision Floating-Point Numbers
d	Double-Precision Floating-Point Numbers
h	Half-Precision Floating-Point Numbers (16 bits per number)
b	16-bit Brain floating-Point Number [40]
c	Single-Precision Complex Numbers (both real and imaginary parts are single-precision)
z	Double-Precision Complex Numbers (both real and imaginary parts are double-precision floating-point numbers)

rocBLAS also supports batched and strided-batched operations. A batched linear algebra operation handles multiple input elements using a single function call. Batched functions are suffixed with **_batched** in the *rocBLAS* function name. For example, *rocblas_sdot_batched* is the batched version of the regular *rocblas_sdot* function, and it calculates the dot product of multiple vector pairs. The output is a vector instead of a scalar value, which is the output type of the regular version of the function.

Strided-batched operations allow functions to perform operations on a subset of the input batch. For example, if the batch size is five, and the stride is two, the function will process the 0th, 2nd, and 4th elements of the input array. These operations add a "strided_batched" suffix to the *rocBLAS* function name.

9.1.3 Asynchronous execution

Earlier, we discussed that GPU kernels are launched as streams during execution – *rocBLAS* kernels are no exception. By default, *rocBLAS* kernels are launched asynchronously to the default NULL stream. Therefore, a programmer should not assume that the results will be ready immediately after the function returns. Instead, proper synchronization using *HIP* APIs, such as *hipDeviceSynchronize* or *hipStreamSynchronize* is required. The benefits of using the default asynchronous execution model is the simplicity of the programming provided, which overlaps CPU execution with *rocBLAS* operations (see Listing 9.4).

Listing 9.4: Overlapped *rocBLAS* execution with CPU execution.

```
1 rocblas_sgemm(arguments...);
2 // CPU work that overlaps with the rocblas_sgemm call.
3 hipDeviceSynchronize();
```

It is also possible to use streams to control API call concurrency. The handle keeps track of the stream using *rocBLAS* API calls. Notably, using multiple streams allows the runtime, driver, and hardware to control overlapped executions. An example is shown in Listing 9.5. The API calls on Lines 10 and 13 (e.g., **rocblas_sgemm**) can execute concurrently if the GPU has sufficient resources.

Listing 9.5: Multi-device and multi-stream *rocBLAS* execution.

```
1  hipStream_t stream1, stream2;
2  rocblas_handle handle;
3
4  hipStreamCreate(&stream1);
5  hipStreamCreate(&stream2);
6
7  rocblas_create_handle(&handle);
8
9  rocblas_set_stream(stream1);
10 // API call 1 that uses stream1
11
12 rocblas_set_stream(stream2);
13 // API call 2 that uses stream2
14
15 hipStreamSynchronize(stream1);
16 hipStreamSynchronize(stream2);
17
18 // Destroy the streams and the handle.
```

9.1.4 *rocBLAS* on MI100

CDNA/CDNA2 GPUs are equipped with matrix units that significantly accelerate matrix multiplication operations. The *rocBLAS* implementations automatically utilize matrix units whenever possible, without the need to turn the matrix unit on or off explicitly.

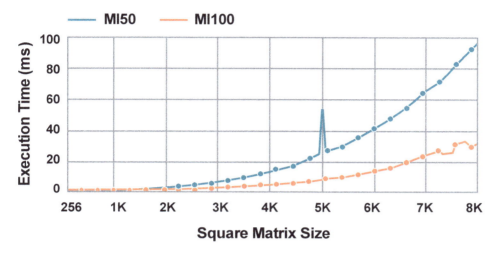

Figure 9.1: Performance comparison of MI100 and MI50.

To understand the performance improvements provided by the matrix unit, we run the *rocBLAS* single-precision general matrix multiplication (SGEMM) API on both the MI100 and MI50s GPUs (see Figure 9.1). Considering the case in which we multiply an 8,192×8,192 matrix with another of the same size, the theoretical number of operations required is $2 \times 8,192 \times 8,192 \times 8,192 \approx 1.1T$. An MI50 GPU computes multiplication in 95.7 ms, achieving a 10.45 TFLOPS effective computing throughput, compared with the theoretical MI50 throughput of 13.41 TFLOPS. Thus, the MI50 GPU already achieves extremely high (81%) utilization. However, the MI100 GPU is 3.14× faster and completes the same multiplication in 30.4 ms. Execution on the MI100 achieves an effective throughput of 32.84 TFLOPS, which is 149% of the theoretical computing throughput, if we only consider SIMD-unit execution. This seemingly impossible utilization is only achievable if the matrix unit is used. We can clearly see that doing so improves the overall performance of linear algebra operations.

9.1.5   Porting from the legacy *BLAS* library

At a high level, there is a one-to-one mapping between legacy *BLAS* library APIs and *rocBLAS* APIs. The mapping is straightforward, as the API names remain the same. The only difference is that *rocBLAS* uses lowercase API names and prefixes each with *rocblas_* entry. Additionally, the argument list requires minor modifications. The *rocBLAS* APIs require the **rocblas_handle** as the first argument of each function. If the legacy API returns a value, it must be passed to a function by referencing the last argument so that the *rocBLAS* API can return **rocblas_status**.

To maintain consistency between the *rocBLAS* and the legacy *BLAS* APIs, *rocBLAS* assumes that the matrices are one-based (i.e., indices begin at one instead of zero) and are column-major. However, this design differs from the *C* programming convention, in which matrix indices are typically zero-based and row-major. Thus, care must be taken when processing matrices created in *C/C++*.

9.2   *rocSPARSE*

Real-world data is sparse, consisting primarily of zero values. Thus, if we use a matrix to represent Facebook user friendship statuses, most elements will be empty as most pairs of users are not friends. The percentage of zeros in the matrix is called "sparsity." A 90% sparsity (10% density) means that the 90% of the elements are zeros. As sparse matrices are widely used to represent real-world data, efficient processing is critical. The uniqueness of sparse matrices suggests that we should not use dense matrix algorithms to process them.

Performing sparse linear algebra operations (e.g., general matrix multiplication (GEMM), using the regular methods provided by *rocBLAS* can be inefficient in terms of memory management and computation. Storing sparse matrices as dense matrices creates vast swaths of wasted memory. Thus, compression is needed. A typical GPU can only perform dense GEMM operations comprising tens-of-thousands of elements per axis. However, real-world sparse datasets can easily contain millions of elements per axis. Hence, GPU memories will be quickly filled if these data are stored in a dense format. Moreover, calculations against zeros are wasteful, as the answer will always be zero. Moreover, the GPU memory hierarchy will consistently transfer large numbers of zeros to the core, which wastes memory bandwidth and cache space.

The *rocSPARSE* and *rocBLAS* libraries provide efficient linear algebra operations using sparse vectors and matrices. Both of these libraries were originally developed for CPUs. In this section, we introduce sparse data representations, followed by *rocSPARSE*-supported linear algebra operations.

9.2.1 Sparse data representation

There are several ways to represent sparse matrices. Each presents advantages and disadvantages, depending on the scenario. Generally, they record the content of matrices using scalar values and vectors containing all the information from the original matrices (i.e., lossless compression). Therefore, converting from a sparse representation to a dense one is possible. Here, we introduce a few commonly used sparse data representations.

The coordinate (COO) representation records both non-zero values and their coordinates. A COO matrix requires three scalar numbers: **m** (i.e., the number of rows), **n** (i.e., the number of columns), and **nnz** (i.e., the number of non-zero elements). The matrix contents are stored as three vectors. The first, **coo_val** includes all non-zero values, sorted by their row and column indices. For each value, the x- and y-coordinates are stored in **coo_col_ind** and **coo_row_ind** vectors, respectively.

For example, the matrix,

$$A = \begin{pmatrix} 1.0 & 2.0 & 0.0 & 3.0 & 0.0 \\ 0.0 & 4.0 & 5.0 & 0.0 & 0.0 \\ 6.0 & 0.0 & 0.0 & 7.0 & 8.0 \end{pmatrix}, \tag{9.1}$$

should be encoded as

$$\begin{aligned} & m = 3, n = 5, nnz = 8 \\ & coo\_val = [1.0, 2.0, 3.0, 4.0, 5.0, 6.0, 7.0, 8.0] \\ & coo\_row\_ind = [0, 0, 0, 1, 1, 2, 2, 2] \\ & coo\_col\_ind = [0, 1, 3, 1, 2, 0, 3, 4] \end{aligned} \tag{9.2}$$

The compressed sparse row (CSR) is efficient in several scenarios, although the COO usually wins in its simplicity. However, the COO takes approximately $3 \times nnz$ to store the data, which may not be efficient enough.

Like COO, CSR requires the same three scalar values, the same non-zero vector, and the same column index vector. The only difference is the row index vector.

CSR uses the **csr_row_ptr** vector to record the offsets in the **csr_val** vector for the first element of each row. The first element in the **csr_row_ptr** vector must be zero because it is also the first element of **csr_val**. If the first row of the matrix has three non-zero elements, the second element in the x will be a three, as the first element on the second row will have an index of three in **csr_val**. If there is no non-zero element in a row, we still need to add the row number to **csr_row_ptr**. In this case, the value will be the index of the next number in **csr_row_ptr**.

Using the same example as above, we should encode the matrix,

$$A = \begin{pmatrix} 1.0 & 2.0 & 0.0 & 3.0 & 0.0 \\ 0.0 & 4.0 & 5.0 & 0.0 & 0.0 \\ 0.0 & 0.0 & 0.0 & 0.0 & 0.0 \\ 6.0 & 0.0 & 0.0 & 7.0 & 8.0 \end{pmatrix}, \tag{9.3}$$

using the CSR representation,

$$\begin{aligned} m &= 4, n = 5, nnz = 8 \\ csr\_val &= [1.0, 2.0, 3.0, 4.0, 5.0, 6.0, 7.0, 8.0] \\ csr\_row\_ptr &= [0, 3, 3, 5, 8] \\ csr\_col\_ind &= [0, 1, 3, 1, 2, 0, 3, 4] \end{aligned} \tag{9.4}$$

The CSR format is suitable for row-by-row processing. Using the example above, if a thread needs to process Row 1, the thread first looks into the **csr_row_ptr** vector for Index 1 (a value of three) and Index 2 (a value of five). The number of non-zero elements in Row 1 can then be easily calculated by subtracting Index 1 from Index 2 ($5 - 3 = 2$). To make this process work on all rows (the last row is special), the **nnz** value must be added to the end of **csr_row_ptr** as an extra element. That is why matrix **A** in the example above has four rows, whereas **csr_row_ptr** includes five numbers. Additionally, Index 1 from **csr_row_ptr** serves as the offsets in **csr_val** and **csr_col_ind** to locate the element's value and column index.

The CSR storage requirement is approximately $2 \times nnz \times m$, which is more efficient than the COO's $3 \times nnz$ space requirement when $m < nnz$. This condition holds for most "not-that-sparse" matrices. However, in extremely sparse cases, COO is more efficient.

The *rocSPARSE* library also supports less-commonly used sparse representations. Interested readers are referred to the official *rocSPARSE* documentation for details.

9.2.2   *rocSPARSE* functions

Like *rocBLAS*, *rocSPARSE* functions are divided into three levels. Level 1 functions describe operations between sparse and dense vectors. Level 2 describes operations between a sparse matrix and a dense vector. Finally, Level 3 describes operations between sparse and dense matrices. Additionally, *rocSPARSE* supports four data types (i.e., single-precision, double-precision, single-precision complex, and double-precision complex), prefixed with **s**, **d**, **c**, **z**, respectively.

Listing 9.6: Example matrix multiplication with *rocSPARSE*. One matrix is represented in CSR and the other as a dense matrix. Error handling and memory-releasing code is ignored for brevity.

```
1  rocsparse_handle handle;
2  rocsparse_mat_descr descr;
3  float alpha, beta;
4  float *dVal;
5  int *dRowPtr, *dColInd;
6
7  rocsparse_create_handle(&handle)
8  rocsparse_create_mat_descr(&descr);
9
10 alpha = 1.0;
11 beta = 0.0;
12
13 // Allocate and fill in dVal, dRowPtr, dColInd.
14
15 rocsparse_scsrmm(
16     handle,
17     rocsparse_operation_none,
18     rocsparse_operation_transpose,
19     size, size, size,
20     nnz, &alpha, descr, dVal, dRowPtr, dColInd,
21     dB, size,
22     &beta, dC, size);
23 hipDeviceSynchronize()
```

We provide an example of using the *rocSPARSE* APIs in Listing 9.6. Like *rocBLAS*, *rocSPARSE* requires a handle object to track the execution context. Note that the handle differs from a *rocBLAS* handle and cannot be mixed if both libraries must be invoked. Each handle works for one device. Thus, using multiple devices (even non-concurrently) requires creating a handle for each device. Additionally, a descriptor (i.e., **descr**, declared on Line 2 of Listing 9.6) is needed to inform the API about the sparse matrix' organization (e.g., zero- or one-based indexing, column- or row-major). By default, the descriptor is set to a zero-base as row-major; hence, there is no need to change it in our example.

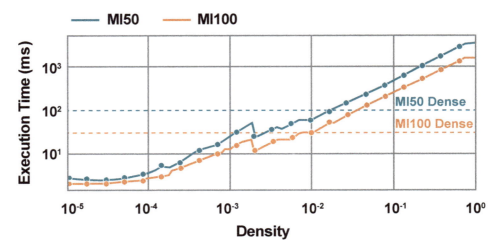

Figure 9.2: Performance benefits of using *rocSPARSE*. This example uses CSR to represent a sparse matrix. The results may differ if another format is used.

The choice to use *rocBLAS* or *rocSPARSE* depends on the problem and the underlying hardware. Generally, *rocSPARSE* outperforms *rocBLAS* on highly sparse matrices. To illustrate the comparison, we multiply an 8,192 × 8,192 matrix with another of the same size using both *rocBLAS* and *rocSPARSE* (see Figure 9.2). We vary the density of the first matrix to see how the change impacts performance. Because the performance of *rocBLAS* is data-independent, we can visualize its performance as horizontal lines. From Figure 9.2, we can see that as the density decreases, the execution time of *rocSPARSE* also decreases, because the actual calculation and data movement decrease with fewer non-zero elements in the matrix. The trend only slows when the density is lower than 1‰. Comparing the performances of dense and sparse matrix multiplications allows us to observe that, when the density is smaller than 5 and 1%, *rocSPARSE* outperforms *rocBLAS* on the MI50 and MI100 GPUs, respectively.

9.3 *rocFFT*

The discrete Fourier transform (DFT) refers to a common digital signal processing operation that converts signals from time to frequency domains. DFT decomposes the signals into amplitudes and phases at different frequencies. The decomposed form then facilitates the analysis of how a filter or processing system alters the signal at different frequencies. Additionally, DFT is commonly used as the first step in convolutional operations, which are essential to CNNs. Convolutions in the time domain are equivalent to multiplications in the frequency domain, and multiplication is far less computationally complex.

A typical DFT formula is shown in Equation 9.5, where x is the input data, $\tilde{x}$ is the output, the $\pm$ sign represents the conversion directions, and $+$ and $-$ indicate the direction of conversion to the frequency or time domains, respectively. The DFT operation can be generalized to 2D and 3D data, as shown in Equation 9.6 and Equation 9.7, respectively. These equations suggest that a direct DFT algorithm has a computational complexity of $O(N^2)$. The outer loop calculates each output element, and the inner loop traverses it all.

$$\tilde{x}_j = \sum_{k=0}^{n-1} x_k exp(\pm i \frac{2\pi jk}{n}) \text{ for } j = 0, 1, ..., n-1, \tag{9.5}$$

$$\tilde{x}_{jk} = \sum_{q=0}^{m-1}\sum_{r=0}^{n-1} x_{rq} exp(\pm i\frac{2\pi jr}{n})exp(\pm i\frac{2\pi kq}{m}) \tag{9.6}$$
$$\text{for } j = 0, 1, ..., n-1 \text{ and } k = 0, 1, ..., m-1,$$

$$\tilde{x}_{jkl} = \sum_{s=0}^{p-1}\sum_{q=0}^{m-1}\sum_{r=0}^{n-1} x_{rqs} exp(\pm i\frac{2\pi jr}{n})exp(\pm i\frac{2\pi kq}{m})exp(\pm i\frac{2\pi ls}{p})$$
$$\text{for } j = 0, 1, ..., n-1 \tag{9.7}$$
$$\text{and } k = 0, 1, ..., m-1$$
$$\text{and } l = 0, 1, ..., p-1.$$

The fast Fourier transform (FFT) is not an algorithm per se; it describes a set of algorithms that perform DFT operations at $O(N \log N)$ complexity, which is far simpler than the $O(N^2)$ complexity of the direct DFT method. FFT algorithmic details are outside the scope of this book, but note that they all produce the exact same output as the direct DFT algorithm. The *rocFFT* function hides the details and provides a simple interface to the programmer for efficient DFT operations.

9.3.1 *rocFFT* workflow

In Listing 9.7, signal processing with *rocFFT* requires the following steps:

First, the *rocfft_setup* function is invoked to initialize the library. Symmetrically, by the end of the program, the *rocfft_cleanup* function must also be called using the *rocfft_setup* function.

Second, an FFT execution plan is required as it describes the key information about the operation's execution data dimensions, layout, and type (e.g., real, complex, single-, or double-precision). We will discuss the FFT plan in more detail shortly. The plan must be destroyed to free resources after the FFT operation is completed.

Third, the buffers required by the FFT algorithm must be provided externally. The *rocFFT* library provides a *rocfft_plan_get_work_buffer_size* function that retrieves the size of the required buffer according to the execution plan. The buffer must be allocated using the *hipMalloc* API and configured using the *rocfft_execution_info_set_work_buffer* API.

Finally, the operation is executed by calling the *rocfft_execute* API. Like other functions that invoke GPU kernels, *rocfft_execute* executes asynchronously and returns prior to operation completion. Hence, before retrieving the results, explicit synchronization via *hipDeviceSynchronize* is required.

Listing 9.7: Example of using the *rocFFT* library.

```
 1  rocfft_setup();
 2
 3  size_t N = 16;
 4  size_t Nbytes = N * sizeof(float2);
 5
 6  // Create \textit{HIP} device buffer
 7  float2 *x;
 8  hipMalloc(&x, Nbytes);
 9
10  // Initialize data
11  std::vector<float2> cx(N);
12  for (size_t i = 0; i < N; i++) {
13      cx[i].x = 1;
14      cx[i].y = -1;
15  }
16
17  // Copy data to device
18  hipMemcpy(x, cx.data(), Nbytes, hipMemcpyHostToDevice);
19
20  // Create rocFFT plan
21  rocfft_plan plan = nullptr;
22  size_t length = N;
23  rocfft_plan_create(&plan,
24      rocfft_placement_inplace,
25      rocfft_transform_type_complex_forward,
```

```
26      rocfft_precision_single,
27      1, &length, 1, nullptr);
28
29  // Check if the plan requires a work buffer
30  size_t work_buf_size = 0;
31  rocfft_plan_get_work_buffer_size(plan, &work_buf_size);
32  void* work_buf = nullptr;
33  rocfft_execution_info info = nullptr;
34  if(work_buf_size) {
35      rocfft_execution_info_create(&info);
36      hipMalloc(&work_buf, work_buf_size);
37      rocfft_execution_info_set_work_buffer(info, work_buf, work_buf_size);
38  }
39
40  // Execute plan
41  rocfft_execute(plan, (void**) &x, nullptr, info);
42
43  // Wait for execution to finish
44  hipDeviceSynchronize();
45
46  // Clean up work buffer
47  if(work_buf_size) {
48      hipFree(work_buf);
49      rocfft_execution_info_destroy(info);
50  }
51
52
53  // Use the results (skipped).
54
55  // Clean up
56  rocfft_plan_destroy(plan);
57  rocfft_cleanup();
```

9.3.2 FFT Execution Plan

From the example above, we can see that the FFT execution plan is key to using the *rocFFT* library as it provides detailed information on the pending operation. Hence, we must describe how to create an FFT plan.

For most cases, the *rocfft_plan_create* API is invoked for plan creation. The first argument is the pointer to the plan. The second describes the placement of results, which can either be **inplace** (i.e., the execution output overwrites the input buffer) or **notinplace** (the output is stored in another buffer). The third argument, **transform_type**, specifies whether the FFT is forward (i.e., time to frequency domain) or inverse (i.e., frequency to time domain), and the data is real or complex. All four permutations, with their respective data types, are possible.

The fourth argument is the floating-point precision level (e.g., single or double) of the data.

The four arguments introduced above describe the FFT operation, and the others describe the data. The following two parameters represent the shape of the data, with the fifth describing the number of dimensions (1, 2, or 3) and the sixth describing the dimension sizes. The input and output data of an FFT operation are always the same size; thus, one group of size parameters is sufficient to describe both the input and output data. The *number_of_transforms* parameter allows for a single invocation of the *rocfft_execution* API to apply the same FFT conversion on multiple groups of data (i.e., batched operations). Finally, the description parameter is typically NULL unless an unusual data layout is needed.

Listing 9.8: Signature of the *rocfft_plan_create* function.

```
1  rocfft_status rocfft_plan_create(
2      rocfft_plan *plan,
3      rocfft_result_placement placement,
4      rocfft_transform_type transform_type,
5      rocfft_precision precision,
6      size_t dimensions,
7      const size_t *lengths,
8      size_t number_of_transforms,
9      const rocfft_plan_description description
10 )
```

9.4 *rocRAND*

Random number generation is essential for several HPC applications. Random numbers are used to inhibit deterministic and predictable outcomes; therefore, they are widely applied to encryption, identification, and privacy preservation functions. This step is a fundamental step in Monte Carlo simulations, as they investigate the impact of stochastic variables on a given system.

The *rocRAND* library provides highly efficient random number generation in large quantities. Listing 9.9 provides an example of the use of *rocRAND*. First, a *rocRAND* generator is created, then a seed is set, and the random number generation function is finally invoked.

Listing 9.9: A *rocRAND* function that generates 1M pseudo-random numbers.

```
1  #include <hip/hip_runtime.h>
2  #include <rocrand.h>
3  #include <stdio.h>
```

```
 4  #include <time.h>
 5
 6  int main() {
 7    size_t n = 1048576;
 8
 9    rocrand_generator gen;
10    float *d_rand;
11
12    hipMalloc((void **)&d_rand, n * sizeof(float));
13
14    // Step 1: Create a random number generator.
15    rocrand_create_generator(&gen, ROCRAND_RNG_PSEUDO_DEFAULT);
16
17    // Step 2: Set a seed.
18    rocrand_set_seed(gen, time(NULL));
19
20    // Step 3: Generate the random numbers.
21    rocrand_generate_uniform(gen, d_rand, n);
22
23    // Use the generated random numbers.
24
25    rocrand_destroy_generator(gen);
26    hipFree(d_rand);
27    return 0;
28  }
```

The *rocrand_generate_uniform* function is among the simplest random number generator variants provided by *rocRAND*. Programmers can call different functions based on the data types involved. *rocRAND* supports chars (8-bit unsigned integers), shorts (16-bit unsigned integers), 32-bit unsigned integers, half-precision floating-point numbers, single-precision floating-point numbers, and double-precision floating-point numbers. The function also supports random number generation following different distribution functions, including uniform, normal, log-normal, and Poisson. The mapping between distributions and data types is listed in 9.2.

These APIs generate pseudo-random numbers, in which each new one is independently generated from the previous one. Hence, some generated numbers may appear numerically close to previous ones. Numerically close random numbers may be undesirable for simulations, as experimenters normally seek diverse or stochastic results. In certain cases, the parameter space should be explored in a more structured fashion; hence, we would need the generated random numbers to spread out and fill the space quickly. This type of number generation is "quasi"-random. A comparison between pseudo- and quasi-random numbers is shown in Figure 9.3.

Table 9.2: *rocRAND* functions for different distribution functions and data types.

API	Data Type	Distribution	Range
rocrand_generate	uint32	Uniform	$[0, 2^{32})$
rocrand_generate_char	uint8	Uniform	$[0, 2^{8})$
rocrand_generate_short	uint16	Uniform	$[0, 2^{16})$
rocrand_generate_uniform	uint32	Uniform	$(0, 1]$
rocrand_generate_uniform	Float	Uniform	$(0, 1]$
rocrand_generate_uniform_double	Double	Uniform	$(0, 1]$
rocrand_generate_uniform_half	Half	Uniform	$(0, 1]$
rocrand_generate_normal	Float	Normal	-
rocrand_generate_normal_double	Double	Normal	-
rocrand_generate_normal_half	Half	Normal	-
rocrand_generate_log_normal	Float	Log-Normal	-
rocrand_generate_log_normal_double	Double	Log-Normal	-
rocrand_generate_log_normal_half	Half	Log-Normal	-
rocrand_generate_poisson	uint32	Poisson	-

rocRAND provides the APIs needed to generate quasi-random numbers. An example is listed in Listing 9.10. These APIs are similar to those used to generate

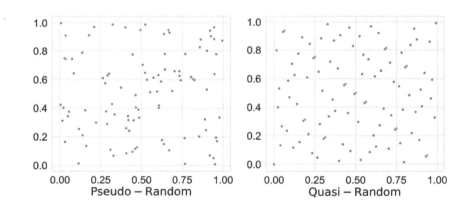

Figure 9.3: Comparison of pseudo- and quasi-random numbers generated along a uniform distribution.

pseudo-random numbers, though there are differences when creating the quasi-random number generator because we use *ROCRAND_RNG_QUASI_DEFAULT*. We must also specify the dimension of the random variable. If the dimension is two, the random generator will generate a group of two random numbers that serve as the x- and y-axes so that the space may be adequately filled.

Listing 9.10: Example of a *rocRAND* program that generates 1M quasi-random numbers.

```
1  #include <hip/hip_runtime.h>
2  #include <rocrand.h>
3  #include <stdio.h>
4  #include <time.h>
5
6  int main() {
7    size_t n = 1048576;
8
9    rocrand_generator gen;
10   float *d_rand;
11
12   h_rand = (float *)malloc(sizeof(float) * n);
13   hipMalloc((void **)&d_rand, n * sizeof(float));
14
15   rocrand_create_generator(&gen, ROCRAND_RNG_QUASI_DEFAULT);
16   rocrand_set_quasi_random_generator_dimensions(gen, 2)
17   rocrand_set_seed(gen, time(NULL));
18   rocrand_generate_uniform(gen, d_rand, n);
19
20   // Use the generated random numbers.
21
22   rocrand_destroy_generator(gen);
23   hipFree(d_rand);
24   return 0;
25 }
```

Finally, the *rocRAND* library ships with a sibling *hipRAND* library. They are designed to be interoperable with both *rocBLAS* and *hipBLAS*. The *hipRAND* library is a thin compatibility layer that supports both rocRAND on AMD platforms and *cuRAND* on NVIDIA platforms. The APIs in the hipRAND library mimic those in *rocBLAS*; hence, we skip the detailed introduction to *hipRAND* in this chapter.

9.5   Conclusion

In this chapter, we demonstrated the capabilities of a few *ROCm* libraries, including *rocBLAS*, *rocSPARSE*, *rocFFT*, and *rocRAND*. These libraries provide a simple and efficient mechanism for programmers to leverage the power of GPUs in their applications. We still recommend that programmers who are beginners with HIP programming write their own kernels. Once a developer starts to work on more complex applications, the availability of these libraries provides an efficient and high-performance solution in many cases. We even encourage programmers to conduct a performance analysis of their own handwritten algorithms, and compare their performance to that of the *ROCm* library implementation of the same algorithm. The programmer can write a matrix multiply kernel and then compare their code against the matrix multiply operation provided in the *rocBLAS* library. This can serve as an educational experience for the programmer. After profiling the differences between the two implementations, the program can use this new knowledge to improve the efficiency of their future HIP programs.

Chapter 10

Multi-GPU Programming

We live in an era where the amount of information produced is growing exponentially. Online services and social media platforms are hard-pressed to maintain the enormous commodity. Moreover, search engines must continually improve their indexing power while mapping the enormity of the data using ML capabilities. As mentioned, GPUs are the platform of choice for many of these data-oriented applications.

Although GPUs process data significantly faster than CPUs, the computing power of a single GPU is constrained. Thus, the application of multiple GPUs to accelerate applications is common. As *ROCm* was built primarily for ultrascale computing, it also provides excellent multi-GPU support out-of-the-box. In this chapter, we examine the commonly used multi-GPU programming approaches available with *ROCm*.

10.1 *HIP* Device APIs

Before exploring multi-GPU programming, we must first learn how to select a specific GPU. When using an API with a single GPU, explicit device selections need not be specified because *HIP* APIs default to GPU 0. A *HIP* example of using an API to run a program on the GPU with the fastest clock is shown in Listing 10.1.

The *hipGetDeviceCount* API is usually the first one called by a *HIP* application that requires specific GPUs. This API checks the number of available GPUs and returns the count. The next step is to use the *hipGetDeviceProperties* API to query the device properties (e.g., model, main memory size, core clock frequency, and concurrent kernel support). A full list of available properties can be found in the *hipDeviceProp_t* structure.

Listing 10.1: Running a GPU program at the highest clock frequency.

```
int main() {
  int device_count;
  hipDeviceProp_t props;

  // Get GPU Count.
  hipGetDeviceCount(&device_count);

  // Find the GPU with the highest clock frequency.
  int fastest_gpu = 0;
  int fastest_gpu_freq = 0;
  for (int i = 0; i < device_count; i++) {
    hipGetDeviceProperties(&props, i);

    if (props.clockRate > fastest_gpu_freq) {
      fastest_gpu_freq = props.clockRate;
      fastest_gpu = i;
    }
  }
  printf("Fastest GPU: %d (%d KHz)\n",
    fastest_gpu, fastest_gpu_freq);

  // Select the GPU.
  hipSetDevice(fastest_gpu);


  // Allocate buffers, copy data, & launch kernels

  return 0;
}
```

The *hipSetDevice* API explicitly selects a specific GPU or group by taking an integer argument. Afterwards, future API calls running on the same thread will use the same GPU unless changed. Kernels can be launched on this GPU, and the device synchronization API helps ensure that all tasks are completed before returning. Recall that the *hipMalloc* API allocates the GPU memory.

To switch to another GPU, the *hipSetDevice* API is called again, and the index of the current GPU is stored as a thread in a local variable. If the program needs to know which device is currently being used, *HIP* provides the *hipGetDevice* API for querying the selected device index. Calling *hipGetDevice* prior to *hipSetDevice* will return the default GPU ID. Additionally, as the device index is a local thread, setting the device will not impact the APIs invoked by other threads.

Multi-GPU computing improves GPU system performance by allowing multiple GPUs to participate in the execution as applicable. At a high level, we must control the GPUs and dispatch tasks in parallel. *ROCm* and *HIP* provide several options for parallel task dispatching on the CPU side. The first option is to use streams, as their tasks can be executed in parallel. Hence, we create a thread for each GPU. Another option is to use threads on the CPU side, with one thread controlling one GPU. Finally, if manually creating and synchronizing threads is too complex, *MPI*-related libraries can be used to reduce complexity significantly. Therefore, in the following three sections, we introduce three multi-GPU programming schemes: stream-, thread-, and *MPI*-based.

Note that the performance of the above-mentioned approaches is generally equivalent, and the choice is usually left up to the programmer's preference and discretion, depending on the type of problem. Notably, these approaches can be combined, such as using two CPU threads to control four GPUs and using stream-based approaches within each of the two CPU threads. This gives programmers the flexibility to write expressive and easy-to-manage multi-GPU programs.

10.2 Stream-Based Multi-GPU Programming

Tasks that are queued in different streams may be executed in parallel. Using this property, the easiest method of parallel GPU programming uses streams. One stream is created for each GPU prior to the execution of any GPU-related tasks. Then, kernels are launched in each queue, most often as a loop, as it is likely that we will launch the same kernel to run on multiple GPUs. Because kernel launching is asynchronous, the program can execute the next iteration while launching other kernels without waiting for the current one to complete. Finally, we wait for the kernels to finish in a synchronized manner.

A simple example that uses multiple GPUs to perform *vector_add* operations is shown in Listing 10.2. Note that there are three separate loops that iterate through GPUs. The first creates queues, allocates memory, and copies memory to the GPU. The second launches kernels. Finally, the third works as a barrier that synchronizes all streams to ensure that all kernels complete their executions at the right time. The first lines in the first and second loops call the *hipSetDevice* API, which selects the GPU to use at each iteration. There is no need to call *hipSetDevice* again in the third loop because the streams are already associated with the desired device.

Listing 10.2: Example of programming multiple GPUs with streams.

```
1  int main() {
2    int device_count;
3    hipDeviceProp_t props;
4    uint64_t length = 1024000000;
5    int block_size = 256;
6    int num_gpus = 8;
7    int length_per_gpu = length / num_gpus;
8    int num_block_per_gpu = (length_per_gpu - 1) / block_size + 1;
9
10   std::vector<float> a, b, c;
11   for (int i = 0; i < length; i++) {
12     a.push_back((float)rand() / (float)RAND_MAX);
13     b.push_back((float)rand() / (float)RAND_MAX);
14   }
15
16   std::vector<float*> d_a, d_b, d_c;
17   std::vector<hipStream_t> streams;
18
19   for (int i = 0; i < num_gpus; i++) {
20     hipSetDevice(i);
21
22     hipStream_t stream;
23     hipStreamCreate(&stream);
24     streams.push_back(stream);
25
26     float *a_ptr, *b_ptr, *c_ptr;
27     hipMalloc((void**)&a_ptr,
28         length_per_gpu * sizeof(float));
29     hipMalloc((void**)&b_ptr,
30         length_per_gpu * sizeof(float));
31     hipMalloc((void**)&c_ptr,
32         length_per_gpu * sizeof(float));
33
34     d_a.push_back(a_ptr);
35     d_b.push_back(b_ptr);
36     d_c.push_back(c_ptr);
37
38     hipMemcpy(a_ptr,
39         a.data() + i * length_per_gpu,
40         length_per_gpu * sizeof(float),
41         hipMemcpyHostToDevice);
42     hipMemcpy(b_ptr,
43         b.data() + i * length_per_gpu,
44         length_per_gpu * sizeof(float),
45         hipMemcpyHostToDevice);
46   }
47
```

```
48    for (int i = 0; i < num_gpus; i++) {
49      hipSetDevice(i);
50      vec_add<<<num_block_per_gpu, block_size, 0, streams[i]>>>(
51          d_a[i], d_b[i], d_c[i], length_per_gpu);
52    }
53
54    for (int i = 0; i < num_gpus; i++) {
55      hipStreamSynchronize(streams[i]);
56    }
57
58    c.resize(length);
59    for (int i = 0; i < num_gpus; i++) {
60      hipSetDevice(i);
61      hipMemcpy(c.data() + i * length_per_gpu,
62          d_c[i],
63          length_per_gpu * sizeof(float),
64          hipMemcpyDeviceToHost);
65    }
66
67    // Use the result and free the GPU memory.
68
69    return 0;
70  }
```

Stream-based multi-GPU programming is convenient when all GPUs run the same kernel, and the program requires frequent synchronization. However, in some applications, GPUs may work on different tasks and only require limited synchronization. Using a stream-based approach to implement these can make programs verbose and challenging to manage. We want each GPU to have its own independent flow of tasks (e.g., memory-copying and kernel-launching) and to synchronize only when necessary. To simplify programming for this purpose, we next introduce thread-based multi-GPU programming.

10.3 Thread-Based Multi-GPU Programming

Thread-based multi-GPU programming is quite straightforward. We first create and launch a thread for each GPU, and each thread calls the *hipSetDevice* API to bind with a particular GPU. Then, we can call other *HIP* APIs for GPU control.

Typically, most thread-based multi-GPU programming requires synchronization. However, this can be done using regular *C/C++* thread synchronization primitives (e.g., joins, mutexes, and conditional variables). Therefore, we do not delve further into this topic.

In Listing 10.3, we provide the same multi-GPU *vector_add* example implemented using the thread-based approach. This time, we dedicate a CPU thread starting from the function named **gpu_thread** to perform GPU-related tasks. The function takes the GPU ID as an argument so that it can associate a specific GPU with the first line of code in the function. The rest of the thread function behaves like a single GPU code.

As we leave all GPU tasks to the thread functionality, the main function does not need to make *HIP* API calls, other than declaring and initializing data. The main function only needs to start the list of threads, one per GPU, followed by synchronizing them all. In this example, we use the *join* function to wait for all threads to exit.

Listing 10.3: Example of programming multiple GPUs with threads.

```
1
2  void gpu_thread(int gpu_id, int length_per_gpu, float* A, float* B, float
       * C) {
3    hipSetDevice(gpu_id);
4
5    printf("gpu_thread %d\n", gpu_id);
6
7    int n = length_per_gpu;
8
9    float *dA, *dB, *dC;
10   hipMalloc(&dA, n * sizeof(float));
11   hipMalloc(&dB, n * sizeof(float));
12   hipMalloc(&dC, n * sizeof(float));
13
14   hipMemcpy(dA, A, n * sizeof(float), hipMemcpyHostToDevice);
15   hipMemcpy(dB, B, n * sizeof(float), hipMemcpyHostToDevice);
16
17   int block_size = 256;
18   int grid_size = (n + block_size - 1) / block_size;
19   vec_add<<<grid_size, block_size>>>(dA, dB, dC, n);
20
21   hipMemcpy(C, dC, n * sizeof(float), hipMemcpyDeviceToHost);
22
23   hipDeviceSynchronize();
24
25   hipFree(dA);
26   hipFree(dB);
27   hipFree(dC);
28  }
29
30  int main() {
31   hipError_t err;
32   int device_count;
33   hipDeviceProp_t props;
```

```
34
35    uint64_t length = 102400;
36    int num_gpus = 8;
37    int length_per_gpu = length / num_gpus;
38    if (length % num_gpus != 0) {
39      fprintf(stderr, "length must be a multiple of num_gpus\n");
40      return 1;
41    }
42
43    std::vector<float> a, b, c;
44    for (int i = 0; i < length; i++) {
45      a.push_back((float)rand() / (float)RAND_MAX);
46      b.push_back((float)rand() / (float)RAND_MAX);
47    }
48    c.resize(length);
49
50    std::vector<std::thread> threads;
51    for (int i = 0; i < num_gpus; i++) {
52      threads.push_back(std::thread(
53          gpu_thread, i, length_per_gpu, a.data() + i * length_per_gpu,
54          b.data() + i * length_per_gpu, c.data() + i * length_per_gpu));
55    }
56
57    for (int i = 0; i < num_gpus; i++) {
58      threads[i].join();
59    }
60
61    // Use the result.
62
63    return 0;
64 }
```

10.4 *MPI*-Based Multi-GPU Programming

The *MPI* Communication Standard is widely used in high-performance multi-core and distributed computing environments. It was originally designed to manage a large number of CPU threads, and it automatically starts those that perform similar tasks, including communication primitives that allow different threads to share data. Owing to the popularity of the *MPI* Standard in the HPC community, *HIP* supports *MPI*-based multi-GPU computing, which is quite similar to thread-based approaches. The only difference is that *MPI* takes care of thread creation, communication, and synchronization, which reduces programmer overhead when managing threads.

We present a simple example (see Listing 10.4) using *MPI* to control multiple

GPUs. Here, we create a random array (Line 25), scatter it to the GPUs (Line 36), calculate the square of each element (Line 49), gather the results back to the root GPU (Line 60), and sum the squared elements (Line 72).

A few lines of code in the example are *MPI*-specific. At the beginning of the main program, we first initialize the *MPI* environment by calling *MPI_Init(&argc, &argv)*. In this example, we assume that the number of processes equals the number of GPUs used. Note that MPI also allows the user to run multiple MPI processes per GPU, though we do not use this capability here. Next, we obtain the current rank number and the total number of ranks using the *MPI_Comm_rank* and *MPI_Comm_size* APIs, respectively. The rank number and count provide the positional information needed so that each process knows which portion of the data to manipulate. The current rank number can also be used to associate the processes with their corresponding GPUs. In this example, we assume that the rank ID of a process equals the ID of the GPU under control.

In the main body of the program, we use several *MPI* communication primitives, including *MPI_Scatter* and *MPI_Gather*. Instead of GPU–GPU communications, they support data transfers between CPU buffers. This implementation is not the most efficient solution, as extra (and unnecessary) CPU–GPU data movements are involved. For example, on Line 51, we copy the squared result to a rank-local buffer so that after we gather the data on Line 60, we can copy the results back to the GPU on Line 67. Ideally, if we could directly aggregate the data in GPU memory, we would avoid these extra memory copies. To make direct GPU–GPU data aggregation possible, we next introduce *ROCm*'s peer-to-peer communication capability (see Section 10.5) and *RCCL* (see Section 10.6).

Listing 10.4: Example using *MPI* for multi-GPU computing.

```
1   // square kernel implementation is neglected
2   // reduction_sum implementation is neglected
3   // create_rand_nums implementation is neglected
4
5   int main(int argc, char** argv) {
6     // Initialize the MPI environment
7     MPI_Init(&argc, &argv);
8
9     // Find out rank, size
10    int world_rank, world_size;
11    MPI_Comm_rank(MPI_COMM_WORLD, &world_rank);
12    MPI_Comm_size(MPI_COMM_WORLD, &world_size);
13
14    int num_elements_per_proc = atoi(argv[1]);
15    int total_elements = world_size * num_elements_per_proc;
16    int data_in_bytes_per_node = num_elements_per_proc * sizeof(int);
```

```
17  int total_data_in_bytes = total_elements * sizeof(int);
18
19
20  // Create a random array of elements on the root process.
21  srand(time(NULL));
22  int *rand_nums = NULL;
23  if (world_rank == 0) {
24    rand_nums = create_rand_nums(total_elements);
25  }
26
27  // For each process, create a buffer that will hold a subset of the
        entire
28  // array
29  int *sub_rand_nums = (int *)malloc(data_in_bytes_per_node);
30  int *results = (int *)malloc(data_in_bytes_per_node);
31
32
33  // Scatter the random numbers from the root process to all processes in
34  // the MPI world
35  MPI_Scatter(rand_nums, num_elements_per_proc, MPI_INT, sub_rand_nums,
36              num_elements_per_proc, MPI_INT, 0, MPI_COMM_WORLD);
37
38  hipSetDevice(world_rank);
39
40  int *d_sub_rand_nums, *d_results;
41  hipMalloc(&d_sub_rand_nums, data_in_bytes_per_node);
42  hipMalloc(&d_results, data_in_bytes_per_node);
43  hipMemcpy(d_sub_rand_nums, sub_rand_nums, data_in_bytes_per_node,
        hipMemcpyHostToDevice);
44
45  int blockSize, gridSize;
46  blockSize = 32;
47  gridSize = (int)ceil((float)num_elements_per_proc/blockSize);
48  square<<<gridSize, blockSize>>>(d_sub_rand_nums, d_results,
        num_element_per_proc);
49  hipDeviceSynchronize();
50  hipMemcpy(results, d_results, data_in_bytes_per_node,
        hipMemcpyDeviceToHost);
51
52  int *aggregated_results = NULL;
53  if (world_rank == 0) {
54    aggregated_results = (int *)malloc(total_data_in_bytes);
55  }
56
57  MPI_Barrier(MPI_COMM_WORLD);
58
59  MPI_Gather(results, num_elements_per_proc, MPI_INT, aggregated_results,
            num_elements_per_proc, MPI_INT, 0, MPI_COMM_WORLD);
60
```

```
61
62
63   if(world_rank == 0) { // Root node to gather the data.
64      int *d_aggregated_results = NULL;
65      hipMalloc(&d_aggregated_results, total_data_in_bytes);
66      hipMemcpy(d_aggregated_results, aggregated_results,
                total_data_in_bytes, hipMemcpyHostToDevice);
67
68      int *d_output;
69      hipMalloc(&d_output, sizeof(int));
70
71      reduction_sum(d_aggregated_results , d_output, total_elements);
72
73      int reduce_sum = 0;
74      hipMemcpy(&reduce_sum, d_output, sizeof(int), hipMemcpyDeviceToHost);
75      printf("Reduce sum %d\n", reduce_sum);
76   }
77
78   MPI_Finalize();
79
80   // Free CPU and GPU memory buffers.
81 }
```

Compiling and running this program requires a few special commands. Assuming that *MPI* libraries are properly installed, the first command is **mpicc –showme**. The compiler, *mpicc*, is a wrapper for the regular **gcc** command but includes special arguments for *MPI*-related inclusion paths and predefined library links. The **–showme** argument reveals the equivalent command when **gcc** is used. On our platform, the output of the command is as follows:

Listing 10.5: Example output of **mpicc –showme**.

```
gcc
    -I/usr/lib/x86_64-linux-gnu/openmpi/include/openmpi
    -I/usr/lib/x86_64-linux-gnu/openmpi/include/openmpi/opal/mca/event/
        libevent2022/libevent
    -I/usr/lib/x86_64-linux-gnu/openmpi/include/openmpi/opal/mca/event/
        libevent2022/libevent/include
    -I/usr/lib/x86_64-linux-gnu/openmpi/include
    -pthread
    -L/usr/lib
    -L/usr/lib/x86_64-linux-gnu/openmpi/lib
    -lmpi
```

To compile a *HIP* program with *MPI* support, we must replace the *gcc* with *hipcc*. Then, the *MPI* library will be linked to the compiled executable.

To run the compiled program, the **mpirun** command is used. The number of processes, which is also the number of GPUs, is provided by the **mpirun** command. Assuming we want to use four GPUs, and the compiled program is **main**, we use **mpirun -n 4 ./main** to start the program.

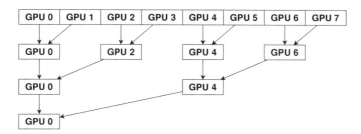

Figure 10.1: GPU-level reduction.

10.5 GPU–GPU Communication

In the examples shown earlier, the CPU distributes the data to the GPUs, which then processes them. However, in many cases, GPUs will need to communicate with one another. For example, a common multi-GPU computing pattern allows each GPU to perform the same operation on different input data independently and store the outputs locally. We then aggregate (e.g., average or sum) the outputs to obtain the final result. Although the first stage, in which each GPU computes independently, does not involve GPU–GPU communications, the second stage (aggregation) does. Copying and aggregating the data back to the CPU is inefficient, as discussed in the *MPI* example.

Typically, aggregating data from multiple GPUs requires a GPU-level reduction algorithm, as shown in Figure 10.1. If the data are distributed across eight GPUs, the reduction requires three iterations ($log_2 8 = 3$). In each, the data on the two GPUs will be aggregated to one. Therefore, the number of active GPUs was reduced by half at each iteration. In the rest of this section, we use a reduction algorithm to demonstrate GPU–GPU communications. Specifically, we average data stored on eight GPUs and store the final result in the input buffer of GPU 0.

With *HIP*, we have two GPU–GPU communication options: regular memory copies or peer-to-peer. *HIP* provides the necessary APIs. The general *hipMemcpy* API specifies the copy direction as *hipMemcpyDeviceToDevice*. For convenience, *HIP* also provides a dedicated API, *hipMemcpyDtoD*, for device-to-device memory copies.

We implement an eight-GPU reduction example in Listing 10.6. For each aggregation step, we first create buffers on the GPUs. For example, with GPUs 0 and 1, we create a buffer on GPU 0. We then use the *hipMemcpyDtoD* API to copy the data from GPU 1 to the newly created buffer on GPU 0. Finally, we launch the average kernel on GPU 0 to aggregate the data. The kernel operates fully on local data, and there is no inter-GPU communication while the kernel runs.

Listing 10.6: Example of using device-to-device memory copy to achieve multi-GPU communication.

```
1  int main() {
2    uint64_t length = 1024;
3    int num_gpu = 8;
4    std::vector<std::vector<float>> h_output(num_gpu);
5    std::vector<float*> output_gpu(num_gpu);
6    float* final_result;
7
8    // Stage 1, calculate the result for otuput_gpu buffers.
9    for (int i = 0; i < num_gpu; i++) {
10     // Neglected
11   }
12   for (int i = 1; i < num_gpu; i = i << 1) {
13     for (int j = 0; j < num_gpu; j += (i * 2)) {
14       int leftGPU = j;
15       int rightGPU = j + i;
16       printf("Calculating average between GPU %d and %d\n", leftGPU,
                rightGPU);
17
18       hipSetDevice(leftGPU);
19
20       float* leftBuf = output_gpu[leftGPU];
21       float* rightBuf;
22       hipMalloc(&rightBuf, (size_t)length * sizeof(float));
23       hipMemcpyDtoD(rightBuf, output_gpu[rightGPU],
24                     (size_t)length * sizeof(float));
25       int block_size = 256;
26       int num_block = (length - 1) / block_size + 1;
27       avg<<<num_block, block_size>>>(leftBuf, rightBuf, length);
28     }
29   }
30   // Use final_result.
31   return 0;
32 }
```

Memory copy-based GPU–GPU communication is a simple, yet effective, solution. It moves data from one GPU to another with predictable performance. When copying a large amount of data, *ROCm* is optimized to utilize the full bandwidth between GPUs. Therefore, this approach is suitable for general use. The only problem is that the compute kernel cannot begin execution until all data have arrived, missing the opportunity to overlap data movements and computations.

The peer-to-peer communication solution allows programmers to control communications and computations at a finer granularity. At a high level, a GPU kernel easily accesses data physically located on another GPU without requiring kernel modifications, thus reflecting peer-to-peer communications. One simply passes the pointer to a remote address as the kernel argument. These mechanisms are provided by *ROCm* on AMD GPUs, and they are fully transparent to the programmer.

In Listing 10.7, we reimplement the same eight-GPU averaging example using peer-to-peer communications. Most of the code, including the kernel that computes the average, remains unchanged. However, there are a few points worth highlighting. First, before using this feature, we must check whether peer-to-peer communication is supported on our platform. This is done by invoking the *hipDeviceCanAccessPeer* API. If this communication utility is not supported, we can fall back to a memory-copy solution or the CPU memory as an intermediate buffer. Second, peer-to-peer communication is not enabled by default; hence, manually enabling this feature with *hipDeviceEnablePeerAccess* is required. Note that enabling peer-to-peer access may reduce GPU performance in some cases and should be turned off with *hipDeviceDisablePeerAccess* or *hipDeviceResult* when the feature is not used.

When using the peer-to-peer communication feature, we can skip the lines that create the intermediate buffers to copy remote data. In this example, peer-to-peer memory copying reduces the number of lines of code and simplifies programming.

Listing 10.7: Example of using peer-to-peer memory access to achieve multi-GPU communication.

```
// Calculate the element-wise average of A and B
// and store the result back in A.
__global__ void avg(float* A, float* B, int n) {
  // Content of the kernel neglected for brevity.
}

int main() {
  uint64_t length = 1024;
  int num_gpu = 8;

  std::vector<std::vector<float>> h_output(num_gpu);
```

```
12   std::vector<float*> output_gpu(num_gpu);
13   float* final_result;
14
15   // Stage 1, calculate the results to store in the output_gpu buffers.
16   for (int i = 0; i < num_gpu; i++) {
17     // Neglected
18   }
19
20   for (int i = 1; i < num_gpu; i = i << 1) {
21     for (int j = 0; j < num_gpu; j += (i * 2)) {
22       int leftGPU = j;
23       int rightGPU = j + i;
24       printf("Calculating average between GPU %d and %d\n", leftGPU,
              rightGPU);
25
26       // Check if peer-to-peer memory access is enabled.
27       int canAccessPeer = 0;
28       err = hipDeviceCanAccessPeer(
29         &canAccessPeer, left_gpu, right_gpu);
30       if (err != hipSuccess) {
31         fprintf(stderr, "Can't access peer device %d\n", right_gpu);
32         exit(EXIT_FAILURE);
33       }
34       printf("Can access peer %d\n", canAccessPeer);
35
36       // Enable peer-to-peer memory access.
37       hipSetDevice(leftGPU);
38       err = hipDeviceEnablePeerAccess(right_gpu, 0);
39       if (err != hipSuccess) {
40         fprintf(stderr, "Can't enable peer access to device %d\n",
                right_gpu);
41         exit(EXIT_FAILURE);
42       }
43
44       // We do the memory copy next.
45       float* leftBuf = output_gpu[leftGPU];
46       float* rightBuf = output_gpu[rightGPU];
47
48       int block_size = 256;
49       int num_block = (length - 1) / block_size + 1;
50       avg<<<num_block, block_size>>>(leftBuf, rightBuf, length);
51     }
52   }
53
54   // Use final_result.
55   return 0;
56 }
```

The performance implications of peer-to-peer methods can become complicated. On the on hand, the *avg* kernel directly issues memory access to remote GPUs. As such, the GPU performs the calculation after a small chunk of data arrives; hence, there is no need to wait for the entire buffer to be copied. Moreover, a long GPU–GPU communication latency may negatively impact overall performance. Additionally, the GPU–GPU bandwidth may not be fully utilized. Without possessing extensive knowledge of peer-to-peer operations or applying performance tuning, programmers should exercise caution using the peer-to-peer memory access feature.

10.6 *RCCL*

In the example introduced in the previous section, we discussed how to aggregate data distributed across multiple GPUs. Given the potential for such operations, *ROCm* provides the ability to greatly simplify data distribution and aggregation across multiple GPUs with the *RCCL*, which is pre-optimized for AMD GPU platforms; hence, programmers can typically expect higher performance over ad hoc implementations. The *RCCL* is the GPU version of an *MPI* primitive, and it avoids the extra memory copies noted in the earlier *MPI* example.

The *RCCL* follows the NVIDIA Collective Communication Library (*NCCL*) API. Therefore, most *RCCL* APIs are prefixed with "nccl." If an existing application is written with the *NCCL*, minimum modifications are required.

The *RCCL* supports a list of communication primitives, including *Broadcast*, *Reduce*, *All Reduce*, *All Gather*, and *Reduce Scatter*. We provide two examples demonstrating the *RCCL*'s utility, one using *Broadcast* and the other using *AllReduce*. Like other multi-GPU programming libraries, the *RCCL* can be used in a stream- or thread/*MPI*-based manner. We demonstrate stream-based *RCCL* calls in the *Broadcast* example and *MPI*-based *RCCL* calls in the *AllReduce* example. Although we only present *Broadcast* and *AllReduce* examples, readers will find that the syntax of other primitives is quite similar.

10.6.1 *Broadcast*

Broadcast is the simplest *RCCL* primitive. As shown in Figure 10.2, it sends a data item from a single GPU to multiple ones. An example of using *Broadcast* is provided in Listing 10.8. At the beginning of this example, we include two header files: the regular *hip_runtime.h* and *rccl.h*. *hip_runtime.h*, which is needed for its memory-, device-, and stream-management capabilities.

Before the *RCCL* communication process begins, we must create a list of buffers

Figure 10.2: *RCCL Broadcast* primitive.

using the *hipMalloc* API. A buffer is allocated to each GPU, and the source buffer (GPU 0) is filled with predefined data to broadcast to all other GPUs. In this example, we create a single buffer for each GPU. For the broadcast root (GPU 0), the source buffer is the same as the destination buffer; hence, there is no need to perform a data copy on the source GPU. However, the *RCCL Broadcast* primitive supports copying to a set of buffers that are different from the sources.

The first step in starting the *RCCL* data transfer is creating a list of communicators. It is commonplace to create one communicator per GPU, and the *RCCL* provides a convenient API, *ncclCommInitAll*, that initializes multiple communicators at once. Because using multiple communicators for one GPU can cause deadlocks, we must carefully design our synchronization strategy; thus, using multiple communicators for one GPU is not recommended.

The broadcast operation is completed using the *ncclBroadcast* API. As we are about to broadcast the data across four GPUs, including the source, the API must be invoked four times in a loop, starting at Line 32.

To indicate to the *RCCL* library that these four API calls belong to one broadcast operation, we call the *ncclGroupStart* API before *ncclBroadcast* and *ncclGroupEnd* API afterwards. Standalone *RCCL* APIs are designed for thread-based multi-GPU programming. Without the *ncclGroupStart* call, *RCCL* waits for all threads to call the *broadcast* API. In a single-threaded environment, this causes deadlocks on the first *Broadcast* call. The APIs notify the *RCCL* that they are about to be called as a single thread and then return without executing. The real execution happens only when *ncclGroupEnd* is called.

ncclBroadcast calls are asynchronous. Thus, we pass in a stream, and the API adds tasks to the stream for execution. At Line 42, all streams are synchronized to ensure that all GPUs receive the data.

Listing 10.8: Example of using peer-to-peer memory access to achieve multi-GPU communication.

```cpp
#include <hip/hip_runtime.h>
#include <rccl.h>


int main(int argc, char* argv[]) {
  const int nDev = 4;
  int size = 1 * 1024;
  int devs[4] = {0, 1, 2, 3};
  std::vector<float> in(size);
  int root = 0;

  // Initialize input.

  // Allocating and initializing device buffers.
  float** buff = (float**)malloc(nDev * sizeof(float*));
  hipStream_t* s = (hipStream_t*)malloc(sizeof(hipStream_t) * nDev);

  for (int i = 0; i < nDev; ++i) {
    hipSetDevice(i);
    hipMalloc(buff + i, size * sizeof(float));
    hipStreamCreate(s + i);
  }

  hipSetDevice(root);
  hipMemcpyHtoD(buff[root], in.data(), size * sizeof(float));

  // Initialize
  ncclComm_t comms[nDev];
  ncclCommInitAll(comms, nDev, devs);

  ncclGroupStart();
  for (int i = 0; i < nDev; ++i) {
    ncclBroadcast((const void*)buff[i], (void*)buff[i], size,
                        ncclFloat, root, comms[i], s[i]);
  }
  ncclGroupEnd();

  // Wait for broadcast to complete.
  for (int i = 0; i < nDev; ++i) {
    hipSetDevice(i);
    hipStreamSynchronize(s[i]);
  }
  // Free allocated CPU and GPU memory buffers.
  return 0;
}
```

10.6.2   *AllReduce*

AllReduce is another common *RCCL* primitive. As seen in Figure 10.3, *AllReduce* aggregates data stored on multiple GPUs and distributes them to all others.

Our *AllReduce* use case involves data-parallel multi-GPU DNN training, which typically begins with various training data distributed across the multiple GPUs. Each GPU then applies forward and backward propagation algorithms to calculate their gradients (i.e., the directions in which each parameter should be updated). Because each GPU uses different training data, the gradients are likely to differ as well. *AllReduce* is used to average the gradients and distribute them to each GPU. After all GPUs receive their averaged gradients, they update their locally stored DNN models independently. After the DNN model is updated, the GPUs can then receive another batch of training data.

In the example of Listing 10.9, we combine *RCCL AllReduce* with *MPI* calls to calculate the element-wise sum of arrays stored on different GPUs. The program begins with regular *MPI* APIs to initialize the environment, obtain the current rank index, and calculate the number of ranks.

Figure 10.3: *RCCL AllReduce* primitive.

This time, rather than using the convenient *ncclCommInitAll* API, we manually initialize the communicators. To do so, we first need to acquire a unique ID, which is used to bind the communicators together and allow the *RCCL* to properly synchronize the processes. To inform the *RCCL* library that the communicators are related, the same unique ID is used during their creation. Hence, we use *MPI Broadcast* primitives to send the unique ID from Rank 0 to all other ranks. Finally, at Line 27, we create the communicators.

Using *RCCL* communication primitives in the thread/*MPI*-based mode is simple, as there is no need to call the group APIs. When one rank calls the *ncclAllReduce* API, the *RCCL* holds the progress of the calling process and waits for all others to call this API. When all the processes arrive at this point, the *RCCL* begins the *AllReduce* calculation.

Listing 10.9: Example of mixing using *MPI* and *RCCL AllReduce*.

```
1  int main(int argc, char* argv[]) {
2    int size = 32 * 1024 * 1024;
3    int myRank, nRanks = 0;
4
5    // initializing MPI
6    MPI_Init(&argc, &argv);
7    MPI_Comm_rank(MPI_COMM_WORLD, &myRank);
8    MPI_Comm_size(MPI_COMM_WORLD, &nRanks);
9
10   ncclUniqueId id;
11   ncclComm_t comm;
12   float *sendbuff, *recvbuff;
13   hipStream_t s;
14
15   if (myRank == 0) ncclGetUniqueId(&id);
16   MPI_Bcast((void*)&id, sizeof(id), MPI_BYTE, 0, MPI_COMM_WORLD);
17
18   // Allocate buffers and create streams
19   hipSetDevice(myRank);
20   hipMalloc(&sendbuff, size * sizeof(float));
21   hipMalloc(&recvbuff, size * sizeof(float));
22   hipStreamCreate(&s);
23
24   // Initializing RCCL
25   ncclCommInitRank(&comm, nRanks, id, myRank);
26
27   // communicating using RCCL
28   ncclAllReduce((const void*)sendbuff, (void*)recvbuff, size,
29                     ncclFloat, ncclSum, comm, s);
30   // Completing RCCL operation by synchronizing on the \textit{HIP}
          stream
31   hipStreamSynchronize(s);
32
33   // Free device buffers
34   hipFree(sendbuff);
35   hipFree(recvbuff);
36
37   // Finalizing NCCL
38   ncclCommDestroy(comm);
39
40   // Finalizing MPI
41   MPI_Finalize();
42   return 0;
43 }
```

Thus with this example, we can understand how to leverage RCCL effectively for certain communication patterns in multi-GPU computing environments.

10.7   Conclusion

In this chapter, we introduced different *HIP*-based multi-GPU programming options for the AMD *ROCm* platform. Overall, *ROCm* and *HIP* provide a high level of flexibility and are feature-rich, enabling programmers to leverage multi-GPU performance scaling. This chapter opened with an explanation of how to use *HIP* APIs to query the number of GPUs and select a specific one for use. We then introduced three multi-GPU programming approaches (i.e., stream-, thread-, and *MPI*-based). These mainly focus on how the CPU dispatches tasks to multiple GPUs. Later, we identified the need for inter-GPU communications and introduced two solutions GPU–GPU solutions: one with memory-copy APIs and another with peer-to-peer memory access. For commonly used multi-GPU communication patterns, the *RCCL* library provides a wide range of communication primitives that enable high-performing, easy-to-use GPU–GPU communications.

Chapter 11

Machine Learning with *ROCm*

GPUs are the platform of choice for accelerating machine learning (ML) applications. To best match the computational demands of ML training and inference, AMD has provided the ML community with high-performance hardware and software ecosystems. On the hardware side, the AMD MI series, particularly the MI300 GPUs, offer impressive performance, providing up to 48 TFLOPS for single-precision (fp32) and 383 TFLOPS for half-precision (fp16).

On the software front, ROCm offers a rich set of application programming interfaces (APIs) and libraries that can harness the computational power of AMD GPUs effectively. AMD's MIOpen library contains optimized kernels for deep neural networks (DNNs), enhancing training efficiency. AMD provides additional highly optimized libraries, such as rocBLAS and rocSPARSE, that implement APIs for performance commonly used operations (e.g., matrix multiplication and sparse matrix multiplication).

Given the rich hardware and software support provided by AMD, ROCm seamlessly integrates with widely used frameworks, such as PyTorch and TensorFlow, across all ROCm-compatible GPUs. AMD abstracts away the underlying complexity of these ML frameworks, allowing developers to use them without significant code modifications. In this chapter, we provide examples of how to use PyTorch and TensorFlow with AMD GPUs.

11.1   *PyTorch* on *ROCm*

PyTorch, which is developed by Facebook Research, is a library designed to efficiently build ML applications on CPUs and GPUs [62]. It allows programmers to define the structure of neural networks with ease through the use of Python-based PyTorch APIs, encompassing various layers, optimizers, and data loaders. The PyTorch backend, which adapts to different hardware platform, leverages optimized functions and kernels for both CPUs and GPUs. Initially, PyTorch exclusively supported a CUDA-based GPU backend. However, PyTorch's flexible interface now enables ROCm to introduce a new backend for AMD GPUs, leveraging the MI-Open library.

The ROCm backend is designed to align with the torch.cuda interface, enabling developers to leverage their past knowledge of using torch.cuda, because it interfaces directly to ROCm. This compatibility ensures a smooth transition and continuity in development practices. For instance, a common function call in many ML applications is torch.cuda.is_available(), which is used to check whether a GPU is available. This function interface remains unchanged in PyTorch when operating on ROCm. This consistency eliminates the need for Python programmers to alter their code for ROCm compatibility. Additionally, for large-scale distributed training, PyTorch running on ROCm leverages the high-performance RCCL library [11], ensuring efficient multi-GPU communication.

11.1.1   Installing PyTorch

To be able to run PyTorch on a ROCm GPU, we first need to install PyTorch on our AMD platform. This can be done easily using the Docker image provided with PyTorch. This will remove the need to manually compile your code and facilitate immediate usage of PyTorch.

Listing 11.1: Command to be used to get the latest PyTorch Docker image.

```
docker pull rocm/pytorch:latest
```

To download the latest PyTorch Docker image, we can execute the above command. This command fetches the most up-to-date version from the public repository. Next, we launch a Docker container using the downloaded PyTorch image.

Listing 11.2: Command to be used to install PyTorch.

```
docker run -it --cap-add=SYS_PTRACE --security-opt seccomp=unconfined --
    device=/dev/kfd --device=/dev/dri --group-add video --ipc=host --shm-
    size 8G rocm/pytorch:latest.
```

The above command creates a Docker container with key parameters set to optimize PyTorch execution. After running this command, we will have access to system-level resources, such as kernel features, security permissions, video devices, and shared memory allocation.

Once the Docker container is installed, we are ready to explore PyTorch's capabilities, experiment with ML models, and execute code effortlessly. The Docker container encapsulates the necessary dependencies and configurations, ensuring a smooth and consistent experience across different systems.

11.1.2 Testing the PyTorch Installation

Before using PyTorch, we need to ensure it is properly installed. First, we can import the torch package in Python, using the command below.

Listing 11.3: Command to be used to test PyTorch installation.

```
python3 -c 'import torch' 2> /dev/null \&\& echo 'Success' || echo '
    Failure'
```

After executing the command, an output of *"Success"* signifies a successful installation, whereas *"Failure"* indicates that troubleshooting is necessary.

Listing 11.4: Command to be used to check GPU availability.

```
python3 -c 'import torch; print(torch.cuda.is_available())'
```

Next, we check if the GPU is accessible from PyTorch. Utilizing torch.cuda, PyTorch's GPU access interface, the **torch.cuda.is_available()** command checks GPU availability for PyTorch operations. An output of True signifies GPU readiness for accelerated computations, whereas False indicates that we need to default and use CPU computations in the absence of an available GPU.

Listing 11.5: Commands to be used to run a set of unit tests for comprehensive PyTorch validation.

```
BUILD_ENVIRONMENT=${BUILD_ENVIRONMENT:-rocm} ./.jenkins/pytorch/test.sh
PYTORCH\_TEST\_WITH\_ROCM=1 python3 test/test\_nn.py --verbose
```

11.1.3 Image Classification using Inception V3

Following the steps outlined earlier, PyTorch should now be operational. In the following discussion, we will run an ML application using ROCm, specifically focusing on the Inception v3 model [69]. This model is frequently utilized for image processing tasks. To streamline the DNN configuration, we will use torchvision [53], a library that provides access to pre-built models and datasets, as well as pre-trained weights.

In this example, our objective is not to train the model from scratch. Instead, we will assess the performance on an image classification task using pre-trained parameters (see Listing 11.6). Our goal is to evaluate how effectively the Inception v3 model handles new, previously unseen images.

Listing 11.6: Image Classification using Inception V3

```
1  import torch
2  import torchvision
3  model = torch.hub.load('pytorch/vision:v0.10.0', 'inception_v3',
       pretrained=True)
4  model.eval()
5  import urllib
6  url, filename = ("https://github.com/pytorch/hub/raw/master/images/dog.
       jpg", "dog.jpg")
7  try:
8      urllib.URLopener().retrieve(url, filename)
9  except:
10     urllib.request.urlretrieve(url, filename)
11
12 from PIL import Image
13 from torchvision import transforms
14 input_image = Image.open(filename)
15
16
17 preprocess = transforms.Compose([
18     transforms.Resize(299),
19     transforms.CenterCrop(299),
20     transforms.ToTensor(),
21     transforms.Normalize(mean=[0.485, 0.456, 0.406], std=[0.229, 0.224,
           0.225]),
22 ])
23
24 input_tensor = preprocess(input_image)
25 input_batch = input_tensor.unsqueeze(0)
26 if torch.cuda.is_available():
27     input_batch = input_batch.to('cuda')
28     model.to('cuda')
29 with torch.no_grad(), torch.autograd.profiler.profile() as prof:
```

```
30    output = model(input_batch)
31 probabilities = torch.nn.functional.softmax(output[0], dim=0)
32 print(probabilities)
33
34 with open("imagenet_classes.txt", "r") as f:
35    categories = [s.strip() for s in f.readlines()]
36 top5_prob, top5_catid = torch.topk(probabilities, 5)
37 for i in range(top5_prob.size(0)):
38    category = categories[top5_catid[i]]
39    probability = top5_prob[i].item()
40    print(f"Category: {category}, Probability: {probability:.4f}")
41
42 print(prof.key_averages().table(sort_by="cuda_time_total"))
```

Listing 11.7: Command to be used to launch a Docker container.

```
docker run -it --mount type=bind,source=/home/yifan/HIP/Deep_Learning,
    target=/var/lib/jenkins --cap-add=SYS_PTRACE --security-opt seccomp=
    unconfined --device=/dev/kfd --device=/dev/dri --group-add video --
    ipc=host --shm-size 8G rocm/pytorch:latest
```

Using the command above, we run the Python script (Listing 11.6) within a Docker container. This command launches a Docker container, specifying that we will use the **rocm/pytorch:latest** image, while presetting a number of configuration parameters and options. Notably, we employ the **--mount** flag to establish a connection between a directory on the host machine and the Docker container. By specifying **type=bind**, we are notifying PyTorch to use a bind mount, which allows easy data sharing and interaction between the host and container environments. The source parameter designates the path to the desired host machine directory to be mounted, while the target parameter specifies the corresponding location within the container where the directory is located.

Upon executing the specified command, the system initiates an interactive session to launch the Docker container. In the container's interactive mode, a text file necessary for image classification can be downloaded using the following command:

wget https://raw.githubusercontent.com/pytorch/hub/master/imagenet_classes.txt.

To process the image classification, run the Python script by executing python3 filename.py. This will produce an output detailing the probabilities for each class, including the top 5 predicted categories.

11.2 *TensorFlow* on *ROCm*

TensorFlow is another popular ML library supported by *ROCm* [1]. *TensorFlow* was originally developed by Google to accelerate model development. Similar to *PyTorch*, *TensorFlow* provides programmers with high-level APIs for building and deploying end-to-end ML models. *ROCm* supports *TensorFlow* with ready-to-use Docker containers, which can ease application development and deployment. On the backend, *Tensor-Flow* uses the *ROCm* libraries (e.g., *MIOpen* and *rocBLAS*) and *HIP* calls to provide high-performance ML capabilities that allow unmodified *TensorFlow* code to execute on *ROCm*-enabled AMD GPUs [5].

11.2.1 Installing Tensorflow

To get started with TensorFlow on ROCm, the initial step involves installing TensorFlow by download the respective Docker image.

Listing 11.8: Command to be used to get the latest Tensorflow Docker image.

```
docker pull rocm/tensorflow:latest
```

Similar to PyTorch, we can pull the TensorFlow Docker image for ROCm by executing the above command.

Listing 11.9: Command to be used to launch the Docker container.

```
docker run -it --network=host --device=/dev/kfd --device=/dev/dri --ipc=
    host --shm-size 16G --group-add video —cap-add=SYS\_PTRACE --security
    -opt seccomp=unconfined rocm/tensorflow:latest
```

Once the image is downloaded, we run the container using the above command. This command launches the container with the specified configuration, allowing us to interact with the TensorFlow environment provided by the ROCm Docker image.

11.2.2 Testing the Tensorflow Installation

After the installation process, it is crucial to confirm that TensorFlow is correctly installed and operational.

Listing 11.10: Command to be used to run the python scipt within a Docker container.

```
python3 -c 'import tensorflow' 2> /dev/null \&\& echo ''Success || echo
    ''Failure
```

To verify this, we import the TensorFlow package in Python with the above command. If TensorFlow is installed correctly, the output will be *"success"*, signaling that

TensorFlow is ready to use. Conversely, a *"Failure"* output suggests the need for further troubleshooting.

11.2.3 Training using TensorFlow

With TensorFlow installed, we run a simple TensorFlow example in a Docker container using the command in Listing 11.11 in the terminal. This command launches the Docker container in interactive mode, allowing the execution of Python files. Upon running this command, the user will enter interactive mode within the Docker container. Once we enter interactive mode, we can execute commands, run Python scripts, and access files within the container. The mounted directory from the host machine can be accessed as the /root directory inside the container, facilitating file sharing and execution between the host and the container.

Listing 11.11: Command to be used to launch a Docker container.

```
docker run -it --mount type=bind,source=/home/yifan/HIP/Deep\_Learning/ex
    \_02,target=/root --device=/dev/kfd --device=/dev/dri --ipc=host --
    shm-size 16G --group-add video --cap-add=SYS\_PTRACE --security-opt
    seccomp=unconfined rocm/tensorflow:latest
```

To execute a Python code for TensorFlow and observe the utilization of the GPU or CPU (Listing 11.12), we will use the following commands:

Listing 11.12: Training using Tensorflow

```
import tensorflow as tf
from tensorflow import keras
(train_images, train_labels), (test_images, test_labels) = keras.datasets
    .cifar10.load_data()
train_images = train_images / 255.0
test_images = test_images / 255.0
model = keras.Sequential([
    keras.layers.Flatten(input_shape=(32, 32, 3)),
    keras.layers.Dense(128, activation='relu'),
    keras.layers.Dense(10, activation='softmax')
])
model.compile(optimizer='adam', loss=tf.keras.losses.
    SparseCategoricalCrossentropy(from_logits=True), metrics=['accuracy'
    ])

if tf.test.is_gpu_available():
    print('Training on GPU')
    with tf.device('GPU:0'):
        model.fit(train_images, train_labels, epochs=10, validation_data
            =(test_images, test_labels))
else:
    print('Training on CPU')
```

```
19    model.fit(train_images, train_labels, epochs=10, validation_data=(
          test_images, test_labels))
20 test_loss, test_acc = model.evaluate(test_images, test_labels, verbose=2)
21 print('Test accuracy:', test_acc)
```

When running the Python code shown in Listing 11.12, the script confirms the availability of a GPU. Additionally, in an evaluation on a test dataset to assess its performance on previously unseen data, the model yielded a test accuracy of approximately 0.4213. This figure reflects the model's ability to generalize to new data. This example highlights how an AMD GPU can be employed to support a basic model's computational process.

11.3   Conclusion

In this chapter, we introduced the reader to the the two most popular ML frameworks, i) *PyTorch* and ii) *TensorFlow*, which are available on *ROCm* systems. Code written using these high-level frameworks will run on *ROCm*-supported GPUs supported by *HIP* libraries.

Chapter 12

ROCm in Data Centers

ROCm provides seamless support in data center and HPC cloud environments where a large set of nodes are shared among multiple users. *ROCm* provides virtual container support for several platforms, including Docker [54], Singularity [46] and, Kubernetes [51]. They allow programmers to deploy microservices via containers on AMD GPU platforms with *ROCm* support. *ROCm* also provides easy integration with job schedulers in cloud environments, using management frameworks such as the Simple Linux Utility for Resource Management (*SLURM*) and Load-Sharing Facility(*LSF*). In this chapter, we examine some of these features, including containers and job schedulers, on a *ROCm* system.

12.1   Containerized *ROCm*

ROCm virtual containers provide an efficient means for programmers to quickly package their code and share it with other programmers. AMD provides ready-to-deploy virtual containers for each new *ROCm* release via Docker and Singularity. Containers are also provided by AMD with preinstalled versions of popular ML libraries such as *PyTorch* and *TensorFlow*. This enables programmers to simply use these containers to run their ML applications without having to perform a time-consuming setup. Figure 12.1 shows how a container platform works with a *ROCm* system. At the basic level, there is a host OS with *ROCm* installed atop *ROCm*-supported hardware. Then, a container platform runs atop the host OS. Finally, various applications (Apps 1, 2, and 3) are executed on the platform, supplied by containers. A container handles all the resource management with the underlying OS, and each application is properly isolated from the others. With this basic understanding, we can leverage a Docker container with *ROCm* support. First, we simply pull (i.e., download) the Docker container from the official AMD docker hub repository [21] which publicly releases different *ROCm* containers. Basic containers, as well as those with preinstalled software libraries, are provided. In our example, we use a Docker container that comes with the *ROCm* installation. Importantly, virtual containers do not virtualize the Linux kernel. Instead, it provides lightweight and fast containerization. The implication of this for the *ROCm* stack is that the *ROCm* kernel and corresponding modules must be installed on the host machine. Because containers share a host kernel, they must also share the *ROCm* kernel driver functions outside the container. In this example, we use the *rocm-terminal* Docker image from the AMD Docker hub repository. To get started, we download the image onto our local system using **docker pull rocm/rocm-terminal**. Then, we simply run the container using the command, **docker run -it –device=/dev/kfd –device=/dev/dri –group-add video rocm/rocm-terminal**, which launches a bash shell inside the *rocm-terminal* container. Finally, we have a working Docker container in a *ROCm* environment that programmers can use to deploy their application as a microservice. They can also use the container to share code bundled with all required dependencies. Readers are encouraged to try out other Docker containers provided by AMD on the Docker Hub.

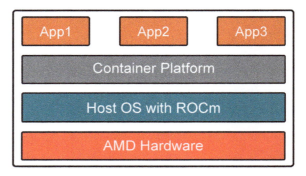

Figure 12.1: How *ROCm* integrates with a container platform for efficient application deployment.

12.2   Managing *ROCm* Containers using Kubernetes

ROCm also provides easy deployment of virtualized containers on the Kubernetes platform. For readers unfamiliar with Kubernetes, it is basically a container orchestration service. For example, if an organization has deployed a large number of containers as microservices, manually managing them is cumbersome. Instead, they can be deployed to Kubernetes, which eases the management and orchestration burden. Kubernetes also provides fault tolerance and scalability features.

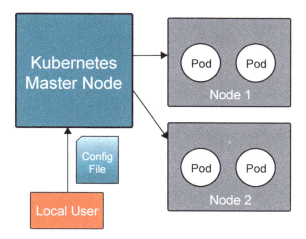

Figure 12.2: High-level architecture of a system using Kubernetes. The user communicates with the master node using a configuration file. The master is responsible for managing and scheduling Pods across nodes.

A group of containers running on Kubernetes is described as a "Pod." The system administrator or programmer describes everything required to manage a Pod, including creating new containers when existing ones terminate and scaling and upgrading the Pods. Figure 12.2 shows the high-level architecture of a Kubernetes system. The local user communicates with the master node using a configuration file describing the containers needed, resource limits, etc. The Kubernetes master node (there can be more than one) then manages and schedules them across the different nodes in the system. In a microservice-based system, Kubernetes scales resources based on calendar demands. There are many advantages to using Kubernetes, but their descriptions are beyond the scope of this book.

To exploit Kubernetes container orchestration, *ROCm* provides support for AMD GPUs [2] so that programmers can take advantage of this technology on *ROCm*-enabled GPUs. AMD provides a Kubernetes device plugin that supports GPU registration via a container cluster for computational purposes on the Docker hub repository [3]. After pulling this plugin from Docker, the programmer must ensure that it executes on all nodes with a *ROCm*-enabled GPU. To simplify this process, the *Daemonset* utility should be used, as it enables Pod copies to be run on all nodes in a cluster. AMD's *Github* repository for Kubernetes device plugins provides a *yaml* file named *k8s-ds-amdgpu-dp.yaml*, which is used for this purpose. A programmer runs the command, **kubectl create -f k8s-ds-amdgpu-dp.yaml**, to pull it. Readers are encouraged to read more about how *Daemonset* works at [45].

With the *Daemonset* running, we deploy a pod that runs the AlexNet [44] benchmark on a GPU. Afterward, the pod goes to sleep. For readers unfamiliar with AlexNet, it is a DNN used to classify images. The *yaml* file for creating this Pod is shown in Listing 12.1. From Line 8, we can see the sections that are responsible for specifying the container name (Line 9) and the Docker image for the container (Line 10). Line 14 identifies the GPU that will run the container, which, in this case, is set to zero. This is followed by the actual AlexNet benchmark script, which will run inside the container. Finally, Lines 17–19 specify the resource limit of the pod, which is a single GPU. To run the yaml file, the programmer will first need to start and run the pod. This can be done with **kubectl create -f alexnet-gpu.yaml**. The status of the pod is checked with **kubectl describe pods**. Finally, to see the results of the AlexNet training script, we run **kubectl logs alexnet-tf-gpu-pod alexnet-tf-gpu-container**, where "alexnet-tf-gpu-pod" refers to the Pod name, and "alexnet-tf-gpu-container" refers to the container name, as specified in the *yaml* file.

This example demonstrates how easy it is to deploy a container using the Kubernetes framework on *ROCm*-enabled GPUs. The reader is encouraged to play around with different parameters by changing the *yaml* file and experimenting with their own prebuilt containers.

Listing 12.1: Configuration file for executing the AlexNet benchmark on a Kubernetes platform.

```
apiVersion: v1
kind: Pod
metadata:
  name: alexnet-tf-gpu-pod
  labels:
    purpose: demo-tf-amdgpu
spec:
  containers:
    - name: alexnet-tf-gpu-container
      image: rocm/tensorflow:latest
      workingDir: /root
      env:
      - name: HIP_VISIBLE_DEVICES
        value: "0" # # 0,1,2,...,n for running on GPU and select the GPUs
           , -1 for running on CPU
      command: ["/bin/bash", "-c", "--"]
      args: ["python3 benchmarks/scripts/tf_cnn_benchmarks/
          tf_cnn_benchmarks.py --model=alexnet; trap : TERM INT; sleep
          infinity & wait"]
      resources:
        limits:
          amd.com/gpu: 1 # requesting a GPU
```

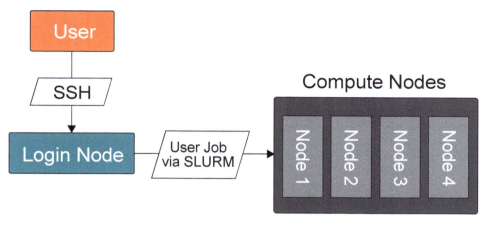

Figure 12.3: High-level overview of how a *SLURM*-based cluster works. Programmers log in to the node and submit jobs via *SLURM*, which are then scheduled and executed on the compute nodes by *SLURM*

12.3   Managing *ROCm* Nodes using *SLURM*

ROCm-enabled GPUs can also be managed using a scheduling utility, such as *SLURM*. Such tools are widely used in HPC centers and academic computing clusters to manage access to shared resources. In this section, we examine some basic *SLURM* functions, including how to request interactive access to a *ROCm* GPU and how to submit jobs to it.

Two important cluster-related terms to understand are "home node" and "compute node." When a user logs into a cluster, its home node is the first location, which is just the login node. From there, the user may issue requests to *SLURM* to access a compute node so that they may run their jobs. Figure 12.3 shows the high-level block diagram of a cluster running *SLURM*.

There are two ways a user can issue requests to *SLURM*. The first is via the *SLURM* interactive mode, which allows users to open a remote terminal on the requested node. From there, the user can perform tasks, such as compiling code, installing libraries, and executing programs. The second is via the batch submission mode, in which the programmer creates a batch script containing the compute and memory resource requests, the command to execute when the resources are available, and the time limits of the job. When using batch mode, the job is submitted to the *SLURM* scheduler, which queues and manages it. The user can also include commands in the batch script that will notify them when their job is complete. We view examples of these modes next.

12.3.1 *SLURM* interactive mode

To run in interactive mode, the command to request a resource is **salloc**. It has several optional parameters, which can be viewed in the official *SLURM* documentation [65] or by simply running **salloc -h**, which lists the options. For our purposes, the three most important parameters include **-N**, the number of nodes, **-p**, the partition requested, and **-t**, the time limit of the job. For example, the command, **salloc -N 2 -p MI100 -t 02:00:00**, means that we are requesting two nodes on partition MI100 for 2 h. This command is of a blocking type, meaning that it will only return when the request is processed by *SLURM*). Then, the user is directly logged into the requested compute node via the terminal. When the time limit has expired, the terminal automatically exits with a timeout message, and the user returns to their home node. If the user finishes the job sooner than the timeout, they can issue **scancel <job_id>**, where the "job_ID" refers to the user's job. The job ID can be found with **squeue -u $USER**.

12.3.2 *SLURM* batch submission mode

In *SLURM*'s batch submission mode, the programmer prepares a script similar to *matmul.bash*, which is shown in Listing 12.2. Here, we specify the cluster partition, number of GPUs, amount of memory, and number of CPU cores. Beyond these details, we specify that the script should load the *ROCm* module so that the environment is correctly set for using all *ROCm*-related libraries. We include the compilation command in Line 18. In this example, we compile *matmul.cpp*, which produces the *matmul* binary. Finally, in Line 20, we specify the script that should execute *matmul*. To request *SLURM* to schedule and execute our job, we simply use the **sbatch** command and pass the filename. In this case, **sbatch matmul.bash** submits the job to the *SLURM* scheduler. If the program prints to **stdout**, the result is stored in the *gpu.out* file (Line 4 of *matmul.bash*).

Listing 12.2: *matmul.bash SLURM* batch submission script.

```
#!/bin/bash

#SBATCH --job-name=matmulgpu    # job name
#SBATCH --output=gpu.out # output log file
#SBATCH --error=gpu.err  # error file
#SBATCH --time=01:00:00  # 1 hour of wall time
#SBATCH --nodes=1        # 1 GPU node
#SBATCH --partition=mi100 # GPU2 partition
#SBATCH --ntasks=1       # 1 CPU core to drive GPU
#SBATCH --gres=gpu:1     # Request 1 GPU
#SBATCH --mem=8Gb.  # Request 8 GB of memory


# Load all required modules below. As an example, we load rocm:
module load rocm
```

```
# Add lines here to run your GPU-based computations.
hipcc mamtul.cpp -o matmul

./matmul
```

12.4   Conclusion

In this chapter, we learned how *ROCm* can be used in data center environments. Whether we use Docker, Kubernetes, or the *SLURM* scheduler, *ROCm* provides the data center with all the service support needed, allowing rapid deployment and scaling of microservices. Furthermore, it eases cluster and data center management for system administrators.

Chapter 13

Third-Party Tools

To support *HIP/ROCm* development, a number of third-party tools have been developed. This chapter briefly describes a few of those tools and provides pointers on where to find additional information.

13.1 *PAPI*

13.1.1 Introduction

High Performance Computing (HPC) application development can be time-consuming and complex. Many programs demand the efficient use and utilization of the underlying hardware and software stack. The efficiency with which different hardware resources are utilized can be quantified with detailed measurements from a wide range of performance counters. The HPC community has relied on the *PAPI* monitoring library to track low-level hardware operations for more than two decades [70]. In addition to tracking traditional CPU counters, which record the number of instructions executed, as well as various events, including floating-point operations, retired instructions, cache accesses and misses, *PAPI*'s latest developments enable the monitoring of counters on GPUs (e.g., AMD, Intel, and NVIDIA), communication networks, input/output (I/O) systems, as well as energy monitoring and power-capping components. *PAPI* enables the collection of performance-counter data from across the entire compute system using a single GUI.

In addition to hardware-based counters, *PAPI* provides access to counters that originate from software layers, tracking software-defined events (SDEs). They allow programmers to export arbitrary information from within their libraries. For example, a task-scheduling runtime might use SDEs to export internal performance related information, such as the "available tasks at different points in time" data item.

```c
#include <stdio.h>
#include <stdlib.h>
#include "papi.h"

int main(){
    int EventSet = PAPI_NULL;
    int tmp=0, i, retval;
    long long values[2];

    if((retval = PAPI_library_init(PAPI_VER_CURRENT)) != PAPI_VER_CURRENT ){
        fprintf(stderr,"Error initializing the PAPI library.\n");
        exit(-1);
    }
    if(PAPI_OK != PAPI_create_eventset(&EventSet)){
        fprintf(stderr,"Error creating eventset.\n");
        exit(-1);
    }
    PAPI_add_event(EventSet, PAPI_TOT_INS);
    PAPI_add_event(EventSet, PAPI_TOT_CYC);
    PAPI_start(EventSet);

    for (i = 0; i < 1000000; i++) // User code here
        tmp = tmp+i;

    PAPI_stop(EventSet, values);
    printf("Total instructions executed: %lld \n", values[0] );
    printf("Total cycles executed: %lld \n",values[1]);
    PAPI_shutdown();

    return 0;
}
```

Figure 13.1: Example of using *PAPI* in a program.

PAPI enables the monitoring of both hardware and software events through the same **PAPI_start()**, **PAPI_stop()**, and **PAPI_read()** GUI-based commands, which allow more efficient tuning of heterogeneous hardware resources and present a complete picture of full application performance. In addition to using *PAPI* directly, programmers can leverage performance frameworks that use *PAPI* for performance-counter monitoring behind the scenes. Such tools employ hardware counter sampling, call path tracking, and binary analysis. As a result, they offer graphical profiles that attribute counter values and time spent on particular application code lines. Examples of integrated performance frameworks include *Arm MAP*, *HPCToolkit*, and *TAU*.

13.1.2 *PAPI* utilities and tests

In addition to APIs used to monitor events, there are some command-line utilities provided with *PAPI* such as:

- **papi_component_avail**. This provides information about components that are configured in Figure 13.2.
- **papi_avail**. This presents information about preset events and their availability on a given machine (see Figure 13.3).
- **papi_native_avail**. This gives information about native events (see Figure 13.4).
- **papi_command_line**. This allows users to test events from the CLI (see Figure 13.5).

```
Compiled-in components:
Name:    perf_event         Linux perf_event CPU counters
Name:    perf_event_uncore  Linux perf_event CPU uncore and northbridge
   \-> Disabled: Insufficient permissions for uncore events. Set /proc/sys/kernel/
perf_event_paranoid to 0.
Name:    rocm               GPU events and metrics via AMD ROCm-PL API
Name:    rocm_smi           AMD GPU System Management Interface via rocm_smi_lib

Active components:
Name:    perf_event         Linux perf_event CPU counters
                            Native: 141, Preset: 17, Counters: 5
                            PMUs supported: perf, perf_raw, amd64_fam17h_zen2

Name:    rocm               GPU events and metrics via AMD ROCm-PL API
                            Native: 343, Preset: 0, Counters: 343

Name:    rocm_smi           AMD GPU System Management Interface via rocm_smi_lib
                            Native: 146, Preset: 0, Counters: 146
```

Figure 13.2: **papi_component_avail**.

```
     Name        Code     Avail Deriv Description (Note)
PAPI_L1_DCM   0x80000000  No    No    Level 1 data cache misses
PAPI_L1_ICM   0x80000001  Yes   No    Level 1 instruction cache misses
PAPI_L2_DCM   0x80000002  No    No    Level 2 data cache misses
PAPI_L2_ICM   0x80000003  No    No    Level 2 instruction cache misses
PAPI_TLB_DM   0x80000014  Yes   No    Data translation lookaside buffer misses
PAPI_TLB_IM   0x80000015  Yes   Yes   Instruction translation lookaside buffer misses
PAPI_BR_TKN   0x8000002c  Yes   No    Conditional branch instructions taken
PAPI_BR_MSP   0x8000002e  Yes   No    Conditional branch instructions mispredicted
PAPI_TOT_CYC  0x8000003b  Yes   No    Total cycles
PAPI_L1_DCA   0x80000040  Yes   No    Level 1 data cache accesses
```

Figure 13.3: **papi_avail**.

```
==================================================================================
Native Events in Component: rocm
==================================================================================
| rocm:::SQ_INSTS_VMEM_WR:device=0                                                |
|             Number of VMEM write instructions issued (including FLAT). (per-si|
|             md, emulated)                                                       |
----------------------------------------------------------------------------------
| rocm:::SQ_INSTS_VMEM_RD:device=0                                                |
|             Number of VMEM read instructions issued (including FLAT). (per-sim|
|             d, emulated)                                                        |
----------------------------------------------------------------------------------
| rocm:::SQ_INSTS_SALU:device=0                                                   |
|             Number of SALU instructions issued. (per-simd, emulated)            |
==================================================================================
Native Events in Component: rocm_smi
==================================================================================
| rocm_smi:::NUMDevices                                                           |
|             Number of Devices which have monitors, accessible by rocm_smi.    |
----------------------------------------------------------------------------------
| rocm_smi:::mem_usage_VRAM:device=0                                             |
|             VRAM memory in use.                                                 |
----------------------------------------------------------------------------------
| rocm_smi:::power_cap:device=0:sensor=0                                         |
|             Power cap in microwatts. Read/Write. Between min/max (see power_ca|
|             p_range_min/max). May require root privilege.                       |
----------------------------------------------------------------------------------
```

Figure 13.4: **papi_native_avail**.

13.1.3 *PAPI* support for AMD GPUs

PAPI version 6.0.0 adds support for several new components, including *ROCm*, which supports performance counters on AMD GPUs, and *rocm_smi*, which monitors power usage. These additions provide programmers with the ability to update power settings and control their utility.

PAPI rocm Component

The *PAPI rocm* component interfaces the AMD *ROCm* profiling library (i.e., *rocProfiler*) and enables the monitoring of hardware performance counters on AMD GPUs. Examples of monitoring features include:
- LDS—LDS events.
- GDS—Global data store events.
- TCP/TA—L1 cache-related counts.
- TCC—L2 cache-related counts.
- SQ—Sequencer: Fetch, decode, schedule instructions.

```
$ papi_command_line CORE_TO_L2_CACHEABLE_REQUEST_ACCESS_STATUS:LS_RD_BLK_C

This utility lets you add events from the command line interface to see if they work.

Successfully added: CORE_TO_L2_CACHEABLE_REQUEST_ACCESS_STATUS:LS_RD_BLK_C

CORE_TO_L2_CACHEABLE_REQUEST_ACCESS_STATUS:LS_RD_BLK_C :          76

----------------------------------
```

Figure 13.5: **papi_command_line**.

- FLAT—Video+Sys+LDS+Scratch: Slower memory instructions using flat address space.
- VMEM—Vector memory storage.
- VMem—Video memory.
- SMEM—Scalar memory storage..
- SFetch—Scalar fetch events
- VFetch—Vector fetch (excludes Flat instructions) events.
- VALU—Vector ALU events.
- SALU—Scalar ALU events (not including floating-point counts).

Figure 13.6 shows the L2 cache hits collected by *PAPI_read()* every 5 ms on the AMD MI100 GPU during the execution of a *rocBLAS* GEMM kernel.

PAPI *rocm_smi* Component

The *PAPI rocm_smi* component interfaces with AMD *SMI* and adds power management support, enabling the monitoring and capping of power on AMD GPUs. This new *PAPI* capability enables scientific application programmers to change run profiles to reduce energy costs. Examples of the monitoring features include:

- Power - monitoring and power capping.
- Temperature - current temperature, maximum critical value, temporary emergency temperature.
- Fan - fan speed in rotations per minute, maximum speed, read/write speed.
- Memory - total VRAM, visible VRAM, graphics translation table (GTT) VRAM.
- PCI - throughput sent, received, maximum packet size.
- Busy percent - percentage of time the device is busy processing.

The example in Figure 13.7 shows fine-grained power usage samples collected by *PAPI_read()* on an AMD MI60 GPU while running the *hipBLAS* GEMM kernel.

13.1.4 Preset Events and Counter Analysis Toolkit (*CAT*)

In addition to enabling access to low-level hardware counters, *PAPI* provides a set of higher-level events that abstract the micro-architectural details while maintaining the

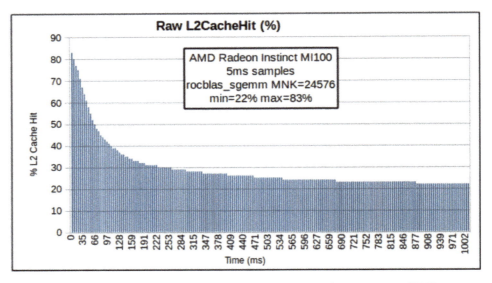

Figure 13.6: L2 cache SGEMM hit rate on the AMD MI100 GPU.

same name across vendors and hardware generations. An example of a preset event is **PAPI_L2_DCR**.

The counters are configured to count the number of read requests to the L2 cache. The importance of preset events is two-fold. First, it is convenient when using portable and intuitive names for events. Second, they are designed to map to performance concepts more readily.

To aid programmers in selecting native events or combinations thereof, a set of examples are available for defining preset events. The *CAT* is available as part of *PAPI*.

```
./cat_collect -in event_list.txt -out OUT_DIR -dcr
```

13.2   *Score-P* and *Vampir*

13.2.1   Overview

Vampir [13] is a commercial tool that visualizes event logs as timelines and statistical charts. Event logs retain the temporal information of each event, supporting the detection of performance problems with changing characteristics over an application's runtime. The *Score-P* [24] measurement infrastructure is a highly scalable and easy-to-use tool suite for profiling and event-tracing HPC applications. *Score-P* is the preferable

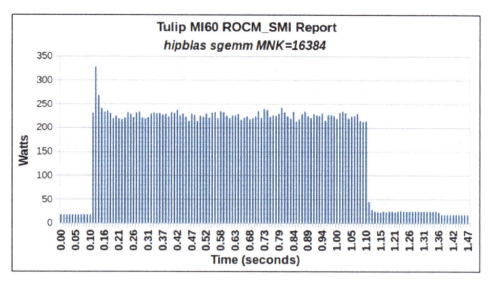

Figure 13.7: Power usage for SGEMM with *PAPI* on an AMD MI60 GPU.

method for generating event logs for *Vampir*. For further details on *Vampir* [77] and *Score-P* [80], please refer to the user manuals available on their respective websites.

AMD *ROCm* provides a comprehensive compute ecosystem for AMD GPUs. In addition to a full toolchain for compiling and running accelerated applications, it provides tools and APIs for debugging and performance analysis. To record the runtime behaviors and performance metrics of an application, it also provides APIs for external tools. *Score-P* utilizes the *rocProfiler* and *rocTracer* libraries from AMD. The *rocTracer* library is callback-based (i.e., the tool registers functions to specific events, which are then triggered by the *ROCm Runtime*). These events include the entry and exit of *HIP* API functions, data movement between the host and device, and kernel launch operations, among others. The *rocProfiler* library is used to regularly sample GPU metrics.

13.2.2 Tracing with *Score-P*

In *Score-P*, only an HPC-focused subset of the *ROCm* tracer APIs is supported, exposing the events reported by this interface as Open Trace Format (*OTF*) version 2 (*OTF2*). The resulting *OTF2* trace files can be analyzed using *Vampir*.

The events currently supported cover the following activities on the host and device:

1. Stream management.
2. Kernel launches.

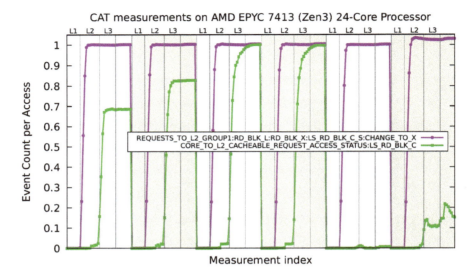

Figure 13.8: Power usage for SGEMM with *PAPI* on the AMD MI60 GPU.

3. Host and device memory allocations.

4. Synchronous and asynchronous memory transfers between host and devices.

5. Device and stream synchronization.

6. Host-side user instrumentation via *rocTX*.

Most of these events are mapped to function entry/exit events in *Score-P*, but some include additional information. *Score-P* provides normal kernel-name filtering capabilities. Thus, a programmer can provide a filtering file to exclude specific kernel invocations. Memory allocations are tracked using separate allocation metrics for the host and device, and data transfers are modeled by one-sided communication events between the host and devices.

A collection of *HIP*-related *Score-P* environment variables allows programmers to select which categories of events are recorded or discarded. By default, everything is recorded. The list of metrics to sample is also controlled by an environment variable and can be queried using *rocProf*, provided by the *rocProfiler* package:

```
$ rocprof --list-basic
$ rocprof --list-derived
```

13.2.3 *Score-P* Usage

Score-P provides a command that enables the instrumentation of applications at compile/link time. Some instances of parallel frameworks (e.g., *MPI* and *OpenMP*) can be automatically detected, whereas some must be enabled explicitly. To use this feature, the application must be rebuilt by prepending all compile/link commands with the *Score-P* instrumenter, **scoreP**.

For example, instead of:

```
$ gcc -c foo.o
```

one is required to execute:

```
$ scorep gcc -c foo.o
```

The same applies to the link command.

ROCm tracer-based instrumentation is enabled by passing the **–hip** option to the *Score-P* instrumenter, **scorep**, in the same manner that one would enable instrumentation for *CUDA* and other accelerator paradigms. The *scorep-hipcc* compiler wrapper passes this flag automatically. For a more detailed example of using *ROCm* instrumentation, please see the *Score-P* documentation.

13.2.4 Profiling the *Quicksilver* Application

Next, we present an example of using *Score-P* and *Vampir* while running the *Quicksilver CORAL* benchmark application [79]. The *Quicksilver* benchmark is a proxy application for the Monte Carlo Transport Code, the Mercury part of the Lawrence Livermore National Laboratory (LLNL) codesign. We use a *ROCm*-enabled version of *Quicksilver* for our demonstration, which is located in the *AMD-HIP* branch of the *GitHub* repository.

Instrumentation

First, we clone the *Quicksilver* repository and check out the *AMD-HIP* branch:

```
$ git clone -b AMD-HIP \
    https://github.com/LLNL/Quicksilver.git
$ cd Quicksilver/src
```

Next, we build the benchmark with *Score-P* instrumentation enabled. To start the build procedure, the standard process must be altered so that the *Score-P* instrumenter can be used. The command to compile and link is **scorep-hipcc**.

```
$ sed -i -e 's,^CXX = $(HIP)/bin/,CXX = scorep-,' Makefile
$ make HIP=/opt/rocm
```

This produces the *qs* binary, which specifies an input size appropriate for this demonstration. The application is run in one process with one AMD GPU, and we collect performance data using an *OTF2* trace:

```
$ SCOREP_ENABLE_TRACING=true \
  SCOREP_TOTAL_MEMORY=4G \
  SCOREP_EXPERIMENT_DIRECTORY=Quicksilver-1x1-Instrumented \
  ./qs
```

The resulting trace file in *Quicksilver-1x1-Instrumented* can now be opened in *Vampir*. Figure 13.9 shows the master timeline for the host process and the accelerator stream, *RocM[0:0]*. The format is the same as that used in *CUDA* traces, including the naming of the accelerator streams, where the numbers in brackets denote the device and stream IDs. Additionally, the figure shows the memory allocation metrics for the host and device in the lower part under "counter timelines." It is easy to identify the host initialization phase, during which the host memory is allocated. The same holds true for the device initialization phase.

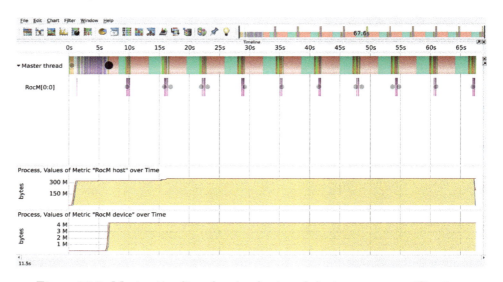

Figure 13.9: Master timeline showing host and device memory utilization.

In Figure 13.10, we show the profiling results of the initialization phase, including transfers of varying durations and sizes. All *Quicksilver* transfers are synchronous. Thus, overlapping these phases is possible.

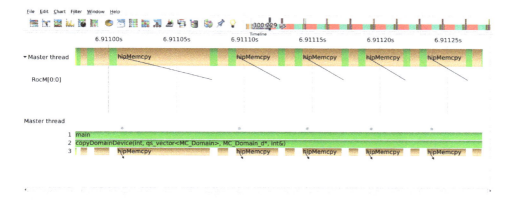

Figure 13.10: Master and process timeline for host/device transfers.

Figure 13.11 provides a snapshot of device memory allocation and includes the master timeline, showing when the data transfers occurred, as indicated by the black circles. This presents a clear pattern of the allocate/fill cycles.

Finally, Figure 13.12 shows the main computation, which involves the execution of a single kernel launch and the subsequent device synchronization while waiting on the results. The trace suggests that for *Quicksilver*, the CPU was idle during most of the kernel execution, following a launch–synchronize–copy results pattern.

13.2.5   Summary

The *Vampir/Score-P* ecosystem fully supports *HIP/ROCm* profiling. We have provided an overview and demonstrated their utility using the *Quicksilver* application. *Vampir/Score-P* tools allow users to profile *ROCm* behaviors, as well as those of applications that leverage parallel frameworks, including *MPI* and *OpenMP*.

13.3   *Trace Compass* and *Theia*

Trace Compass

Trace Compass is a tool that provides visualization and analysis for several trace formats. Trace analysis takes several steps:

1. Each event is fed into one or more analysis modules to model the state of the system (e.g., a table of processes and threads, the state of each thread, and GPU

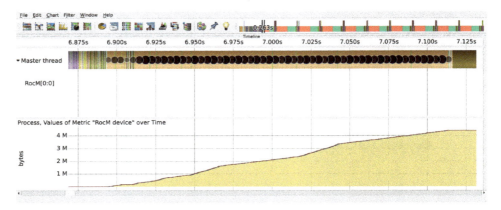

Figure 13.11: Master timeline showing device memory utilization.

compute kernels). A **process_create** event will add a new process and thread to the process table, whereas a scheduling event will change the state of the current and upcoming thread based on the relevant core. The database of the modeled state over the duration of the trace is called the "State History."

2. Traces from different nodes actively exchanging network packets can be synchronized by matching the send and receive events of the different nodes and computing the clock drift and offset.

3. The content of individual events can be displayed as a detailed event list. Higher-level views and analyses typically query the *State History* database for fast navigation through the trace.

The following sections present two HPC trace formats of interest supported by *Trace Compass*, followed by a case study. Other advanced *Trace Compass* features are used to synchronize traces collected on different nodes or compute the critical path of a distributed program's execution, with all views synchronized temporally.

Theia

Theia is an open and extensible cloud and desktop integrated development environment (IDE) platform. It is similar to *Visual Studio* and uses many of the same underlying modules, protocols, and extension APIs. Its GUI is also similar, and support for various programming languages is delegated to external modules through the language server protocol (LSP). Thus, through the *LLVM clangd* language server, the *Theia* editor supports not only *C/C++* but also several related languages, such as *OpenCL*. Similarly,

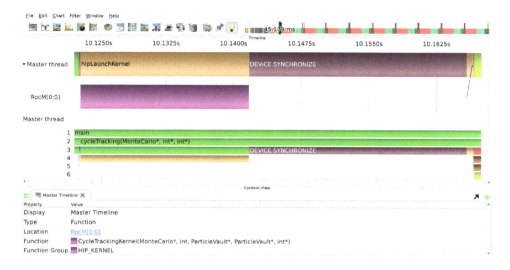

Figure 13.12: Master timeline with kernel launch and device synchronization.

Theia supports advanced debugging via the debugger adapter protocol (DAP) to communicate with the *GDB*.

Trace Compass was rebuilt to separate its GUI frontend from the trace reading and analysis backend. The backend server now feeds its classic GUI frontend using *Eclipse*, or it interfaces *Theia*. The trace server protocol (TSP), which is similar to the LSP and DAP, was created to connect the TSP to the *theia-trace-extension* plugin. These traces can then be directly analyzed from within the *Theia* IDE.

Common Trace Format (*CTF*)

CTF [23] is a binary trace format designed to minimize tracing overhead. It is generic so that programmers can define their own event types, and the payload format is defined in a metadata file that is parsed to convert the trace content into a high-level representation.

CTF provides a plugin that supports GPU tracing programs using *ROCm* with *rocProfiler* and *rocTracer*. The plugin sorts the *HIP* and *HSA* events from their occurrence using priority queues and writes them into *CTF* streams using *barectf* [49]. The resulting traces are then analyzed and displayed in *Trace Compass*.

OTF2

OTF2 [61, 28] is a common binary trace format used to trace massively parallel computer systems. Such traces often lead to the generation of massive trace files, sometimes spanning several gigabytes or even terabytes of data. Nevertheless, *OTF2* is optimized to generate compact and efficient results [81].

To produce a *ROCm* trace in *CTF*:

- Download the *rocProfiler* and *rocTracer* plugins from the *GitHub* site.
  `https://github.com/dorsal-lab/rocprofiler_ctf_plugin`
  Once installed, to produce a *CTF* trace:

  - Export the plugin path using the *CTF_PLUGIN* environment variable:
    `$ export CTF_PLUGIN=/path/to/plugin.`

  - Run the **rocprof** command with the options **--ctf-format** and **-d** to specify the trace directory:

  `rocprof --ctf-format --hip-trace -d /path/to/my/trace ./my_program.`

  - If the plugin version is "rocm-4.2.x-interval," "rocm-4.3.x," or above, run this command:

  `python $CTF_PLUGIN/scripts/post_processing.py /path/to/my/trace.`

  - Your trace is now available in the *CTF_trace* directory in a subdirectory specified with the "-d" option.

  These instructions may change in the future. Up-to-date instructions can be found at `https://github.com/dorsal-lab/rocprofiler_ctf_plugin`

- To generate an *OTF2* trace, follow these steps:

  - Install *Score-P* and *OTF2* installed:
    `https://www.vi-hps.org/projects/score-p/.`

  - Install the *OTF2*-to-*CTF* converter: `https://github.com/dorsal-lab/OTF2-to-CTF-converter.`

  - Trace the program in *OTF2* format:
    * Compile the program with *Score-P*.
    * Enable tracing:
      `$ export SCOREP_ENABLE_TRACING=1.`
    * Run the compiled program to obtain the *scorep-<identifier>* directory containing an *OTF2* trace.

– Convert the *OTF2* trace to *CTF*:

* Export the path to the converter in the *OTF2_CONVERTER* environment variable:
  `$ export OTF2_CONVERTER=/path/to/converter`.
* Convert the trace with the following command.

`$ OTF2_CONVERTER/otf2_converter. /path/scorep/trace/traces.otf2`

* Now, you should have a *CTF* trace in the *converted_otf2_<identifier>* directory.

Sample traces and code can be found at:
`https://github.com/dorsal-lab/OTF2_testcases`

Theia Trace Extension

The *Theia Trace Extension* is provided as a ready-to-build open source or hosted in *GitPod*. To locate the repository, visit:
`https://github.com/theia-ide/theia-trace-extension`
`https://github.com/dorsal-lab/tracevizlab/tree`
`/master/labs/304-rocm-traces`
We use a *ROCm* trace to demonstrate the utility of this framework.

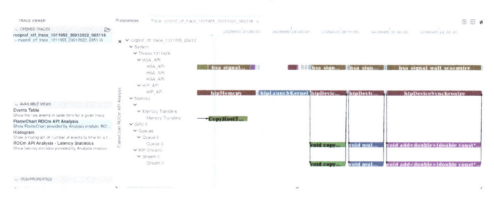

Figure 13.13: Visualization using the *Theia Trace Extension*.

Figure 13.13 presents a detailed view of a *HIP* program execution. The *add4 HIP* kernel was taken from the *HIP-Examples* [7] repository. This trace contains events from the execution of four different compute kernels in succession. In the figure, the top-left menu shows the different traces opened, the middle-left shows the available analyses, the bottom-left shows details of user selection, and the main view contains a flame-chart analysis of the program. From top to bottom, we see the system threads with per API type (i.e., *HIP* and *HSA*) and memory transfers. At the bottom, the GPU kernels are shown. A lane shows the kernels per queue, and another shows the kernels per *HIP* stream. Each kernel is assigned a specific color, and the arrows represent the dependencies between the *HIP* API call and the actual GPU kernel execution. Note that the first execution is more time-consuming than the others owing to the initialization occurring at this step.

Theia.cpp Debug Extension

The *Theia.cpp* debug extension provides a debugging view for *C/C++* and related programming languages [72]. It is based on DAP [55] and uses the machine interface protocol to communicate with the *GDB*. As *rocgdb* extends *GDB* features for *ROCm*, the extension handles several new commands and displays *ROCm*-related GPU information, such as queues, agents, dispatches, and lanes.

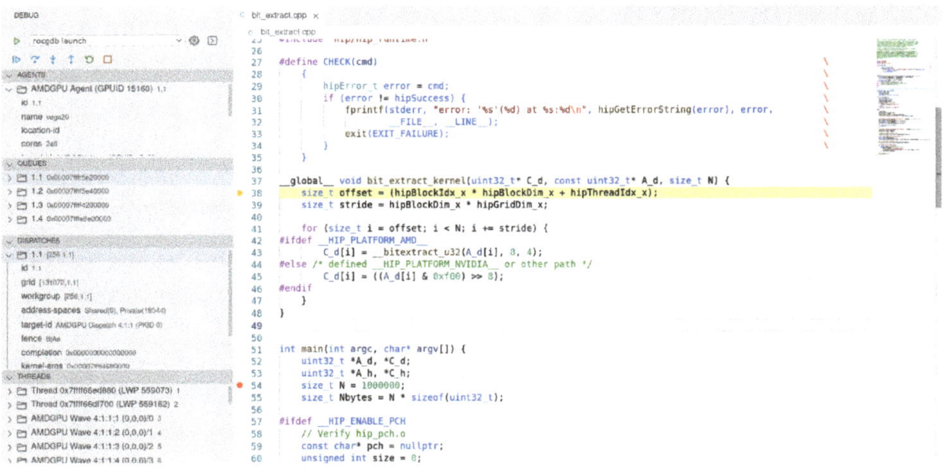

Figure 13.14: *rocgdb* debug view in *Theia*.

To use the *Theia.cpp* debug extension, after installation, simply specify the *GDB* parameter during program launch. Breakpoints can be used to stop the program while having access to *rocgdb* information in the GPU debug view.

Trace Compass

Multiple traces can be visualized using *Trace Compass*. For installation, follow the instructions on *GitHub* [75]. The only *ROCm*-specific requirement is that, during the third step, *ROCm* plugins must be installed.

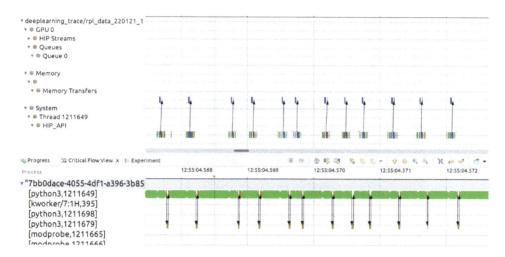

Figure 13.15: Multiple synchronized traces in *Trace Compass*.

In Figure 13.15, we present the execution of a deep learning program alongside its *Linux* kernel trace analysis. To generate a *Linux* kernel trace, we use the *Linux Trace Toolkit: Next Generation* [50] with a few trace points activated. The tracer records *Linux* kernel events, such as system calls, memory allocations, and thread preemptions, which are useful for debugging multithreaded applications. GPU API calls sometimes do not provide a complete picture. In this case, combining multiple trace sources allows programmers to closely follow program behaviors. The analysis shown here is the same as that in the *Theia-trace-extension* section, as it is merely a different frontend to the same *Trace Compass* server backend.

The bottom part, the "critical flow" view, shows the critical path of the program's main thread under study. The critical path analysis begins at the end of the thread and moves back through the dependency chain, identifying the longest path based on resource contentions. We can thus determine when processes must wait for semaphores or I/O operations. In the figure, we can see the relationship between threads 1,211,649 and 1,211,698, where the first waits for the second to complete an operation.

13.4   *TAU*

The *TAU Performance System®* [64] is a parallel performance evaluation toolkit that supports profiling and tracing modes of measurement. It can be applied to unmodified binaries and identifies where the application spends its time alongside other system resources. *TAU* is available open-source at: `http://tau.uoregon.edu`.

    TAU leverages support from various libraries and technologies, such as *rocProfiler* [73] and *rocTracer* [74] for *HIP/ROCm* measurements, *GNU binutils* [31] for symbol resolution and demangling, *PAPI* for hardware performance counting [71], and *OTF2* [27] for scalable distributed trace collection [27]. *TAU* also utilizes the support provided by parallel programming models to integrate performance measurement callbacks from libraries and runtimes, including *MPI* [30], *OpenMP* [59], *OpenACC* [58], and *Kokkos* [76]. When instrumentation and/or callbacks are unavailable, *TAU* performs periodic sampling on the CPU, interrupting programs and capturing counters to build statistical profiles. When collecting samples, optional call-stack unwinding is performed to capture the full sample context.

    For the asynchronous tasking of programming models lacking conventional call stacks, such as *High Performance ParalleX* [39] or applications and libraries that support dynamic runtime adaptation, *TAU* includes an alternative called the Autonomous Performance Environment for eXascale (*APEX*) measurement library [36]. While *APEX* can be used for profiling any program, the captured performance data is represented from a task dependency perspective rather than a call-stack. Dynamic runtime adaptation is provided by a policy engine that periodically or on-demand evaluates the performance state and applies policy rules to adjust control parameters.

13.4.1   Profiling *HIP* Programs Using *TAU*

TAU supports the profiling and tracing of *HIP* programs using the *rocProfiler* and *rocTracer* APIs. *rocTracer* provides *TAU* instrumentatiofn in *HIP* and *HSA* runtime system events, in addition to those provided by *rocProfiler*. To generate performance data, a user typically launches the application using the *tauexec* utility. *TAU* is installed using third-party libraries, such as *binutils* and *libdwarf* [20], which translates program-counter values with source-code locations (e.g., file name, function name, and line number), *libunwind*, which unwinds the system call stack, and *OTF2*, which generates *OTF* trace files. *TAU* supports a download option in which it automatically installs these libraries using the correct flags (e.g., **-fPIC**) to generate position-independent code. A typical *TAU* installation is shown below:

```
./configure -rocm=<dir> -rocprofiler=<dir> \
-bfd=download -unwind=download -dwarf=download
-otf=download \
-iowrapper ...
make install
```

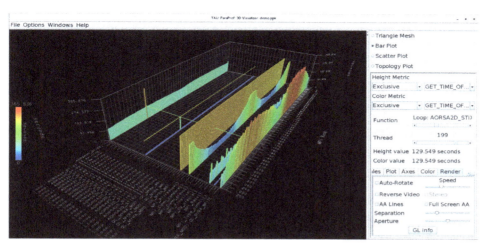

Figure 13.16: 3D visualization using *TAU*'s *ParaProf* tool, revealing the profile shape.

This generates the *tauexec* tool used to launch applications using the above configuration with tags of **-rocm** and **-rocprofiler**, as follows:

```
tau_exec -T rocm,serial,rocprofiler -ebs -rocm ./a.out
```

When *MPI* is not configured for *TAU*, a serial configuration tag is chosen while launching the execution using *tauexec*. It preloads the *TAU* dynamic shared object in the address space of the executing application, generates callbacks, and intercepts system calls. Optionally, when the **-ebs** option is used, *TAU* uses event-based sampling (EBS) to periodically interrupt the application and generate detailed profile data that maps to the source-code location. Using the callbacks from *rocProfiler* and *rocTracer* APIs, *TAU* gathers timestamp information of executing kernels on the GPU and data-transfer information. However, the pairs of timestamps may not appear in order, which poses a problem for the accurate generation of trace files that require monotonically increasing system timestamps. The GPU timestamps must also be correlated with CPU timestamps to produce a consistent global view of the performance data. *TAU* uses a novel sliding-window algorithm to buffer–kernel timestamp pairs and flush them to disk when full. By delaying the commitment of the trace data to disk, the system can handle out-of-order kernel timestamps. Via trial-and-error, the current window size was chosen as 128K pairs of start/stop kernel execution events. Kernel events recorded in profile files are saved in a separate execution thread for each queue. Figure 13.17 shows the time spent for each kernel in a given queue for the *rochpcg* application in the *ParaProf* tool. *TAU*

TAU: ParaProf: Statistics for: node 0, thread 6 - /Users/sameer/ppk/amd/hpcg_rocm.ppk

Name	Exclusive ...	Inclusive ...	Calls	Child ...
void kernel_symgs_sweep<128u>(int, int, int, int, int, int const*, double const*, double const*, double const*, doubl	9.19	9.19	175,620	0
void kernel_backward_sweep_0<128u>(int, int, int, int, int const*, double const*, int const*, double*) [clone .kd]	3.484	3.484	116,928	0
void kernel_forward_sweep_0<128u>(int, int, int, int, int const*, double const*, int const*, double const*, double*) [	3.156	3.156	117,199	0
void kernel_fused_restrict_spmv<1024u>(int, int const*, double const*, int, int, int const*, double const*, doubl	0.678	0.678	12,564	0
void kernel_waxpby<512u>(int, double, double const*, double, double const*, double*) [clone .kd]	0.315	0.315	8,502	0
void kernel_symgs_halo<128u>(int, int, int, int, int const*, int const*, double const*, double const*, int const*, doul	0.304	0.304	12,564	0
void kernel_dot2_part1<256u>(int, double const*, double const*, double*) [clone .kd]	0.23	0.23	8,420	0
void kernel_fused_waxpby_dot_part1<256u>(int, double, double const*, double, double*, double*) [clone .kd]	0.159	0.159	4,208	0
void kernel_gather<128u>(int, double const*, int const*, int const*, double*) [clone .kd]	0.131	0.131	29,366	0
void kernel_spmv_halo<128u>(int, int, int, int, int const*, double const*, int const*, double const*, double const*, double*)	0.099	0.099	4,298	0
void kernel_prolongation<1024u>(int, int const*, double const*, double*, int const*, int const*) [clone .kd]	0.082	0.082	12,546	0
void kernel_pointwise_mult<256u>(int, double const*, double const*, double*) [clone .kd]	0.059	0.059	16,747	0
void kernel_dot_part2<256u>(double*) [clone .kd]	0.028	0.028	8,502	0
void kernel_fused_waxpby_dot_part2<256u>(int, double*) [clone .kd]	0.014	0.014	4,203	0
__amd_rocclr_copyBuffer.kd	0.007	0.007	363	0
__amd_rocclr_fillBuffer.kd	0.004	0.004	125	0
void kernel_jpl<27u, 16u>(int, int const*, int, int, char const*, int const*, int*) [clone .kd]	0.003	0.003	16	0
void kernel_setup_halo<27u, 16u>(int, int, int, int, int, int, int, bool, bool, bool, int, int, long long, long long, lon	0.002	0.002	4	0
void kernel_to_ell_val<27u, 32u>(int, int, double const*, double*) [clone .kd]	0.002	0.002	4	0
void kernel_perm_cols<32u, 16u>(int, int, int const*, int*, double*) [clone .kd]	0.002	0.002	4	0
void kernel_permute_ell_rows<1024u>(int, int const*, double const*, int const*, int*, double*) [clone .kd]	0.002	0.002	108	0
void kernel_dot1_part1<256u>(int, double const*, double*) [clone .kd]	0.002	0.002	88	0
void kernel_generate_problem<27u, 16u>(int, int, int, int, int, long long, long long, long long, long long, long long, l	0.002	0.002	4	0
void rocprim::detail::sort_and_scatter_kernel<256u, 15u, 6u, false, long long*, long long*, int*, int*>(long long*, lon	0.001	0.001	72	0
void kernel_to_ell_col<27u, 32u>(int, int, int const*, int*, int*) [clone .kd]	0.001	0.001	4	0
void rocprim::detail::sort_and_scatter_kernel<256u, 15u, 7u, false, long long*, long long*, int*, int*>(long long*, lon	0.001	0.001	48	0
void rocprim::detail::fill_digit_counts_kernel<256u, 15u, 6u, false, long long*>(long long*, unsigned int, unsigned int	0.001	0.001	72	0

Figure 13.17: Kernel events from the *rochpcg* application, as shown in *TAU*'s *ParaProf* profile browser.

supports CPU and GPU profiling using EBS. A code region executing on the CPU can also be highlighted without recompiling the source using performance instrumentation. Figure 13.18 shows the time spent with the *computeDistance* method in the Quantum Monte Carlo Package (*QMCPack*) application across multiple execution threads. Here, we can observe how an application region performs across multiple threads on the CPU side. Note that a single kernel's execution may be tracked across multiple GPUs, as shown in Figure 13.19. Although these two-dimensional displays are informative, *TAU*'s *ParaProf* profile browser also includes a 3D visualizer that shows the exclusive time spent in a code region mapped across threads (ranks) and functions in an interactive 3D display, enabling users to view the profile shape. Figure 13.16 shows a 3D window in which cross-hairs represent functions, and threads represent sliders, which allow users to accurately pinpoint a single thread.

13.4.2 Tracing *HIP* Programs Using *TAU*

Although profiling provides aggregate summary statistics (e.g., total execution time for a kernel across multiple invocations), tracing can highlight temporal variations. *TAU* generates trace files in its native *TAU* format and in *OTF2*. Traces in the *TAU* format can be merged and converted to Jumpshot's *SLOG2* and *JSON* formats for visualization using *Google Chrome*'s **chrome://tracing** or the *Perfetto* trace browser [32].

TAU also supports the *Kokkos* [76, 63] profiling interface, which provides a performance-

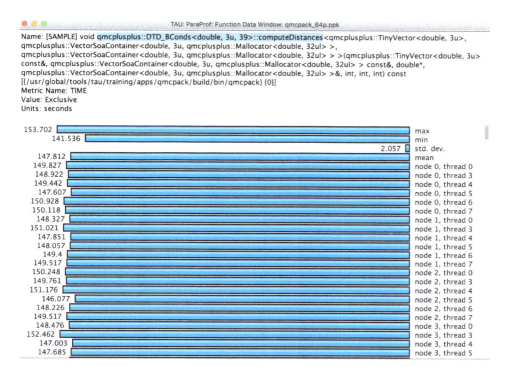

Figure 13.18: EBS applied to *QMCPack* helps pinpoint computationally expensive code regions.

portable method of expressing parallelism in applications using *C++ Lambda* functions for parallel operations, such as **for**, **scan**, and **reduce** operations. These *lambda* functions are internally transformed to GPU backends (e.g., *HIP*). The first argument of these parallel operations is an optional character string that represents meaningful source constructs. *TAU* interfaces with *Kokkos* and tracks these high-level abstractions and maps the kernel execution to them. In the absence of user annotations, template instantiations are used. Figure 13.22 shows a timeline display of kernel execution in the *Vampir* trace visualizer from T.U. Dresden [43]. With *TAU*'s *OTF2* trace generation capabilities, the trace file does not require processing (e.g., merged or converted) after the unmodified code is launched using *tauexec* and the appropriate commands (i.e., **export TAU_TRACE=1** or **export TAU_TRACE_FORMAT=otf2**).

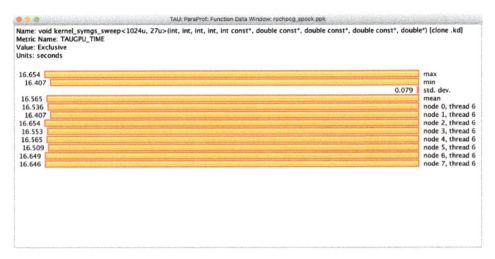

Figure 13.19: *TAU*'s *ParaProf* tool shows the execution of a single kernel across multiple GPU queues.

13.4.3   Using *APEX* to Measure *HIP* Programs

APEX provides a profiling tool like *tauexec*, called *apexexec*, which automatically preloads the *APEX* measurement library and sets the appropriate environment variables for profiling supported runtimes. For example, to execute a sample *HIP* program (e.g., *Matrix-Transpose_hip*), the user prefixes the program with **apexexec** and any *APEX*-related arguments prefixed with **–apex**. In this example, several options are enabled to make things more interesting:

```
apex_exec --apex:hip --apex:hip_metrics   \
--apex:monitor_gpu  --apex:period 10000   \
--apex:ompt --apex:ompt_details --apex:gtrace
```

In this example, the program performs a matrix transpose on an $8,192 \times 8,192$ matrix 10 times, and the result is compared to a reference CPU execution each time. To make the example even more interesting, the CPU execution and its validation use *OpenMP* for concurrency. *APEX* measures the *HIP* CPU and GPU activity using the *rocTracer* library and periodically captures GPU status counters using *rocProfiler* and *ROCm SMI* [22]. The period is specified as 10,000 μ or 100 Hz. The data are written to a *JSON* trace-event [33] file for visualization using *Perfetto*[32], and the task tree is written to machine- and human-readable text files. The *hipcc* compiler and runtime also include support for the *OpenMP* profiling interface; thus, *OpenMP* Tools (*OMPT*)-

Figure 13.20: *APEX* task dependency tree rendered by *Perfetto*. In this example, the first CPU thread is located at the top of the trace, and the worker CPU threads are located at the bottom. The *HIP* GPU activity is just below the three worker threads. *APEX* also captures *ROCTX* instrumentation calls and markers. A flow event, highlighted by the red arrow, indicates the flow of control from a *HIP* API call to the GPU device activity.

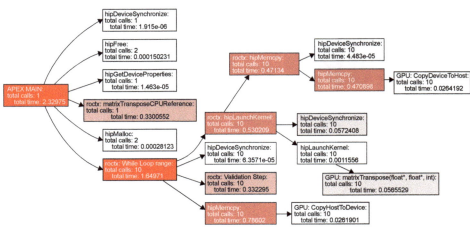

Figure 13.21: *APEX* task dependency tree rendered by Graphviz. The red color indicates the relative time spent in each node of the task graph. Note that some tree nodes have more accumulated time than the total execution wall-clock time owing to their having been executed on multiple threads or devices concurrently. *HIP* API calls and device activities are captured in the dependency tree, and *APEX* captures *ROCTX* instrumentation calls and markers.

related options are enabled. Figure 13.21 displays the task tree when rendered with the *dot* utility from Graphviz[14]. This run is executed without *OMPT* support to make the graph easier to read.

The trace file is rendered by *Perfetto* in Figure 13.20. Several host- and device-side metrics are periodically captured, including power and temperature, memory usage, GPU and GPU memory utilization, and others. Flow events are visualized by the red arrow between CPU Thread 0 and the *HIP* activity, revealing the control-flow dependency relationship between resources. *APEX* also captures CPU instrumentation ranges and markers added using the *ROCTX* API provided by the *ROC-Tracer* library.

13.4.4   Summary of *TAU*

With its extensive capabilities, *TAU* provides a holistic view of low-level CPU and GPU kernel event performance, as well as data transfers between the host and device and

Figure 13.22: *TAU*'s *OTF2* trace data visualized using the *Vampir* commercial trace visualizer.

across the network with support for *OpenMP*, *OpenACC*, *OpenCL*, *MPI*, and *Kokkos*. Support for asynchronous execution is found in *TAU*'s *APEX* measurement layer, and support for profile and trace visualization and data capture and storage performance is found in its *TAUdb* database system. For cross-experiment analysis and data mining perspectives, support is found in *TAU*'s *perfexplorer* [35], which supports scaled performance engineering.

13.5 *TotalView* Debugger

The *TotalView* for the *HPC* debugger from Perforce Software was developed over a period of 30 years. It has supported the *HPC* community during this period by providing debuggers for AMD, Cray, HP, IBM, Intel, SGI, Sun, and other hardware vendors. *TotalView* runs on *Unix*, *Linux*, *macOS*, and custom kernels, and it has continually adapted to the ever-changing HPC landscape, supporting new architectures, languages, and technologies over time.

Today, *TotalView* is a feature-rich debugger that supports *C*, *C++*, and *Fortran* programming languages, including multi-language applications built with these and *Python*. It also supports hybrid mixtures of parallel programming paradigms, such as *MPI*, *OpenMP*, *pthreads*, *HIP*, *CUDA*, Open Accelerators (*OpenACC*), *Unified Parallel C*, *Coarray Fortran*, *Global Arrays*, and *Symmetric Hierarchical Memory*.

TotalView provides an easy-to-use GUI (see Figure 13.23) and command-line in-

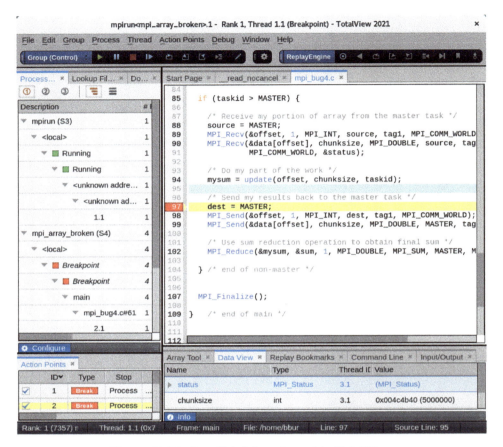

Figure 13.23: Parallel debugging with *TotalView*.

terface (*CLI*) for interactive debugging. Programmers can debug many processes and threads consisting of multiple languages and parallel programming paradigms, all from a single control center. Standard debugging features include starting and stopping threads, processes, and groups. Source- and instruction-level step and step-over methods are supplied, as are breakpoints and conditional breakpoints. Source code, variables, arrays, memory blocks, and registers are displayed, and the program state can be modified. The *CLI* is a programmable tool command language interpreter that supports the creation of user-defined utilities to extend debugger functionality and provides a scripting language that enables automated operations. *TotalView* can be driven in script mode through its *TVScript* and *MemScript* frameworks, which enable non-interactive batch debugging using an event-action model in which the programmer defines a series of events that may occur within the program and the actions to be taken when they occur. Data are logged to a set of output files for review when batch jobs are done.

TotalView offers several other debugging features, including *C*, *C++*, and *Fortran* expression evaluators, data watchpoints, *C++ Standard Template Library* element visualizers (e.g., map, set, array, list, string, etc.), process and thread display aggregators, memory debuggers, core file debuggers, asynchronous thread controllers, reverse debuggers, heterogeneous debuggers, and built-in help and documentation utilities.

These features and capabilities of *TotalView* enable programmers to understand how their complex applications are running and identify potential logic errors. In addition to finding software bugs, *TotalView* is helpful with understanding new code, as its dynamic analysis capabilities allow programmers to experience how programs run with visualized data.

TotalView has a modest list of requirements, including X11 support for GUI clients, a full-featured process and thread-tracing interface (e.g., *ptrace* or the */proc* file system), a compiler that produces accurate debugging information, (e.g., the Executable and Linkable Format (*ELF*), Debugging With Arbitrary Record Formats (*DWARF*), or *Symbol Table Strings*), the *MPI-and-Rationals* interface, the *libpthread_db* thread-level tracing interface, transport control protocol/internet protocol (TCP/IP) sockets and remote shell support (e.g., secure shell) for debugging multiple nodes, the AMD *GPU Debug* API, and the NVIDIA *CUDA Debug* API.

TotalView delivers advanced GPU debugging support for both AMD and NVIDIA GPUs. Programmers can easily debug multiple GPUs on a cluster of nodes within the same session. Using *TotalView*'s advanced GPU capabilities, programmers can easily understand how their code is running, step through lines of code, examine GPU-specific data, and debug CPU and GPU code. *TotalView* supports several common languages that target GPUs, including *CUDA*, *HIP*, *OpenCL*, and *OpenMP*.

TotalView supports the debugging of heterogeneous applications involving a mix of processor architectures (e.g., PowerPC, x86_64, and various GPUs). *TotalView*'s address-space model supports processes containing multiple heterogeneous address spaces, in which various threads run in their own GPU device contexts, or they may share a process address space with other threads (e.g., *pthreads*). As programming languages are extended to accommodate accelerator devices (e.g., *OpenMP* target constructs), the address space model allows *TotalView* to more accurately reconstruct the conceptual model in which a process is a container for a CPU or GPU.

TotalView provides comprehensive support for debugging *HIP* applications running on AMD GPUs. Debugging a *HIP* or any AMD GPU application under *TotalView* is like debugging other kinds of applications. Most commands and actions that apply to CPUs also apply to GPUs. The programmer is able to:

- Launch, attach-to, and detach-from processes, including *MPI* processes.

- Display SGPR, VGPR, general purpose, and special registers.

- Display disassembled machine instructions.
- Create, delete, enable, and disable breakpoints.
- Trace source- and instruction-level code via single-stepping.
- Unwind stacks.
- Display variables (within the limits of the debug information produced by the compiler).

HIP applications should be compiled with the **ggdb** and **O0** debugging options. Linking with the **-Wl,-R/opt/rocm/hip/** option allows an application to automatically find the *HIP* shared libraries.

Listing 13.1: Example compiling a *HIP* program for *TotalView*.

```
hipcc -O0 -ggdb -c bit_extract.cpp -o  bit_extract.o
hipcc -Wl,-R/opt/rocm/hip/ bit_extract.o -o bit_extract
```

A debugging session is launched by simply running the target application under *TotalView* or attaching to an already running program. The *TotalView* **-rocm** option ensures that AMD GPU debugging is enabled.

Listing 13.2: Example *HIP* debugger launch in *TotalView*.

```
totalview -rocm -args bit_extract
```

TotalView displays a unified view of source-code and -line breakpoints across all image files (e.g., executables, shared libraries, and GPU *ELF* images), and all source files. Thus, any code that is dynamically loaded at runtime, including AMD GPU *ELF* images, is unified in the source display. Setting a breakpoint on a source line will result in stopping at or near that line when executed by the CPU or GPU, regardless of whether the machine code for the source has been loaded. A programmer can set pending breakpoints in code that are dynamically loaded, including shared libraries and GPU image files. To set a pending breakpoint, simply select the line number in the source display, and *TotalView* will arrange to stop the program as close as possible to that source line.

By default, the *HIP* runtime defers GPU code loading until the first kernel is launched; hence, all breakpoints added in the *HIP* source code must be set beforehand as pending breakpoints. However, if setting *HIP_ENABLE_DEFERRED_LOADING* (*HIP's* environment variable) to zero will disable deferred GPU code-loading, thus ensuring that the GPU code is loaded before the application enters the *main* function. When deferred GPU code-loading is disabled, the GPU source line information will become available upon entering the *main* function before the first kernel is launched, making it easier to set a source-level breakpoint in the GPU code.

TotalView assigns a negative debugger thread ID (DTID) to each GPU agent (device) within the process. For example, a process using two GPU devices will have two debugger

GPU agent threads (e.g., −1 and −2). A programmer can focus on a specific device by selecting the GPU agent thread within the process. *TotalView* maintains separate address spaces for the *Linux* CPU process address space and that of each GPU agent thread.

These address spaces are placed into the same *TotalView* share group that contains all processes created and shared by a program. Breakpoints are created and evaluated within the share group and are applied to all image files (e.g., executables, shared libraries, and GPU *ELF* images) in the share group. Thus, a breakpoint can be applied to both CPU and GPU code, allowing breakpoints to be set on source lines in the host code that are then planted in the GPU images at the same location after the GPU code is loaded.

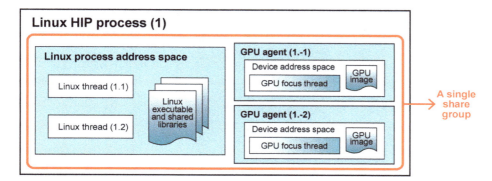

Figure 13.24: *TotalView*'s *HIP* debugging model.

If we have a *Linux* process consisting of two *pthreads* and two GPU agent threads, the GPU debugging model can be summarized as follows:

- A *Linux* process address space, containing a *Linux* executable and a list of *Linux* shared libraries.

- A collection of *Linux* threads that:

  - are assigned a positive DTID.

  - share the *Linux* process address space with other *Linux* threads.

  - share a collection of GPU agent threads that:

    * are assigned a negative DTID.

    * has its own address space separate from the *Linux* process address space and separate from those of other GPU agent threads.

    * has a GPU focus thread that attends to a specific hardware lane within the GPU agent thread.

The above *TotalView HIP* debugging model is reflected in the *TotalView* GUI and CLI. Additionally, *ROCm*-specific CLI commands allow programmers to inspect GPU agent threads, change the focus to a specific lane, and display the status of GPU agents, queues, dispatches, workgroups, wavefronts, and work items.

13.6   *HPCToolkit*

Rice University's *HPCToolkit* performance tools support the measurement and analysis of GPU-accelerated applications by recording call-path profiles and traces of both CPU and GPU activity [83]. To help programmers understand how GPU operations are used by an application, the *HPCToolkit* provides metrics for each GPU operation and attributes the contributions of the calling context in which it is invoked. To supplement the timing and semantic information recorded for GPU operations, *HPCToolkit* also measures GPU operations using hardware performance counters.

HPCToolkit supports multiple CPU architectures (e.g., x86-64, Power, and ARM), GPUs from different vendors (e.g., AMD, Intel, and NVIDIA), and various programming models for offloading computations to GPUs (e.g., *CUDA* [56], *HIP* [4], *Raja* Portability Suite [15], *Kokkos* [26], *OpenMP* [60], and *Data Parallel C++* [37]. We next describe the workflow of the *HPCToolkit* and provide two examples that demonstrate how it analyzes the performance of applications accelerated by AMD GPUs.

13.6.1   *HPCToolkit*'s Workflow

Figure 13.25 shows *HPCToolkit*'s workflow used to analyze the performance of GPU-accelerated applications. *HPCToolkit*'s *hpcrun* measurement tool uses sampling to measure CPU activity and collects GPU performance metrics with profiling APIs from GPU vendors. *hpcrun* measures programs that employ one or more GPU programming models. As a program loads GPU binaries during execution, *hpcrun* records them for later analysis. For GPUs that provide APIs for fine-grained measurement, *hpcrun* collects instruction-level characterizations of GPU kernels using hardware support or binary instrumentation. *hpcrun*'s output includes profiles and optional traces of CPU and GPU activities. Each profile contains a calling context tree in which each call path, represented by a tree node, is associated with a set of metrics (e.g., execution time and instructions executed). Each trace file contains a sequence of call paths and timestamp pairs for a CPU thread or GPU stream.

hpcstruct analyzes CPU and GPU binaries to recover static information about procedures, inline functions, loop nests, and source lines. There are two important aspects of this process: recovering information about line mappings and inlined compiler-recorded information from binaries and analyzing machine code to recover information about loops.

hpcprof and *hpcprof-mpi* correlate performance metrics gathered during GPU-accelerated program execution with source-code contexts using information produced

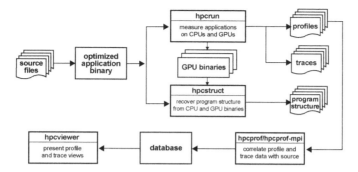

Figure 13.25: *HPCToolkit*'s workflow for analyzing GPU-accelerated applications.

by *hpcstruct*. *hpcprof* uses a single node to aggregate profiles and traces to relate measurements associated with machine instructions back to the CPU and GPU source code. *hpcprof-mpi* employs distributed memory parallelism to accelerate the performance analysis of extreme-scale executions.

Finally, *hpcviewer* interprets and visualizes databases produced by *hpcprof* and *hpcprof-mpi*. In its profile view, *hpcviewer* presents a heterogeneous calling context tree that spans both CPU and GPU contexts, annotated with measured or derived metrics to help users assess code performance and identify bottlenecks. In its trace view, *hpcviewer* displays CPU and GPU activities over time, which can help programmers understand the time-varying behaviors of applications as they execute.

13.6.2 Analyzing *PIConGPU* with *HPCToolkit*

PIConGPU [16] is a fully relativistic, manycore, 3D3V particle-in-cell (*PIC*) code. In the next section, we demonstrate how to use *HPCToolkit* to measure the performance of *PIConGPU* running on 16 *MPI* ranks and 16 MI100 GPUs.

13.6.3 Collecting and Analyzing Profiles and Traces

The first step measures *PIConGPU*'s performance using *hpcrun*, as shown in Listing 13.3.

Listing 13.3: Example of the **hpcrun** command.

```
hpcrun -t -e REALTIME -e gpu=amd -o picgongpu.m picongpu
```

In the command shown above, **-t** directs *hpcrun* to collect traces. **-e REALTIME** indicates that *hpcrun* should sample the execution of each CPU thread at equal intervals of real time, which causes samples to be recorded, even when threads are idle. **-e gpu=amd** specifies the collection of GPU profiles with AMD's *ROCm* support, and **-o picgongpu.m** directs *hpcrun* to store measurement data in the *picgongpu.m* directory.

The second step recovers the program structure using *hpcstruct*, as shown in Listing 13.4.

Listing 13.4: Example of the **hpcstruct** command.

```
hpcstruct picgongpu.m
```

By default, *hpcstruct* uses half the hardware threads available on the current node to perform concurrent and parallel analysis of the application's executable, shared libraries, and GPU binaries to recover their program structures. By inspecting the contents of the *picgongpu.m* measurement directory recorded by *hpcrun*, *hpcstruct* knows what GPU and GPU binaries it should analyze and augments the measurement directory with the results.

The third step uses *hpcprof* to interpret the performance measurements using program structure information recovered by *hpcstruct*, as shown in Listing 13.5.

Listing 13.5: Example of the **hpcprof** command.

```
hpcprof -o picgongpu.d picgongpu.m
```

The **-o** option specifies the name of the output directory to which *hpcprof* should write its analysis results.

The final step is using *hpcviewer* to examine the profiles and traces collected by *HPCToolkit*, as shown in Listing 13.6.

Listing 13.6: Example of the **hpcviewer command.**

```
hpcviewer picgongpu.d
```

Figure 13.26 shows a top-down profile view of a hot kernel in *PIConGPU*. The scope pane on the bottom left shows its unified CPU–GPU calling context, which consists of three parts: the CPU calling context of the *HIP* API that launches the kernel, a placeholder frame (i.e., <**gpu kernel**>) that represents the transition from the host to device, and the GPU calling context. Presently, the GPU calling context on AMD GPUs includes only the GPU kernel, as there is no support for fine-grained measurements within kernels. Figure 13.26 shows GPU kernel execution times, and the bottom-right pane presents columns of performance metrics. *HPCToolkit* can also present metrics for copy operations in and out of GPU memory. The source pane at the top shows the

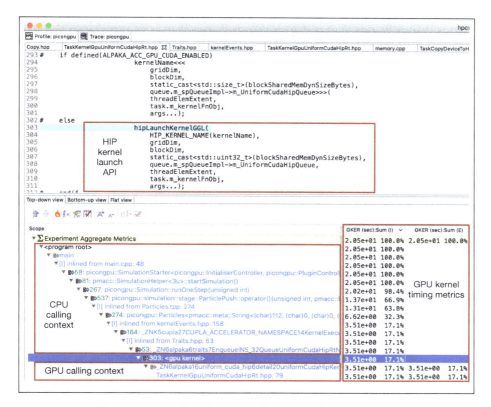

Figure 13.26: Top-down profile view of *PIConGPU*.

source line of a *HIP* API, *hipLaunchKernelGGL*. The user can navigate the source code of a function in the calling context by simply clicking on it.

Figure 13.27 shows a bottom-up profile view of GPU memory copy operations. The bottom-up calling context of a function in the scope pane shows one or more contexts in which the function is invoked. In the figure, the GPU memory copy operation represented by the placeholder frame, **<gpu copy>** was invoked in two different calling contexts that correspond to instantiations of different templates. In this case, the top context was responsible for nearly all GPU copy costs.

In this example, we only need to inspect the top call path to understand where most of the GPU copy operations were incurred. Generally, the costs of an operation are typically split more evenly among invocations according to multiple calling contexts. The bottom-up view makes it easy to understand this by grouping all invocation contexts

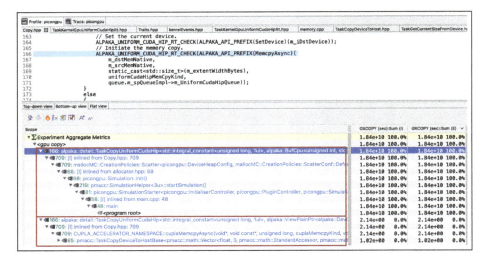

Figure 13.27: Bottom-up profile view of *PIConGPU*.

from an operation.

Figure 13.28 shows a unified CPU–GPU trace view. The trace lines from the top to the bottom represent a CPU thread and a GPU stream for *MPI* ranks 1–16. Each *MPI* rank of the execution also employs an *MPI* helper thread; we use *hpcviewer*'s *Filter* menu to hide these threads in the trace view, as they are idle throughout execution. From the trace view, we can see that during the first third of the execution, the GPU trace lines are white, indicating that they were idle. This period represents the initialization phase of the application. During the remaining execution, we see scattered operations along each GPU trace line, which indicates that the GPUs were not entirely utilized. Thus, the programmer should closely examine the CPU threads to understand what they are doing when the GPUs are idle.

13.6.4   Measurement Using Hardware Counters

HPCToolkit uses the University of Tennessee's *PAPI* [71] toolkit, as discussed earlier in this chapter, to measure GPU activity with hardware counters. Currently, the only way tools can associate hardware counter measurements with individual GPU kernels using existing vendor APIs is to serialize the kernels and read data from counters before and after each execution. Serializing kernels slows execution and may alter program behaviors.

We use *FloydWarshall*, a *HIP* sample code [7], to illustrate *HPCToolkit*'s ability

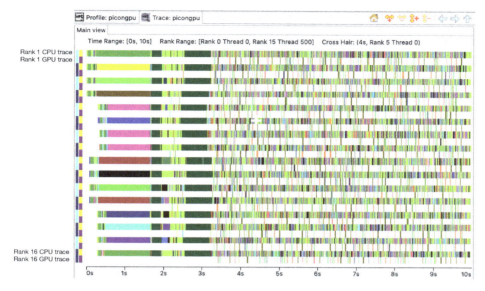

Figure 13.28: Trace view.

to measure the characteristics of an application's performance using GPU hardware counters. The following command directs *HPCToolkit* to use *PAPI* to measure hits and misses in the TCC of an AMD GPU. Recall that the TCC serves as a shared L2 cache for GPU CUs. The command is shown in Listing 13.7.

Listing 13.7: Command for collecting the TCC miss counter for the *FloydWarshall* application using *HPCToolkit*.

```
hpcrun -e gpu=amd -e rocm:::TCC_HIT_sum:device=0  -e rocm:::TCC_MISS_sum:
    device=0 ./FloydWarshall -q -i 100
```

As before, we analyze the resulting measurement database with *hpcstruct* and *hpcprof*.

Figure 13.29 shows the resulting database with hardware counter metrics associated with GPU calling contexts. Using the metric filtering capabilities in *hpcviewer*, we hide columns with exclusive hit and miss metrics and compute the TCC miss rate as 100 × misses/(hits + misses). Figure 13.29 shows that the TCC miss rate was only 6.87% for the *FloydWarshallPass* kernel, but it was 100% for a pair of *hipHostMalloc* operations on Line 356. This information can be quite useful for identifying GPU code contexts that exhibit poor memory hierarchy utilization.

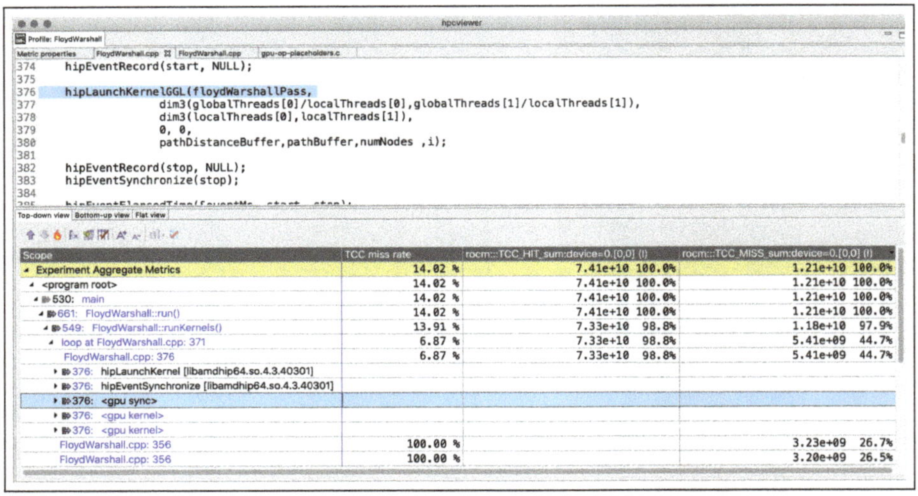

Figure 13.29: Associating hardware counter metrics with GPU operations in their calling contexts.

13.7 Debugging and Profiling with Linaro Forge

Linaro Forge combines Linaro DDT for parallel high-performance application debugging, Linaro MAP for performance profiling and optimization advice, and Linaro Performance Reports for summarizing and characterizing both scalar and MPI application performance. Linaro Forge supports many parallel architectures and models, including MPI, CUDA and OpenMP. Linaro Forge is a cross-platform tool, with support for the latest compilers and C++ standards, and Intel, 64-bit Arm, AMD, NVIDIA GPU and AMD GPU hardware.

Linaro Forge provides everything you need to debug, fix, and profile programs at any scale. One common interface makes it easy to move between Linaro DDT and Linaro MAP during code development. Linaro Forge provides native remote clients for Windows, Mac OS X, and Linux. Use a remote client to connect to your cluster, where you can debug, profile, edit, and compile application files.

To download Linaro Forge, see:

https://www.linaroforge.com/downloadForge/

For more information on Linaro Forge, see:

https://docs.linaroforge.com/latest/html/forge

13.7.1 Linaro DDT

Linaro DDT is a powerful graphical debugger that is suitable for different development environments, including:

- single process and multi-threaded software,
- OpenMP,
- parallel (MPI) software,
- heterogeneous software (e.g., GPU software),
- hybrid code mixing paradigms (e.g., MPI with OpenMP, MPI with HIP, MPI with CUDA), and
- multi-process software including, client-server applications.

Linaro DDT helps you find and fix problems in a single thread, or across hundreds of thousands of processes. Linaro DDT supports static analysis to highlight potential code problems, as well as integrated memory debugging, to perform array-based bounds checking on reads and writes, and integration with MPI message queues.

13.7.2 Linaro MAP

Linaro MAP is a parallel profiler enables the programmer to identify the most time-consuming lines of code in their application. Linaro MAP also attempts to explain why those lines of code are costly. Configuring Linaro MAP is straightforward, allowing users that may not have experience with profiling tools to leverage its full power. Linaro MAP supports:

- MPI, OpenMP, CUDA, ROCm, single- and multi-threaded programs,
- small data files - all data are aggregated on the cluster and only a few megabytes are written to disk, regardless of the size or duration of the program execution,
- sophisticated source code viewing, enabling you to analyze performance across individual functions,
- both interactive and batch modes for gathering profile data,
- a rich set of metrics, providing data on memory usage, floating-point calculations, and MPI usage across processes, including:
  - percentage of vectorized instructions, including AVX extensions, used in each part of the code,
  - time spent in memory operations, and how it varies over time and processes, to identify any cache bottlenecks,
  - a visual summary across aggregated processes and cores, to highlight any region of imbalance in the code, and
  - GPU metric collection and GPU kernel detection.

13.7.3   Linaro Performance Reports

Linaro Performance Reports is a low-overhead tool that produces one-page text and HTML reports summarizing and characterizing both scalar and MPI application performance. Linaro Performance Reports provides the most effective way to characterize and understand the performance of HPC application runs. A one-page HTML report answers a range of vital questions for any HPC user, including:

- Is this application optimized for the system it is running on?
- Does it benefit from running at this scale?
- Are there I/O or networking bottlenecks affecting performance?
- What hardware, software or configuration changes can be made to improve performance?

Linaro Performance Reports is based on the Linaro MAP adaptive sampling technology that minimizes data storage requirements and application overhead. Some of the key features of Linaro Performance Reports include:

- the ability to run transparently on optimized production-ready codes by simply adding a single command to your scripts, and
- the introduction of less than 5% application slowdown during sampled runtime, even when sampling thousands of MPI processes.

13.7.4   GPU Debugging Using Linaro DDT

Linaro DDT can be used to debug programs that use AMD GPU devices. The code running on the GPU is debugged simultaneously using the code on the host CPU. The AMD ROCm software stack is supported by Linaro DDT.

To debug GPU programs using Linaro DDT, you need a GPU-enabled license key. This is an additional option. If GPU support is not included with your DDT license, the GPU options will be disabled on the Run dialog.

When using AMD's ROCm hipcc compiler, kernels must be compiled with the -g flag. Using the syntax below enables generation of symbol information for debuggers in kernels, and disables some optimizations that will hinder debugging.

```
$ hipcc -g -O0 -o program_name source_file.cpp
```

To start Linaro DDT:

```
$ ddt --rocm <program_name> [arguments]
```

Ensure that ROCm is selected on the Run dialog before you click Run/Submit. To control GPU threads, use the standard play, pause, and breakpoint controls. They all work for controlling execution of GPU kernels. However, because GPUs have a different

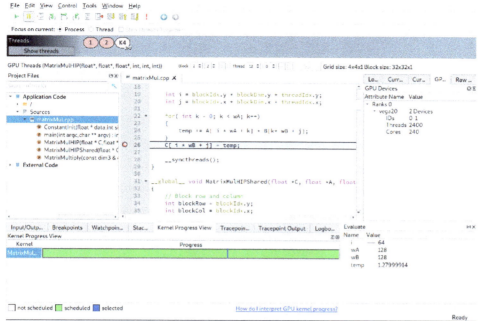

Figure 13.30: Debugging a HIP Application with Linaro DDT.

execution model from that of a CPU, there are a few behavioral differences, as described below.

GPU breakpoints can be set in the same way as other breakpoints. Right-click in the Source Code viewer where you want to place a breakpoint, then choose to add a breakpoint. Breakpoints affect all GPU threads, and cause the program to stop when a thread reaches the breakpoint.

The GPU execution model is noticeably different from that of the host CPU. In the context of stepping operations, that is, step in, step over, or step out, there are critical differences to note. The smallest execution unit on a GPU is a wavefront, which on current AMD GPUs is 64 threads. All threads in a wavefront execute in lockstep, which means that you cannot step each thread individually. Click Play/Continue to run all GPU threads. It is possible to use conditional breakpoints to pause execution at specific blocks, wavefronts, or threads. However, all of the threads in this wavefront will stop for this example. Click Pause to pause a running kernel.

When working with GPUs, most of the user interface is unchanged from regular MPI or multithreaded debugging. However, there are a number of enhancements and additional features that have been added to help debug GPU programs.

The Thread Selector enables you to select your current GPU thread. The currently selected thread is used for the variable evaluation windows, along with the various GPU stepping operations.

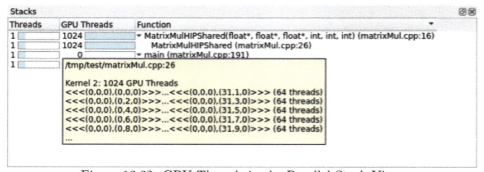

Figure 13.31: The GPU Thread Selector.

In Figure 13.31, the first entry specifies the block index. The subsequent entries specify the 3D thread index inside that block. Changing the current thread updates the local variables, the evaluations, and the current line displayed, as well as the source code displayed, providing a lens into the state of the GPU kernel. The Thread Selector also displays the dimensions of the grid and blocks in your program. It is only possible to inspect/control threads in the set of blocks that are loaded into the GPU. If you attempt to select a thread that is not currently loaded, a message is displayed. The Thread Selector is only visible when there is a GPU Kernel active.

As shown in Figure 13.32, the Parallel Stack View displays the location and number of GPU threads. Click an item in the Parallel Stack View to select a GPU thread at this frame, update the variable display components accordingly, and move the Source Code viewer to the appropriate location. To see which individual GPU thread ranges are at a specific location, and to view the size of each range, hover over an item in the Parallel Stack View.

Figure 13.32: GPU Threads in the Parallel Stack View.

Kernel Progress View

As shown in Figure 13.33, a Kernel Progress View tab will be displayed at the bottom of the user interface by default whenever a kernel is in progress. This view provides the necessary detail to help you decide whether the array data is fresh or stale (i.e., is the array associated with the active thread) during debugging.

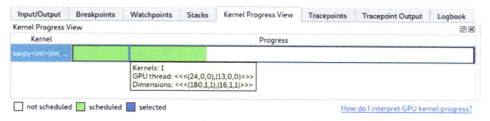

Figure 13.33: GPU Threads in the Kernel Process View.

For a simple kernel that calculates an output value for each index in an array, it is not easy to check whether the value at a particular position x in an array has been calculated, or whether the calculating thread has been scheduled. This contrasts sharply with scalar programming, where if the counter of a (up-)loop exceeds x, then the value of index x can be taken as being the final value. The Kernel Progress View (see Figure 13.33) identifies the kernels that are in progress. The number of kernels is provided and the numbers are grouped by different kernel identifiers across processes. The identifier is the kernel name. A colored progress bar shows which GPU threads are in progress. The progress bar is a projection onto a straight line of the GPU block and thread indexing system. It illustrates the sizes of the kernels operating in the program.

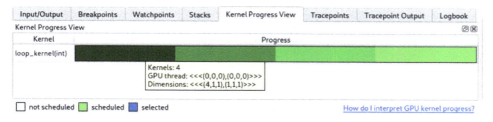

Figure 13.34: GPU Threads in the Kernel Process View.

Click the color-highlighted sections of the progress bar to select a thread that closely matches the click location.

- Blue represents the selected GPU thread.
- Green GPU threads are threads that are scheduled to run. Multiple scheduled threads display in different shades of green to differentiate them.
- White areas of the progress bar represent inactive items. They are inactive either because they have already run or are not scheduled to run.
- Kernels with the same name are stacked, and the shade of green becomes darker (see Figure 13.34).

- Kernels with different names display on separate rows.

Source Code Viewer

The Source Code viewer helps you visualize the program flow through your source code by highlighting lines in the current stack trace. When debugging GPU kernels, it applies color to highlight lines with available GPU threads and displays the GPU threads in a similar manner to that of regular CPU threads and processes. To display a summary of the GPU threads on a highlighted line, hover over the line in the Source Code viewer.

GPU Device Information

One of the challenges of GPU programming is discovering device parameters, such as the device type and whether a device is present. The GPU Devices tab, shown in Figure 13.35, lists the GPUs that are present and in use across a program, and groups the information scalably (grouping information based on similar characteristics, such as GPU model) for multi-process systems.

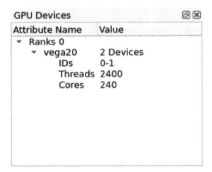

Figure 13.35: GPU Devices Tab

13.7.5   GPU Profiling using Linaro MAP

You can use the Linaro MAP GPU profiling capabilities when working with AMD ROCm programs. AMD GPU profiling is initialized by default when the ROCm libraries are detected. In a program using an AMD ROCm CPU, time spent waiting for GPU kernels to complete is displayed in purple. In Figure 13.36, an example of a mixed MPI and HIP application is observed, with two processes each executing a HIP kernel on a GPU, and a single process executing serially.

Figure 13.36: Profiling a HIP Application with Linaro MAP.

To see the source code in Linaro MAP, compile your program with the debug flag, as shown below. Do not use a debug build. When profiling using Linaro MAP, always keep optimization flags turned on.

```
$ hipcc -g -O3 -o program_name source_file.cpp
```

To start Linaro MAP,

```
$ map <program_name> [arguments]
```

If you have Linaro Forge Professional, the AMD ROCm GPU accelerator metrics are enabled by default. These metrics can be selected using a preset menu option for AMD ROCm. An example of these is shown in Figure 13.37.

Metrics include:

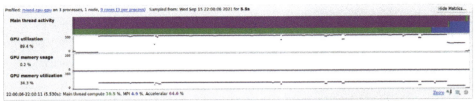

Figure 13.37: ROCm GPU Metrics View in Linaro MAP.

- GPU utilization - the percentage of time that the GPU was in use, with one or more kernels executing on the GPU card. If multiple cards are present on a compute node, this value is the mean across all the cards in a compute node.

- GPU memory usage - the memory allocated on the GPU, as a percentage of the total available GPU memory.

- GPU memory utilization - the percentage of time that the GPU memory was in use. If multiple cards are present on a compute node, this value is the mean across all the cards in a compute node.

When profiling AMD GPU programs, GPU kernels that can be tracked will be displayed in the GPU Kernels tab, as shown in Figure 13.38.

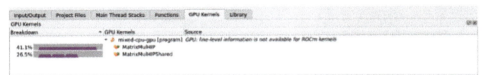

Figure 13.38: GPU Kernels Tab in Linaro MAP.

This lists the GPU kernels that were detected in the program, alongside graphs indicating their time when active. If multiple kernels are identified in a process within a particular profiled sample, they are given equal weighting in this graph. Selecting a single GPU Kernel results in the Source Code viewer jumping to this kernel if debug information is available.

13.7.6 GPU Performance Reports

To generate a report using the Linaro Performance Reports:

```
$ perf-report <program_name> [arguments]
```

The program runs as normal. After the program completes, a performance report is saved to the current working directory, using a name based on the application executable, in both html and text formats. Accelerator metrics and advice are visible in the report for AMD ROCm applications, as shown in Figure 13.39.

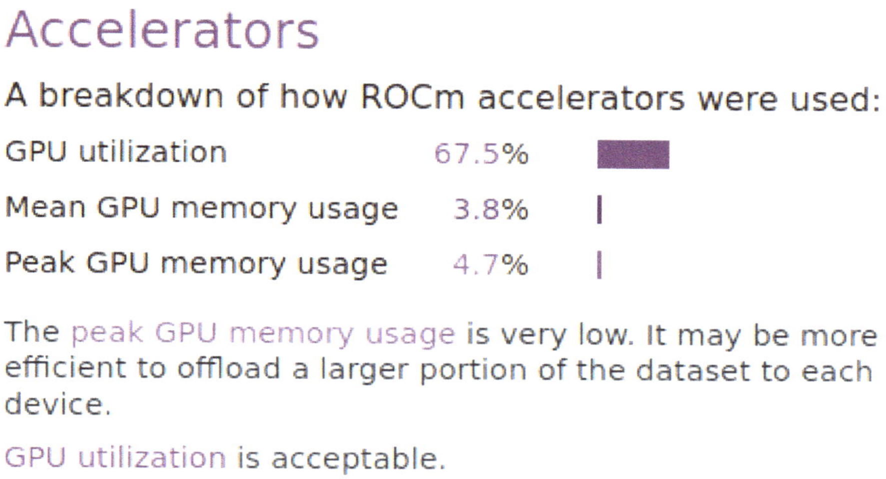

Accelerators

A breakdown of how ROCm accelerators were used:

GPU utilization   67.5%

Mean GPU memory usage   3.8% |

Peak GPU memory usage   4.7% |

The peak GPU memory usage is very low. It may be more efficient to offload a larger portion of the dataset to each device.

GPU utilization is acceptable.

Figure 13.39: Accelerator metrics report.

The metrics reported include:

- GPU utilization - the percentage of time during which one or more kernels were executing on the GPU, averaged across the available GPUs.

- Mean GPU memory usage - the average amount of memory in use on the GPU cards.

- Peak GPU memory usage - the maximum amount of memory in use on the GPU cards.

Downloads and further information about Linaro Forge can be found at: https://www.linaroforge.com/

13.8   *E4S* - The Extreme Scale Scientific Software Stack

The *E4S* [52] is a curated collection of software products based on the *Spack* package manager [25]. It includes full-featured and base-container images available for download

```
% singularity run --rocm ./e4s-rocm-22.05.sif
Singularity> which hipcc
/usr/bin/hipcc
Singularity> which spack
/spack/bin/spack
Singularity> which mpicc
/spack/opt/spack/linux-ubuntu20.04-x86_64/gcc-9.4.0/mpich-4.0.2-ssbmd2ccbxzkbxk7fzrlekupe23rokw2/bin/mpicc
Singularity> spack find +rocm amdgpu_target=gfx90a
==> 17 installed packages
-- linux-ubuntu20.04-x86_64 / gcc@9.4.0 ----------------------------
amrex@22.05  camp@0.2.3  gasnet@2022.3.0  heffte@2.2.0  kokkos@3.6.00  petsc@3.17.1  slepc@3.17.1  superlu-dist@7.2.0  upcxx@2022.3.0
arborx@1.2    chai@2.4.0  ginkgo@1.4.0    hpx@1.7.1      magma@2.6.2   raja@0.14.0  strumpack@6.3.1  umpire@6.0.0
Singularity> python
Python 3.9.7 (default, Sep 16 2021, 13:09:58)
[GCC 7.5.0] :: Anaconda, Inc. on linux
Type "help", "copyright", "credits" or "license" for more information.
>>> import tensorflow
>>> tensorflow.__version__
'2.8.0'
>>> tensorflow.config.list_physical_devices('GPU')
[PhysicalDevice(name='/physical_device:GPU:0', device_type='GPU')]
>>> import torch
>>> exit()
Singularity> module avail

------------------------------ /spack/share/spack/lmod/linux-ubuntu20.04-x86_64/mpich/4.0.2-ssbmd2c/Core ------------------------------
   adios/1.13.1                      geopm/1.1.0-openmp            openpmd-api/0.14.4            slepc/3.17.1-rocm-gfx90a
   adios2/2.8.0                      globalarrays/5.8             papyrus/1.0.2                slepc/3.17.1-rocm-gfx908
   alquimia/1.0.9                    h5bench/1.2                  parallel-netcdf/1.12.2       slepc/3.17.1                    (D)
   amrex/22.05-rocm-gfx90a           hdf5/1.10.7                  paraview/5.10.1              strumpack/6.3.1-openmp
   amrex/22.05-rocm-gfx908           heffte/2.2.0-rocm-gfx90a     parsec/3.0.2012             strumpack/6.3.1-rocm-gfx90a-openmp
   amrex/22.05             (D)       heffte/2.2.0-rocm-gfx908     petsc/3.17.1-rocm-gfx90a     strumpack/6.3.1-rocm-gfx908-openmp (D)
   arborx/1.2-rocm-gfx90a            heffte/2.2.0        (D)      petsc/3.17.1-rocm-gfx908 (D) sundials/6.2.0
   arborx/1.2-rocm-gfx908            hpctoolkit/2022.04.15-rocm   phist/1.9.5-openmp           superlu-dist/7.2.0-rocm-gfx90a
   arborx/1.2              (D)       hpctoolkit/2022.04.15 (D)    plumed/2.6.3                superlu-dist/7.2.0-rocm-gfx908  (D)
   ascent/0.8.0-openmp               hpx/1.7.1-rocm-gfx90a        precice/2.4.0               tasmanian/7.7-openmp
   axom/0.6.1-openmp                 hpx/1.7.1-rocm-gfx908        pruners-ninja/1.0.1         tau/2.31.1-rocm
   bricks/r0.1                       hpx/1.7.1           (D)      pumi/2.2.7                  tau/2.31.1                      (L,D)
   butterflypack/2.1.1               lammps/20220107-openmp       py-cinemasci/1.7.0          unifyfs/0.9.2
   cabana/0.4.0                      libnrm/0.1.0                 py-libensemble/0.9.1        upcxx/2022.3.0-rocm-gfx90a
   caliper/2.7.0                     mercury/1.1.0                py-petsc4py/3.17.1          upcxx/2022.3.0-rocm-gfx908
   datatransferkit/3.1-rc3           metall/0.20                  py-warpx/22.05-dims2        upcxx/2022.3.0                  (D)
   dyninst/12.1.0-openmp             mfem/4.4.0                   py-warpx/22.05-dims3        veloc/1.5
   exaworks/0.1.0                    mpifileutils/0.11.1          py-warpx/22.05-dimsRZ (D)   vtk-m/1.7.1-openmp
   faodel/1.2108.1                   nccmp/1.9.0.1                rempi/1.1.0                 wannier90/3.1.0
   flecsi/1.4.2                      nco/5.0.1                    scr/3.0rc2
   fortrilinos/2.0.0                 omega-h/9.34.1               slate/2021.05.02-openmp

------------------------------ /spack/share/spack/lmod/linux-ubuntu20.04-x86_64/Core ------------------------------
   aml/0.1.0                         flit/2.1.0                   kokkos/3.6.00-openmp         py-jupyterhub/1.4.1
   archer/2.0.0                      flux-core/0.38.0             legion/21.03.0              qthreads/1.16
   argobots/1.1                      gasnet/2022.3.0-rocm-gfx90a  loki/0.1.7                  raja/0.14.0-rocm-gfx90a
   bolt/2.0                          gasnet/2022.3.0-rocm-gfx908  magma/2.6.2-rocm-gfx90a     raja/0.14.0-rocm-gfx908 (D)
   chai/2.4.0-rocm-gfx90a            gasnet/2022.3.0       (D)    magma/2.6.2-rocm-gfx908 (D) superlu/5.3.0
   chai/2.4.0-rocm-gfx908            ginkgo/1.4.0-openmp          mpark-variant/1.4.0         swig/4.0.2-fortran
   chai/2.4.0              (D)       ginkgo/1.4.0-rocm-gfx90a-openmp  mpich/3.4.3             umap/2.1.0
   charliecloud/0.26                 ginkgo/1.4.0-rocm-gfx908-openmp (D)  mpich/4.0.2   (L,D) variorum/0.4.1
```

Figure 13.40: *E4S* Singularity image showing the list of installed HPC and AI/ML tools supporting an MI210 AMD GPU.

and customization. These container images support Docker and Singularity [68] container runtimes. In addition to packaging over 100 HPC tools and numerical libraries, the *E4S* image contains *ROCm* complete with compilers (*hipcc*) and *Python*-based artificial intelligence (AI) and ML tools. These tools include *PyTorch* and *TensorFlow*, which target AMD GPUs. The *E4S* base image contains just *ROCm* and *MPI*. *Spack* may be used to build custom container images. *E4S* also includes a unique tool (i.e., *e4s-cl* [52]) that is commonly used to launch *MPI* applications. The *MPI* library resides in the container image and can be replaced with the corresponding library on the system. Substituting *MPI* unmodified binaries at runtime enables programmers to leverage high-performance networks, such as InfiniBand, for fast internode communications between datacenter nodes. *E4S* is a growing suite of tools and libraries aimed at lowering the barriers to entry for HPC and AI/ML programmers. *E4S* allows new users to easily leverage the benefits of *ROCm* at scale by leveraging ready-to-use *E4S* containers.

The latest *E4S* version 22.05 release provides both full-featured and base images with support for *ROCm* version 5.1.1 and gfx90a (MI210/MI250X+, as well as gfx908 (MI100) architectures. Figure 13.40 shows a session in which both HPC and AI/ML packages (i.e., *TensorFlow* version 2.8.0 and *PyTorch* version 1.11.0) are configured to use AMD GPUs. Tools can be installed in this Singularity image using the *Spack* package manager, which provides modules and the *Spack* CLI. *MPI*, numerical libraries and tools, compilers, build tools (e.g., *cmake* and *autotools*), and GUI tools are included in the container image. The latest versions of performance evaluation tools (e.g., *PAPI* [70], *TAU* [64], and *HPCToolkit* [83]) provide support for AMD GPUs using *rocProfiler* and *rocTracer* instrumentation interfaces. These tools are very effective when run inside the container environment. The *E4S* full-featured image includes more than 100 packages built using *Spack*, *ROCm*, *MPI*, and other build tools. Alternatively, the *E4S* base image includes just *Spack*, *ROCm*, *MPI*, and build tools, but none of the other AI/ML or HPC packages. Nevertheless, programmers have great flexibility in building customized and compact container images from this base image. These derived images can then be launched using Docker, Singularity, or Shifter container runtimes. *E4S* aims to enable all HPC and AI/ML programmers to build their own applications and deploy commonly used tools and libraries with *E4S* containers that support GPUs. These images may be deployed on workstations or large-scale HPC systems in datacenters, providing a consistent development and deployment environment for applications that use the latest AMD GPUs.

Appendix A

ROCm Installation

In this chapter, we cover the installation process of ROCm. Installing ROCm is typically the initial step needed to leverage your AMD GPUs. As such, it helps if programmers are familiar with the installation of the ROCm environment before embarking on the development or execution of GPU programs.

In this chapter, we cover the installation process of ROCm v5.4 on the Ubuntu 20.04 LTS operating system. ROCm is under active development; therefore, we focus on the basic commands needed and highlight the results after issuing these commands. As new versions of ROCm keep being released, some of the contents of this chapter may become dated. Therefore, it is important for readers to refer to the installation documentation before starting the installation process. Installation documentation for ROCm can be found at: https://docs.amd.com.

A.1 Prerequisite

We will demonstrate the ROCm installation process on a Ubuntu 20.04 LTS operating system, ROCm does support a wide range of different Linux operating systems. Currently, ROCm does not support the Microsoft Windows operating system, though Windows support may arrive soon.

The ROCm-supported operating systems are listed in Table A.1. Overall, ROCm supports the Red Hat Enterprise Linux (RHEL), SUSE Linux Enterprise Server (SLES), and Ubuntu distributions. For each distribution, a minimum kernel version (e.g., 5.14, 4.18) is required. Additionally, a few software packages, including `wget`, `gnupg2`, `gawk`, and `curl`, need to be installed on top of the operating system because they are required by the ROCm installation script.

Operating system users who want to run GPU programs need to be added to proper user groups. The `groups` command can be used to check the groups to which the

Table A.1: Currently supported Linux distributions and the Linux kernel versions.

OS	Kernel Version
RHEL 9.1	5.14
RHEL 8.7	4.18
RHEL 8.6	4.18
SLES15 SP4	5.14.21
Ubuntu 20.04.5 LTS	5.15
Ubuntu 22.04.1 LTS	5.15, OEM 5.17

current user belongs. To use GPUs, one has to be added to either the `render` or `video` (recommended) group. To add a user to a certain group, the command `sudo usermod -a -G [group_name] [user_name]` can be used.

Before purchasing GPU hardware, you should confirm that the GPU you intend to purchase is supported by the ROCm platform (see Table A.2).

Table A.2: GPUs that are supported by ROCm.

Family	GPU	GFX ID
GCN GPUs	AMD Radeon Instinct™ MI50 AMD Radeon Instinct™ MI60 AMD Radeon™ VII AMD Radeon™ Pro VII	GFX906
RDNA GPUs	AMD Radeon™ Pro W6800 AMD Radeon™ Pro V620	GFX1030
CDNA GPUs	AMD Instinct™ MI100 AMD Instinct™ MI200	GFX908 GFX90a

A.2 Understanding the ROCm Packages

ROCm is a complex ecosystem that includes many software packages. A full list of packages can be found in Figure A.1. These packages may have complex dependency relationships. To avoid requiring users to install packages one by one, ROCm groups these packages into meta-packages (for a full list, see Table A.3). Users are more likely to install meta-packages rather than individual packages.

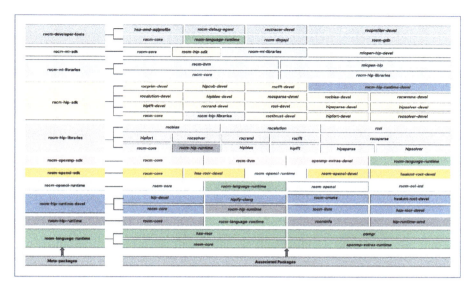

Figure A.1: A list of ROCm meta-packages and the individual packages that are included in the meta-packages.

A.3 Installation

In this overview, we cover two different ways to install ROCm, including the Installer Script Method and the Package Manager Method.

A.3.1 Installer Script Method

The installer script method automates the installation process for the AMDGPU and ROCm stack. The installer script handles the complete installation process for ROCm, including setting up the repository, cleaning up the file system, updating and installing the desired drivers and meta-packages. With this approach, the system has more control over the ROCm installation process. Thus, those who are less familiar with standard Linux standard commands can choose this method for ROCm installation. The installer can be downloaded and installed using the following commands:

Listing A.1: Commands to be used to install ROCm with the installer script.

```
sudo apt-get update
wget https://repo.radeon.com/amdgpu-install/5.4.3/ubuntu/focal/amdgpu-
    install_5.4.50403-1_all.deb
sudo apt-get install ./amdgpu-install_5.4.50403-1_all.deb
```

The commands above should install a program named **amdgpu-install**, that can help manage the ROCm packages. To install ROCm, we can perform execution using `sudo ./amdgpu-install`. Additionally, users can install specific use cases using commands such as `sudo amdgpu-install --usecase=rocm`. Additionally, if the user wants to install multiple use cases at one time, the **usecase** argument can accept multiple values, separated by commas. For example, the command `sudo amdgpu-install --usecase=rocm,hiplibsdk` will install both the ROCm and the **hiplibsdk** use cases. A full list of use cases can be shown using `sudo amdgpu-install --list-usecase`.

A.3.2   Package Manager Method

The package manager method gives users more flexibility on what to install, but requires more user input during the installation process. It is recommended to only be used by advanced users. Overall, installing ROCm with a package manager includes the following six steps:

Step 1: install the Linux kernel header and development packages. One prerequisite of using the package manager method is to install the proper Linux kernel headers and development packages.

One can use the command `sudo dpkg -l | grep linux-headers` to check the version of the installed kernel headers. For example, the output can be `ii linux-headers-5.15.0-41-generic 5.15.0-41.44 20.04.1 amd64 Linux kernel headers for version 5.15.0 on 64 bit x86 SMP`. Similarly, the development packages can be listed using the command `sudo dpkg -l | grep linux-modules-extra` and the output on the authors' system include `ii linux-modules-extra-5.15.0-41-generic 5.15.0-41.44 20.04.1 amd64 Linux kernel extra modules for version 5.15.0 on 64 bit x86 SMP`

If the current version of the Linux header does not satisfy the requirement listed in Table A.1, the user need to install the linux headers using the command `sudo apt install linux-headers-`uname -r` linux-modules-extra-`uname -r``

Step 2: Install the AMD GPU driver. Next, we install the AMD GPU driver using the package manager. The package manager requires the packages to be encrypted; therefore, we need to install a GNU Privacy Guard (GPG) key. The command to install the GPG key is:
`curl -fsSL https://repo.radeon.com/rocm/rocm.gpg.key | sudo gpg --dearmor -o /etc/apt/trusted.gpg.d/rocm-keyring.gpg`.

Next, we add the AMD GPU stack repository to Ubuntu's package manager, using:

    echo 'deb [arch=amd64 signed-by=/etc/apt/trusted.gpg.d/rocm-keyring.gpg]
https://repo.radeon.com/amdgpu/5.4.3/ubuntu focal main' | sudo
tee /etc/apt/sources.list.d/amdgpu.list . Do not forget to run sudo
apt-get update after adding the new repository so that the package manager can
retrieve the package information.

Finally, we install the AMD GPU driver with sudo apt install amdgpu-dkms.
A reboot after the installation is required.

Step 3: Install the ROCm environment. To install the ROCm environment,
we need to add external sources to Ubuntu's package manager with the command:

    echo 'deb [arch=amd64 signed-by=/etc/apt/trusted.gpg.d/rocm-keyring.gpg]
https://repo.radeon.com/rocm/apt/5.4.3 focal main' | sudo tee
/etc/apt/sources.list.d/rocm.list.

This command creates the rocm.list with URLs that provide the packages.

Next, we need to modify a preference with the command:

    echo -e 'Package: *\nPin: release o=repo.radeon.com\nPin-Priority:
600' | sudo tee /etc/apt/preferences.d/rocm-pin-600.

By assigning the ROCm packages a higher pin priority, we can stay with a stable
version of Ubuntu when we updating packages. Still, we need to run sudo apt-get
update after adding the package sources and editing the preference.

A.3.3 Verification of the Installation Process

Regardless of which installation method is used, we need to verify if the installation was
successful. In case of any execution errors, a user should also first check if the ROCm
installation was corrupted.

First, we can check if the directory /opt/rocm contains intended executable files,
such as the rocm-smi, and ROCm libraries, such as librocblas.so. Second, we can
check if the driver is working properly. The command dkms status can check the currently running drivers. For example, on our system, we see the command generate the following output: amdgpu, 5.16.9.22.20-1438746~20.04, 5.4.0-121-generic,
x86_64: installed. This output suggests that the driver was properly installed and
is currently working.

Third, we should check if a program can detect the GPU hardware
and retrieve GPU properties. We can run /opt/rocm/bin/rocminfo or
/opt/rocm/opencl/bin/clinfo to retrieve hardware properties. If these two programs run without error and can display the GPUs installed in the system, the ROCm
environment is properly installed and working. Finally, we can install the meta-packages
using the regular Ubuntu package installation commands. The command is sudo apt
install <package-name>. For example, if we want to install the most commonly
used ROCm features, we can use sudo apt install rocm.

A.4   Upgrading ROCm

It is important to keep your version of ROCm updated, as the tools and libraries keep receiving new feature updates, bug fixes, performance improvements, and security patches. Similar to the installation process, users can either use the installer or the package manager provided by the Linux distribution.

To use the installer method, the first step is to install the installer, as described in Section A.3.1. Then, upgrading the package version is the same as a fresh installation. To upgrade a particular use case, the command is `sudo amdgpu-install --usecase=<usecase name>`.

Upgrading ROCm with the package manager requires many more commands. We first need to update the external sources of the AMD GPU driver packages using the command:

`echo 'deb [arch=amd64 signed-by=/etc/apt/trusted.gpg.d/rocm-keyring.gpg <amdgpu baseurl> focal main' | sudo tee /etc/apt/sources.list.d/amdgpu.lis`

A `sudo apt-get update` is required after altering the source list. Then, we can upgrade the driver using the command `sudo apt install amdgpu-dkms`. Again, a reboot is required.

Finally, we need to repeat the process for ROCm packages. With the commands `echo 'deb [arch=amd64 signed-by=/etc/apt/trusted.gpg.d/rocm -keyring.gpg] <rocm baseurl> focal main' | sudo tee /etc/apt/sources.list.d/rocm.list` and `echo -e 'Package: *\nPin: release o=repo.radeon.com\nPin-Priority: 600' | sudo tee /etc/apt/preferences.d/rocm-pin-600`, where we alter the external sources. Then, we can use the package manager to update the ROCm packages, using the command `sudo apt install --only-upgrade <meta-package>`.

A.5   Uninstalling ROCm

To install ROCm, we can still either use the installer (the uninstaller, in this case) or the Linux distribution's package manager. In the case where ROCm was installed with the installer, an uninstaller is available alongside the installer. Then reinstalling ROCm can be as simple as `sudo amdgpu-uninstall`. Ubuntu's package manager can be used to easily uninstall ROCm or specific use cases. The command is `sudo apt autoremove <package-name>`.

Table A.3: ROCm meta-packages.

Meta-Package	Description
rocm-hip-libraries	rocm-hip-libraries installs HIP libraries optimized for AMD platforms.
rocm-hip-runtime	rocm-hip-runtime is intended to install packages necessary to run an application written in HIP for the AMD platform.
rocm-hip-runtime-devel	rocm-hip-runtime-devel meta-package contains packages to develop an application on HIP or port it from CUDA.
rocm-hip-sdk	rocm-hip-sdk installs packages necessary to develop/port applications using HIP and libraries for AMD platforms.
rocm-language-runtime	rocm-language-runtime meta-package installs the ROCm runtime.
rocm-ml-libraries	rocm-ml-libraries install packages for key Machine Learning libraries, specifically MIOpen.
rocm-ml-sdk	rocm-ml-sdk installs packages necessary to develop and run Machine Learning applications with Machine Learning primitives optimized for AMD platforms.
rocm-opencl-runtime	rocm-opencl-runtime installs packages required to run OpenCL-based applications on the AMD platform.
rocm-opencl-sdk	rocm-opencl-sdk installs packages required to develop applications in OpenCL for the AMD platform.
rocm-openmp-runtime	rocm-openmp-runtime installs packages necessary to run OpenMP-based applications for AMD platforms.
rocm-openmp-sdk	rocm-openmp-sdk installs packages necessary to develop OpenMP-based applications for AMD platforms.

Appendix B

CDNA Assembly

AMD's *CDNA* GPUs execute *CDNA* instructions to carry out computing tasks. This chapter introduces the *CDNA* instruction set and assembly language, which provides a human-readable version of your program.

Developing a good understanding of assembly language will improve a programmer's ability to master GPU programming for several reasons:

1. It fosters a deeper appreciation of how GPUs work for performance tuning.

2. Debugging a GPU program often requires working at the instruction level rather than the source-code level. Understanding the assembly language helps the programmer find and remove errors during debugging.

3. Writing code directly into the assembly is often the best possible method for attaining performance.

In this chapter, we start by reviewing the basic tools used to convert a *HIP* program to assembly. Then, we present the *CDNA Application Binary Interface*, which provides a basic understanding of how the information stored in a *CDNA* binary is loaded into the hardware. The main body of the chapter introduces the *CDNA* instruction set and its mapping to high-level *HIP* programs.

B.1   Using *CDNA* Assembly Code

The ability to extract *CDNA* assembly code from a *HIP* program is necessary. In this section, we introduce the tools used for this purpose. We first extract GPU binaries from *HIP* executable files and convert them into human-readable assembly code.

257

B.1.1   Retrieve *HIP* Kernel Binary

One of the easiest ways to extract *CDNA* assembly is to use the *ROCm* debugger introduced in Section 7.3. A programmer sets a breakpoint in the GPU kernel and uses the **disassemble** command to provide a listing of the instructions around the breakpoint. However, this method requires executing the target program. In many cases, doing so is impractical and time-consuming. Therefore, we need another way to achieve this.

The *HIP* compiler, *hipcc*, compiles GPU programs as fat binaries, which include both the host and GPU binaries. To inspect the GPU assembly, we first must check the GPU programs embedded in the compiled *HIP* binary. *ROCm* provides the *roc-obj-ls* tool, which lists the embedded programs. For example, if we run **roc-obj-ls main**, where *main* is the executable used in the image gamma correction task in Section 8.1, we will obtain output in which each line will include a description of the embedded program (e.g., **hipv4-amdgcn-amd-amdhsa–gfx908**) with a universal resource identifier (URI; e.g., universal resource identifier *file://main#offset=24576&size=9936*). The URI provides the location and size of the embedded program. Next, we use the *roc-obj-extract* tool provided by *ROCm* to extract the GPU program as a standalone file. This requires the URI from *roc-obj-ls* to specify which embedded item to extract. In this example, we use the command, **roc-obj-extract "file://main#offset=24576&size=9936"**. The output is stored in the *main-offset24576-size9936.co* file. It is also possible to combine these two steps. *ROCm*'s *roc-obj* tool dumps all embedded GPU programs from a *HIP* executable.

On a system with the default *ROCm* installation, the aforementioned tools, including *roc-obj-ls*, *roc-obj-extract*, and *roc-obj*, can be found under the */opt/rocm/bin* directory.

The output files, regardless of whether they are generated by *roc-obj-extract* or *roc-obj*, are *ELF* functions. The GPU instructions are stored in the *text* section, and the metadata (e.g., how many registers are required) are stored in the *note* section.

B.1.2   Disassembling a *CDNA* Binary

Thus far, we have shown how a GPU-executable file is represented in a binary. However, it is not yet human-readable and can be difficult to analyze. Hence, we must disassemble the binary file into an assembly file. *ROCm* provides the *llvm-objdump* tool for this purpose. With its standard installation, the *llvm-objdump* utility is available under */opt/rocm/llvm/bin*. Assuming that the GPU executable file is *bin.co*, we can use **llvm-objdump –mcpu=gfx908 –disassemble bin.co** to disassemble the binary.

B.2   *CDNA* Registers

The *CDNA* assembly language allows programmers to use a large array of registers, including SGPRs, VGPRs, and special-purpose registers. Each SGPR or VGPR is 4 B in size. The representation of a general-purpose register comprises both the type and the index. For example, registers **s0** and **v0** represent the 0th register of each of the SGPRs and VGPRs. When specifying register names, the *CDNA* assembly language is not case-sensitive.

To specify wider (e.g., 8- and 16-B) data ranges, up to four adjacent registers can be combined. For example, **v[0:3]** declares that we will use four registers and 16 B of data, which are fed into the ALU units and processed together.

Scalar registers are shared by the entire wavefront, whereas vector registers belong to each work item. For example, if both work item 0 and work item 1 access **s0** concurrently, they will guarantee to get the same data. However, reading **v0** from work item 0 and from work item 1 will mostly result in different values.

CDNA uses a few special-purpose registers to facilitate wavefront execution, including **PC**, **EXEC**, **VCC**, **SCC**, **VMCNT**, and **LGKMCNT**. Note that all these registers are at the wavefront-level. Each wavefront has its own **PC**, **EXEC**, and etc. They can be considered as specialized scalar registers. **PC** stores an 8-B address that points to the next instruction for execution. **EXEC** is the 64-bit execution mask that holds predicates for predicated execution of work items in a wavefront. If a bit in **EXEC** is zero, the execution of the instructions from the corresponding work item will not take effect. Additionally, **VCC** and **SCC** are 8-B and 1-bit registers designed to collect comparison results from vector and scalar comparison instructions, respectively. Finally, **VMCNT** and **LGKMCNT** are memory-access counters. We introduce these later in Section B.4.

Note that the registers discussed here are logical types that differ from physical registers on a GPU chip. When a GPU program executes, the SPI dynamically maps the hardware registers to logical ones similar to how the OS allocates virtual memory. By performing dynamic allocation, wavefronts can collocate on a single CU without causing a register conflict. If each wavefront uses fewer registers, its CU can handle more wavefronts, potentially increasing performance. Finally, the special registers (e.g., **PC**, **VCC**, and **SCC**) are not dynamically allocated; they are physically located in wavefront slots in the Sequencer Block (SQ) (see Section 6.5).

B.3 Instruction Types

The *CDNA* instruction set classifies a small number of instructions, and those of different classes typically require different hardware units for execution:

Scalar instructions represent integer operations shared by all work items in a wavefront. Execution of a scalar instruction only processes a single data item, and scalar instructions can only access scalar registers. **s_add_u32 s0, s1, s2** is an example that adds two unsigned integers stored in **s1** and **s2** and stores the result back to **s0**.

Vector instructions are the most important type as they perform most of the GPU computing. They are executed in a SIMD pattern. Executing a single instruction can process up to 64 data items (the wavefront size on CDNA is 64 work-items). An example is **v_add_f32 v0, v1, s1**, which adds a single-precision floating-point number to **v1** and **s1** and stores the result in the **v0**. Note that a single execution of an instruction can add

64 different numbers stored in **v1** to those stored in **s1**. The resulting 64 numbers are stored back to the 64 registers specified by **v0**.

Scalar memory instructions load data from GPU memory to scalar registers. Executing one scalar instruction only loads one data item, and this is commonly used to fetch kernel arguments, addresses, or global information (e.g., workgroup size).

Vector memory instructions read or write to/from main memory. A single vector memory instruction execution loads different data for different work items.

LDS instructions read or write to/from the LDS memory.

Branch instructions manipulate the PC and redirect control flows.

Internal instructions are special ones that do not need to be executed. Most are responsible for supporting different types of synchronization (e.g., barriers) or execution control tasks (e.g., sleeps and wake-ups).

B.4   Memory Access Instructions

Memory instructions are scalar or vector. The most common memory types are load and store types. Atomic operations are also considered memory instructions.

GPU memory operations typically involve long latencies, which rely on thread-level parallelism to hide the cost of memory access. When one wavefront waits for memory access, the CU can execute instructions from another wavefront. However, in many cases, the degree of thread-level parallelism may not be sufficient, and the CU may become idle. To avoid this, the MI100 GPU leverages instruction-level parallelism. An MI100 CU executes other types of instructions from the same wavefront while waiting for memory accesses to return.

MI100 GPUs mainly rely on the compiler and a few counters (e.g., *VMCNT*, *LKGM-CNT*) to determine which instructions can overlap. For example, when a CU executes a **global_load** instruction, after passing through the instruction pipeline but before returning the loaded data, *VMCNT* is incremented. The CU can potentially execute more instructions from the wavefront without waiting for the load to complete. When the data from the **global_load** return, *VMCNT* is decremented.

The compiler must explicitly add a **waitcnt** instruction to synchronize with the memory access, and the instruction must specify the counter for which it is waiting and the target value. For example, if we want to use data loaded from the **global_load**, **waitcnt vmcnt(0)** must be inserted before the instruction that depends on the previous load.

The target value of the counter gives the CU better control to overlap in-flight loads so as to increase memory level parallelism. We provide the following pseudocode as an example:

Listing B.1: Pseudocode for memory loads.

```
1  global_load [data1]
2  global_load [data2]
3  # Some calculation
4  waitcnt vmcnt(1)
5  # Use [data1]
6  waitcnt vmcnt(0)
7  # Use [data2]
```

After executing Lines 1 and 2, *VMCNT* contains values 1 and 2, respectively. We can then execute other instructions. Prior to using **data1**, we insert an instruction on Line 4 that waits for the *VMCNT* value to become equal to or less than 1. When the *VMCNT*'s value is 1, only **data1** becomes available; **data2** has not yet been retrieved. At this moment, we can finish processes **data1**, and there is no need to wait for **data2**. Finally, at Line 6, we wait for the *VMCNT* to return to 0 so that we can use **data2**. This mechanism allows detailed synchronization control at the cost of requiring the memory accesses from one wavefront to return in-order.

B.5   Example: Shifted Copy

To show how a *HIP* kernel generates *CDNA* instructions, we use a shifted copy (see Listing B.2 and Listing B.3).

Listing B.2: Shifted copy kernel.

```
1  __global__ void shifted_copy (float *in, float *out) {
2      size_t gid = blockDim.x * blockIdx.x + threadIdx.x;
3      out[gid] = in[gid+4];
4  }
```

Listing B.3: Assembly code generated from the shifted copy kernel.

```
1  s_load_dwordx4 s[0:3], s[4:5], 0
2  v_lshlrev_b64 v[2:3], 2, v[2:3]
3  s_waitcnt lgkmcnt(0)
4  s_add_u32 s0, 16, s0
5  s_addc_u32 s1, 0, s1
6  v_mov_b32 v5, s1
7  v_add_co_u32 v0, s0, v2
8  v_addc_co_u32 v1, v5, v3
9  global_load_dword v4, v[0:1]
```

```
10  v_mov_b32 v5, s3
11  v_add_co_u32 v0, s2, v2
12  v_addc_co_u32 v1, v5, v3
13  s_waitcnt vmcnt(0)
14  global_store_dword v[0:1], v4
15  s_endpgm
```

Before the wavefronts are executed, some of the registers will be initialized with specific values. Here, **s[4:5]** should hold the address of kernel arguments. Line 1 loads 16 B of data using a scalar memory instruction, resulting in **s[0:1]** and **s[2:3]**, which store the addresses of the **in** and **out** buffers, respectively.

v[2:3] stores the global thread ID, Line 2 shifts the value left by 2 bits (integer multiplication by four) to convert the global thread ID to the required memory offset, and the ALU operation performed by the instruction on Line 2 does not depend on the data loaded on Line 1. Thus, when Line 2 executes, Line 1 may not be finished. The program, thus, waits for the memory read started at Line 1 using the **s_waitcnt** instruction on Line 3 because the **s0** value will be used on Line 4.

Lines 4 and 5 add 16 to the values stored in **s0** and **s1**, where **s[0:1]** is the **in** buffer). This step calculates the address offset of **in[gid+4]** in the source code. Here, Lines 4 and 5 present good examples of how *CDNA* GPUs use two 32-bit integer instructions to process a 64-bit integer. We can see the same pattern again in Lines 7–8 and 11–12. Note that the first instruction is an **add** and the second is an **addc**. **addc** differs, in that it considers the carry from the previous **add**.

Next, Lines 6–8 add an offset to the base address, storing it for **v[0:1]** load operation. It is necessary to copy the address to the vector register, as the memory copy operation will eventually use the address stored in the vector register. Line 9 reads the data, and while they are in flight, Lines 10–12 calculate the address in the output buffer. Finally, after guaranteeing that the loaded data return by synchronization at Line 13, the data are stored back to the output buffer in Line 14. The whole wavefront terminates with the **s_endpgm** instruction.

B.6   Example: Branching

Because GPUs issue instructions at the granularity of a wavefront, they provide a special mechanism that can be used to handle code branches, especially when wavefront threads diverge to follow different branch paths. At a high level, the *CDNA* instruction set relies on both predicated execution and branch instructions to handle branches and divergent behavior.

Listing B.4: Conditional memory copy kernel.

```
1  __global__ void conditional_copy (double *in, double *out) {
2    size_t gid = blockDim.x * blockIdx.x + threadIdx.x;
3    if (in[gid] > 0) {
4      out[gid] = in[gid];
5    }
6  }
```

Listing B.5: Assembly compiled from the shifted copy kernel.

```
1        s_load_dwordx4 s[0:3], s[4:5], 0
2        v_lshlrev_b64 v[2:3], 3, v[2:3]
3        s_waitcnt lgkmcnt(0)
4        v_mov_b32 v6, s1
5        v_add_co_u32 v0, s0, v2
6        v_addc_co_u32 v1, v6, v3
7        global_load_dwordx2 v[4:5], v[0:1]
8        s_waitcnt vmcnt(0)
9        v_cmp_lt_f64 vcc, 0, v[4:5]
10       s_and_saveexec_b64 s[4:5], vcc
11       s_cbranch_execz BB0_2
12       v_mov_b32 v6, s3
13       v_add_co_u32 v0, s2, v2
14       v_addc_co_u32 v1, v6, v3
15       global_store_dword v[0:1], v[4:5]
16  BB0_2:
17       s_or_b64 exec, exec, s[4:5]
18       s_endpgm
```

Here, we use an example (see Listing B.4) to demonstrate how the *HIP* compiler handles branches. In this kernel, we perform a condition copy operation in which we copy the element from the input array to the output array only if the element is positive. The corresponding assembly is provided in Listing B.5.

Most instructions in Listing B.5 are the same as those in Listing B.3. Therefore, we focus only on the differences.

On Line 9, the instruction checks if the value is less than zero by specifying **lt** in the instruction. The result of the comparison is stored in *VCC*. If the value in **v[4:5]** is positive, the corresponding bit in *VCC* is set to one; otherwise, it is set to zero.

The **s_and_saveexec_b64** instruction applies the result of the comparison to the execution mask stored in the **EXEC** register. This instruction first stores the current execution mask value in **s[4:5]**; then, it updates the execution mask using **EXEC = VCC**

& **EXEC**. Combining Lines 9 and 10, we can see that the program disables execution for those threads with negative values in **v[4:5]** by setting the corresponding bit in the **EXEC** to zero.

A special case occurs when all threads hold negative values. Line 11 checks if all the bits in the execution mask, **execz**, are zero; if so, we skip executing the instructions on Lines 12—15. Hence, **PC** will update **BB0_2**.

The threads that diverge must eventually converge. In this example, the convergence point is Line 17. Using **EXEC** OR **S[4:5]** and storing the execution mask before diverging, the execution mask recovers its original state, and all non-affected threads (execution mask bit is zero) continue their execution.

B.7   Comparing CDNA2 and CDNA3

Following the debut of the MI100 GPU, AMD has steadily improved upon its GPU microarchitecture with the introduction of the MI200 (CDNA2) and MI350 (CDNA3) series GPUs. In addition to these enhancements, AMD also extended the GPU's instruction set. Although these changes to the Instruction Set Architecture (ISA) are not fully backward compatible with the CDNA1 ISA, the extensions do not significantly impact the principles discussed earlier in this chapter. AMD decided to optimize these GPUs to serve as compute-only designs; therefore, the designers of the CDNA GPUs have gradually phased out graphics-related instructions in favor of a more comprehensive instruction set. As a result, these AMD GPUs can perform powerful data manipulation and compute operations.

The MI200 series, as part of AMD's CDNA2 architecture, is a compute-optimized GPU design. A key feature introduced involves the simplification of IMAGE (MIMG) operations. The architecture retains only a core set of opcodes, such as `IMAGE_LOAD`, `IMAGE_STORE`, and various `IMAGE_ATOMIC` operations, streamlining image-related instructions to focus on common operations present in compute tasks.

The CDNA2 microarchitecture changes the registers provided on the GPU. For the CDNA1 architecture, Accumulation Vector General-Purpose Registers (ACCVGPRs) were introduced as a separate set of registers. They are specifically designed to accelerate matrix operations that are used by the accumulator unit. These ACCVGPRs are physically located on a dedicated register file, distinct from the regular Vector General-Purpose Registers (VGPRs). Because they are disjoint from the VGPRS, the ACCVG-PRs cannot be directly written into with standard SIMD instructions. Transitioning to CDNA2, the ACCVGPRs share the same physical register pool, allowing the ACCVG-PRs to serve as a destination operand for memory load instructions, simplifying data handling and improving the efficiency of accumulator operations.

The CDNA2 ISA enhances specialized arithmetic instructions that provide new computational capabilities, added matrix operations, Data Parallel Primitives (DPP), and Packed Math instructions. Matrix instructions utilize the new matrix cores added to the CDNA GPUs. They perform multiplications for a small matrix in a single instruction. CDNA2 adds support for additional matrix sizes (see Table B.1). The DPPs are modifiers to existing instructions, allowing threads to access registers from other threads within the save wavefront. CDNA2 added DPP support for 64-bit data types. Additionally, AMD expanded the Packed Math instructions (enabling them to perform multiple operations in a single instruction), adding new support for single-precision operations (previously, only lower-precision math operations were supported).

Table B.1: Newly supported matrix sizes in CDNA2 by the matrix core. The first matrix has dimension M × K and the second has dimension K × N.

Input Type	Output Type	M × N × K
BF16	F32	$4 \times 4 \times 4$
BF16	F32	$16 \times 16 \times 4$
BF16	F32	$16 \times 16 \times 16$
BF16	F32	$32 \times 32 \times 4$
BF16	F32	$32 \times 32 \times 8$
BF16	F32	$16 \times 16 \times 16$
F64	F64	$16 \times 16 \times 4$
F64	F64	$4 \times 4 \times 4$

The CDNA3 instruction set continues to reduce support for graphics-related features and add new computing capabilities. For example, for the CDNA3 generation, AMD removed all of the image and sampling instructions. Meanwhile, several new memory and compute-related features have been added. A major enhancement was the addition of matrix operations within the CDNA architecture, which introduced new instructions such as V_MFMA_F32_16X16X16_XF32 and V_MFMA_F32_32X32X8_XF32. For AMD, this marks a pivotal shift towards supporting low-precision multiplication, operations commonly found in neural network models. These instructions, while operating on single-precision floating-point numbers, can substantially lower both latency and energy consumption. Additionally, to accommodate applications with less stringent precision requirements, but still demand high performance, the matrix cores now extend support to 8-bit floating-point numbers, including BF8 (with a 5-bit exponent and 2-bit mantissa) and FP8 (featuring a 4-bit exponent and 3-bit mantissa). Furthermore, the CDNA3 ISA introduces support for sparse matrix operations through the innovative SMFMA instructions, broadening the scope for efficiency and performance in specialized computational tasks.

B.8   Conclusion

In this appendix, we briefly introduced the use of *CDNA* assembly language and explored some of the instructions of the newer *CDNA* ISA. We saw that *ROCm* provides good support for working with assembly code and allows programmers to extract assembly from a *HIP* program easily. We also highlighted how GPU assembly language is unique in many respects, such as its vector registers, dynamic register allocation, explicit memory access synchronization, and predicated execution. This chapter offers readers a head start on writing *CDNA* assembly code, while offering *HIP* programmers some familiarity with *CDNA* assembly instructions, which is also helpful when debugging with the ROCm debugger *rocgdb*.

Appendix C

OmniTools

In Chapter 7, we introduced rocTracer and rocProfiler, powerful tools from the ROCm stack that provide essential capabilities for collecting performance data during HIP program execution. However, althrough these tools can gather raw performance metrics, they offer limited analytical capabilities.

To address this gap and offer a more robust set of tools for performance analysis, AMD has developed Omnitrace and Omniperf. It is important to note that these tools are not part of the standard ROCm stack. Instead, they are research projects initiated by AMD to support the community with advanced tooling options. As a result, instead of discussing them in Chapter 7, we introduce these powerful tools in this appendix chapter.

At a high level, both Omnitrace and Omniperf facilitate performance analysis. Omnitrace offers traces of CPU and GPU execution, helping users understand execution patterns and pinpoint potential performance bottlenecks. Omniperf, on the other hand, delves into GPU kernel performance, assessing hardware utilization. Users should start with Omnitrace to identify problematic kernels and then proceed with Omniperf for deeper insights into kernel performance issues.

C.1 Omnitrace

Omnitrace is an open-source project by AMD Research designed to facilitate performance analysis for software running on AMD heterogeneous systems. Omnitrace can profile and trace parallel applications across various languages such as C, C++, Fortran, HIP, OpenCL, and Python. It offers multiple features, including binary instrumentation (CPU only) and call-stack sampling, to collect traces to support performance analysis. The trace can then be used in interactive visualization mode or to generate a high-level profile.

In this book, we will skip walking through the installation process for these tools, because instructions can be found in the open-source location of Omnitrace at https://github.com/ROCm/Omnitrace. More detailed documentation can also be found at https://amdresearch.github.io/Omnitrace/.

C.1.1 Omnitrace Configuration File

The Omnitrace configuration files determine the default behavior of the Omnitrace command line tools. The configuration file can be generated with a command line tool called `omnitrace-avail`, using the following command:

```
omnitrace-avail -G ./omnitrace.cfg
```

The generated file should be self-documenting. If we want a more detailed description about the options listed in the file, the `--all` argument can be used. We can add this argument to a command to dump extra information, providing more details. To use the configuration file, the path should be added to the environment variable named `OMNITRACE_CONFIG_FILE`.

C.1.2 Collect Traces

Omnitrace offers two trace collection methods: 1) call-stack sampling and 2) binary instrumentation. The choice between these methods depends on the user's needs. Call-stack sampling is suitable for collecting traces from all functions (see Figure C.1a). In contrast, binary instrumentation is designed for targeting specific functions, as it reduces tracing overhead and trace size, and provides more precise profiling results (see Figure C.1b). Besides their differences, these two methods can be used together, recording a trace of all the functions using call-stack sampling, while providing a high-precision timestamped recording for specific functions using binary instrumentation.

Regardless of the chosen method, it is recommended that the user compile the executable with optimization enabled (`-O2` or higher), asserts disabled (`-DNDEBUG`), and debug information included (specifying `-g1` or higher).

Call-stack sampling. Call-stack sampling can be activated using an executable `Omnitrace-sample`. For example, if the GPU program to be executed is called `foo`, the following command runs `foo` using call-stack sampling.

```
omnitrace-sample -- foo
```

The `Omnitrace-sample` executable uses the general LLM-style command line argument syntax. All arguments before the double hyphen `--` are for Omnitrace, and all arguments after `--` are for the program.

Binary instrumentation. Binary instrumentation can be executed using the `omnitrace-instrument` executable, which modifies the host program to insert trace collection code. By default, the `omnitrace-instrument` both instruments and executes the program. Its syntax mirrors that of `omnitrace-sample`, with the

(a) Call-stack sampling.

(b) Binary instrumentation.

Figure C.1: Comparing the traces generated by call-stack sampling and binary instrumentation when running the recursive Fibonacci number calculation program. The call-stack sampling methods have limited resolution and cannot capture precise function start and end times.

`omnitrace-instrument` arguments and the program arguments separated by a double hyphen `--`.

Alternatively, `omnitrace-instrument` can either attach to a running process or generate an instrumented binary for later execution. To attach to an existing process, use the `-p` argument, followed by the process ID (PID), as in the command:

```
omnitrace-instrument <omnitrace-options> -p <PID> --
<exe-name>
```

To create an instrumented binary, use the `-o` argument to specify the output file name, as shown in the following command:

```
omnitrace-instrument <omnitrace-options> -o
<name-of-new-exe-or-library> -- <exe-or-library>
```

As the reader may have noticed, we did not specify which functions we used to collect traces. This is because Omnitrace has a default rule of selecting the functions to instrument. By default, all functions are instrumented, unless they have: 1) dynamic call-sites (i.e., function pointers) or 2) fewer than 1024 instructions [1].

The `omnitrace-instrument` tool offers three sets of arguments to customize instrumentation for specific modules (libraries) and functions. The `--module-include` and `--function-include` arguments enable users to add modules and functions (respectively) beyond the default instrumentation rules. These values accept regular expressions to match module and function names. Conversely, the `--module-restrict` and `--function-restrict` arguments override the default selections and only include modules and functions that match the provided regular expressions. Finally, the `--module-exclude` and `--function-exclude` arguments enable users to refine the selection by excluding certain default modules and functions from instrumentation.

C.1.3 Output and Visualization

The output of Omnitrace is stored at:

`<OUTPUT_PATH>[/<TIMESTAMP>]/[<PREFIX>]<DATA_NAME>`
`[<OUTPUT_SUFFIX>].<EXT>`

By assigning values to a few environment variables, we can specify the output location and file names for data traces. For example, the `OMNITRACE_OUTPUT_PATH` environment variable is used to specify the directory for storing output files. Within this path, users can insert special placeholders to detail the context of the trace collection. These placeholders include `%argt%`, `%ppid%`, `%pid%`, and `%rank%`, representing the basename of the executable, the parent process ID, the process ID, and the MPI rank, respectively. To find a comprehensive list of options, including their descriptions, users can run the command `omnitrace-avail —list-keys —expand-keys`.

For each Omnitrace run, a file named `perfetto-trace.proto` will be generated. The file can be opened using the perfetto visualizer, which is available at: `ui.perfetto.dev` (see Figure C.2 for an example).

C.2 Omniperf

In contrast with Omnitrace, which focuses on profiling functions called in the host program, Omniperf provides kernel-level profiling features. Built on top of rocProf, Omniperf profiles ML and HPC workloads running on AMD Instrict MI GPUs (e.g., MI100, MI200, and MI300 series GPUs).

Omniperf's comprehensive features allow for an in-depth analysis through a variety of panels which include System Speed-of-Light and Memory Chart Analysis. This tool supports both command-line and GUI analysis, providing versatility to accommodate different user preferences and enhancing overall access to performance data.

---

[1] More rules can prevent the functions from being instrumented. Please refer to the Omnitrace documentation for more information.

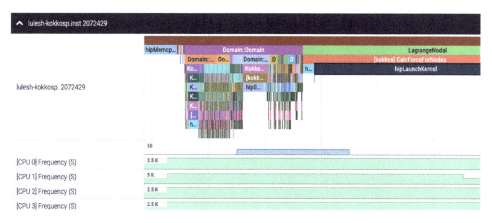

Figure C.2: Example visualization of the trace generated with Omnitrace.

C.2.1 Profiling Programs with Omniperf

Central to Omniperf is a command line tool that can launch the program in profile mode. Assuming our GPU program is named **vcopy**, the following command can collect all the available counters on all the kernels in the program:

```
omniperf profile -n vcopy_data -- ./vcopy -n 1048576 -b 256
```

Similar to Omnitrace, the double hyphen separates the arguments for Omniperf and the name of the program we want to profile. The **-n** argument for Omniperf defines the output directory name. In this case, the output will be stored in the directory **./workloads/vcopy_data/MI200**. Note that Omniperf appends the accelerator name as the last level of the directory unless the output path is overridden using the **-p/--path** option.

Collecting traces for all kernels is time-consuming. Often, owing to the limited number of hardware performance counters, kernels need to be replayed many times to collect all the metrics. To reduce the execution time for a desired set of metrics, Omniperf provides a few arguments, including:

- **-k/--kernel** can filter kernels by kernel name.
- **-d/--dispatch** can filter kernels by dispatch ID (i.e., n-th kernel dispatched)
- **-b/--block** can filter metrics by the hardware component blocks.

Besides debugging typical performance bottlenecks, Omniperf can be used to generate metrics for roofline analysis [82]. Omniperf can be run without collecting profiling metrics for roofline analysis by specifying the **--no-roof**. Alternatively, we can choose to only profile metrics for roofline analysis by including the **--roof-only** arguments.

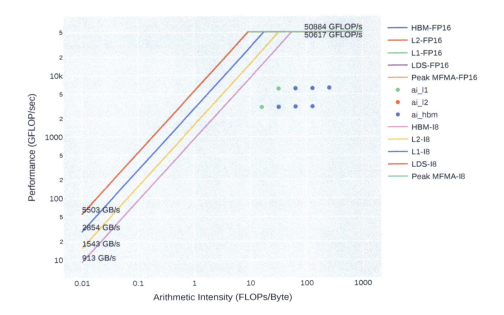

Figure C.3: Roofline analysis chart for 8-bit integer and 16-bit floating-point operations.

Using an empirical roofline model, users can visually compare the measured performance of the application against the machine's attainable peak performance. The roofline analysis feature of Omniperf directly generates roofline visualizations in PDF format (see Figure C.3 and Figure C.4).

C.2.2 Analysis with CLI

The raw profile data collected are not easily decipherable by most users. To address this, Omniperf offers an analysis tool that processes the data to ease interpretation. The analysis tool is also built into the **omniperf** command line tool. To start, we can use the following command:

```
omniperf analyze -p workloads/vcopy/MI200/
```

Here, the **-p** argument requires the path that contains the raw metrics collected by the profiling stage.

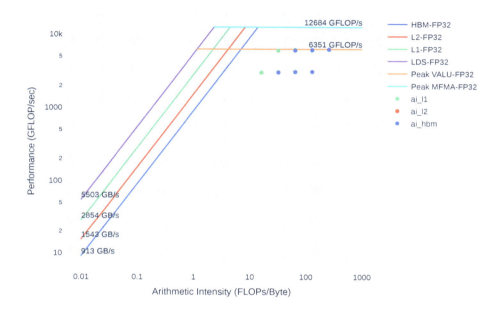

Figure C.4: Roofline analysis chart for 32-bit and 64-bit floating-point operations.

The analysis tool prints the processed data as tables in the command line interface (see Figure C.5). The output typically contains three parts, including the high-level status (kernels and their execution times), system information, and system Speed-of-Light analysis (i.e., derived performance metrics). The derived performance metrics are generally self-explanatory, but users can still refer to the Omniperf documentation for more detailed explanations. [2]

Additionally, Omniperf's CLI-based analysis tool can also support comparing two different executions. Suppose that the raw profile output is stored in **workload1/path** and **workload2/path**, we can use the following command to compare them.

`omniperf analyze -p workload1/path -p workload2/path`

Omniperf's analysis tool can be used to print the derived performance metrics side by side, for easy comparison (see Figure C.6).

---

[2]https://rocm.github.io/omniperf/performance_model.html

```
0. Top Stats
0.1 Top Kernels
```

	Kernel_Name	Count	Sum(ns)	Mean(ns)	Median(ns)	Pct
0	vecCopy(double*, double*, double*, int, int) [clone .kd]	1.00	34240.00	34240.00	34240.00	100.00

```
0.2 Dispatch List
```

	Dispatch_ID	Kernel_Name	GPU_ID
0	0	vecCopy(double*, double*, double*, int, int) [clone .kd]	2

Figure C.5: Beginning of the output generated by the CLI-based analysis tool.

Abs Diff	Sum(ns)	Sum(ns)	Mean(ns)	Mean(ns)	Median(ns)	Median(ns)
0.00	34240.00	34720.0 (1.4%)	34240.00	34720.0 (1.4%)	34240.00	34720.0 (1.4%)

Figure C.6: The output of the Omniperf's analysis tool when comparing two executions. Fields, such as Count, Sum, Mean, and Median, are printed twice, with the second one representing data for workload 2. The relative difference is also listed in the cells for the second workload.

C.2.3   Analysis with Web-Based GUI

To provide a more user-friendly performance analysis interface, Omniperf can start a Flask [34]-based web server. Users can then examine the results using a web browser. The requirement is to append a `--gui` argument to the `omniperf analysis` command, as is done in the following command:

    `omniperf analyze -p workloads/vcopy/MI200 --gui`

The URL that opens the web-based interface is printed in the terminal (e.g., `http://127.0.0.1:8050`). By default, Omniperf uses the 8050 port.

The web interface (see Figure C.7) includes a control panel (top), memory analysis panel (middle), and roofline analysis panel (bottom). Users can use the dropdown menus to filter analysis results for particular kernels and/or kernel dispatches of interest.

C.2.4   Analysis with Grafana

Although the simple web-based GUI provides a more user-friendly interface for performance analysis, the data presented are limited. For a full-scale GUI-based performance analysis, Omniperf employs Grafana [17], a popular data visualization framework. Grafana requires the data to be stored in a MongoDB database. Therefore, Omniperf

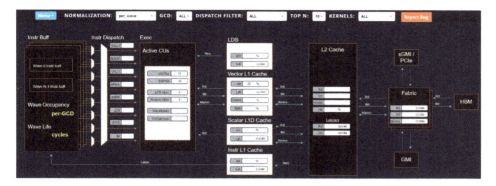

Figure C.7: Interface of the web-based Omniperf analysis GUI.

provides a tool that can import the raw metrics to a MongoDB database with the following command:

```
omniperf database --import -H 127.0.0.1 -u temp -t asw -w
workloads/vcopy/mi200
```

Here, -H and -u accept the host IP address and the username, respectively, of the MongoDB instance. The -t (team) and -w (workload) are arguments that help determine the database name. By default, the database is named:

`omniperf_<team>_<workload>_<soc>` (e.g., `omniperf_asw_vcopy_mi200`).

The Grafana-based analysis tool features 18 panels, each representing different types of data to meet various user needs. In this section, we demonstrate two different views: 1) the Instruction Mix Panel and 2) the L1 Cache Panel. The Instruction Mix Panel (see Figure C.8a) displays the average number of each type of instruction per wavefront, and the L1 Cache Panel (see Figure C.8b) shows the L1 cache hit rate and bandwidth utilization. For more detailed information and instructions, readers can refer to Omniperf's Grafana setup guide [3].

C.3 Summary

In this appendix chapter, we introduced two advanced performance analysis tools: 1) Omnitrace, and 2) Omniperf. They extend the functionality of the built-in ROCm tools, rocTracer and rocProfiler, by offering capabilities to capture program execution traces and performance metrics. Omnitrace and Omniperf offer additional analysis and visualization options, simplifying the process of optimizing program performance.

---

[3]https://rocm.github.io/omniperf/installation.html#setup-grafana-instance

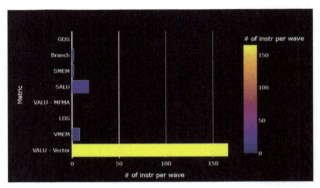

(a) The Instruction Mix Panel displays the average number of each type of instruction in each wavefront.

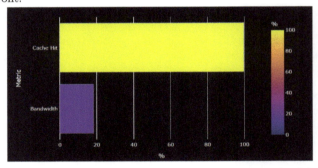

(b) The L1 Cache panel shows the cache hit rate and the bandwidth utilization.

Figure C.8: Example views that are provided by the Grafana-based analysis tool provided by Omniperf.

Bibliography

[1] Martín Abadi. Tensorflow: Learning functions at scale. In *Proceedings of the 21st ACM SIGPLAN International Conference on Functional Programming*, pages 1–1, 2016.

[2] Advanced Micro Devices. GPU Device Plugin for Kubernetes. https://github.com/RadeonOpenCompute/k8s-device-plugin.

[3] Advanced Micro Devices. GPU Device Plugin for Kubernetes. `https://hub.docker.com/r/rocm/k8s-device-plugin/`.

[4] Advanced Micro Devices. HIP Programming Guide, Version 4.3. `https://rocmdocs.amd.com/en/latest/Programming_Guides/Programming-Guides.html`, November 2020.

[5] Advanced Micro Devices. Deep-Learning-With-ROCm. `https://rocmdocs.amd.com/en/latest/Deep_learning/Deep-learning.html`, February 2021.

[6] Advanced Micro Devices. HIP. `https://github.com/ROCm-Developer-Tools/HIP`, February 2021.

[7] Advanced Micro Devices. HIP-Examples. `https://github.com/ROCm-Developer-Tools/HIP-Examples`, February 2021.

[8] Advanced Micro Devices. HIP-Supported-API. `https://github.com/ROCm-Developer-Tools/HIPIFY#-supported-cuda-apis`, February 2021.

[9] Advanced Micro Devices. HIPIFY Tools. `https://github.com/ROCm-Developer-Tools/HIPIFY`, February 2021.

[10] Advanced Micro Devices. Introducing AMD CDNA Architecture, 2021.

[11] Advanced Micro Devices. RCCL. `https://github.com/ROCm/rccl`, February 2021.

[12] Advanced Micro Devices. ROCm-SMI-Lib. `https://github.com/RadeonOpenCompute/rocm_smi_lib`, February 2021.

[13] Andreas Knüpfer and others. The Vampir Performance Analysis Tool-Set. In *Proc. of the 2nd Int. Workshop on Parallel Tools for High Performance Computing*, 2008.

[14] The Graphviz Authors. Graphviz. `https://graphviz.org`, 2021. [Online].

[15] David A. Beckingsale, Jason Burmark, Rich Hornung, Holger Jones, William Killian, Adam J. Kunen, Olga Pearce, Peter Robinson, Brian S. Ryujin, and Thomas RW Scogland. RAJA: Portable performance for large-scale scientific applications. In *2019 IEEE/ACM International Workshop on Performance, Portability and Productivity in HPC (P3HPC)*, pages 71–81, 2019.

[16] Michael Bussmann, H. Burau, T. E. Cowan, Alexander Debus, Alex Huebl, Guido Juckeland, Thomas Kluge, Wolfgang E. Nagel, Richard Pausch, Felix Schmitt, Ulrich Schramm, Joseph Schuchart, and René Widera. Radiative signatures of the relativistic Kelvin-Helmholtz instability. In *Proceedings of the International Conference on High Performance Computing, Networking, Storage and Analysis*, SC '13, pages 5:1–5:12, New York, NY, USA, 2013. ACM.

[17] Mainak Chakraborty and Ajit Pratap Kundan. Grafana. In *Monitoring Cloud-Native Applications: Lead Agile Operations Confidently using Open Source Software*, pages 187–240. Springer, 2021.

[18] Shuai Che, Michael Boyer, Jiayuan Meng, David Tarjan, Jeremy W Sheaffer, Sang-Ha Lee, and Kevin Skadron. Rodinia: A benchmark suite for heterogeneous computing. In *International Symposium on Workload Characterization (IISWC)*, pages 44–54. IEEE, 2009.

[19] Clang. Clang JSON Compilation Database, 2018.

[20] The DWARF Standards Committee. The DWARF Debugging Standard. `https://dwarfstd.org`, 2021. [Online].

[21] Community Repository. ROCM. `https://hub.docker.com/u/rocm`.

[22] Advanced Micro Devices. ROCm System Monitoring Interface. `https://github.com/RadeonOpenCompute/ROC-smi`, 2021. [Online].

[23] Diamon Workgroup. A Common Trace Format: A Flexible, Binary, Trace Format. https://diamon.org/ctf/.

[24] Dieter An Mey et al. Score-P: A Unified Performance Measurement System for Petascale Applications. In Christian Bischof, Heinz-Gerd Hegering, Wolfgang E. Nagel, and Gabriel Wittum, editors, *Competence in High Performance Computing*. Springer Berlin Heidelberg, 2012.

[25] E4S. The Extreme-scale Scientific Software Stack. `https://e4s.io`, 2022.

[26] H Carter Edwards, Christian R Trott, and Daniel Sunderland. Kokkos: Enabling manycore performance portability through polymorphic memory access patterns. *Journal of Parallel and Distributed Computing*, 74(12):3202–3216, 2014.

[27] Dominic Eschweiler, Michael Wagner, Markus Geimer, Andreas Knüpfer, Wolfgang E Nagel, and Felix Wolf. Open Trace Format 2: The Next Generation of Scalable Trace Formats and Support Libraries. In *Applications, Tools and Techniques on the Road to Exascale Computing*, pages 481–490. IOS Press, 2012.

[28] Dominic Eschweiler, Michael Wagner, Markus Geimer, Andreas Knüpfer, Wolfgang Nagel, and Felix Wolf. Open trace format 2: The next generation of scalable trace formats and support libraries. *Advanced in Parallel Computing*, 22:481 – 490, 2012.

[29] Stijn Eyerman and Lieven Eeckhout. The Benefit of SMT in the Multi-Core Era: Flexibility towards Degrees of Thread-Level Parallelism. In *Proceedings of the 19th International Conference on Architectural Support for Programming Languages and Operating Systems*, ASPLOS '14, pages 591—606, New York, NY, USA, 2014. Association for Computing Machinery.

[30] MPI Forum. MPI: A Message-Passing Interface Standard Version 4.0. https://www.mpi-forum.org/docs/mpi-4.0/mpi40-report.pdf, 2021.

[31] Free Software Foundation, Inc. GNU Binutils. `https://www.gnu.org/software/binutils/`, 2021. [Online].

[32] Google. System profiling, app tracing and trace analysis. `https://perfetto.dev`, 2021. [Online].

[33] Google. Trace Event Format. `https://docs.google.com/document/d/1CvAClvFfyA5R-PhYUmn5OOQtYMH4h6I0nSsKchNAySU/edit#`, 2021. [Online].

[34] Miguel Grinberg. *Flask Web Development*. O'Reilly Media, Inc., 2018.

[35] Kevin A. Huck, Allen Davis Malony, Sameer Suresh Shende, and Alan Morris. Knowledge Support and Automation for Performance Analysis with PerfExplorer 2.0. *Journal of Scientific Programming*, 16(2-3):123–134, 2008. (special issue on Large-Scale Programming Tools and Environments).

[36] Kevin A. Huck, Allan Porterfield, Nick Chaimov, Hartmut Kaiser, Allen D. Malony, Thomas Sterling, and Rob Fowler. An autonomic performance environment for exascale. *Supercomputing Frontiers and Innovations*, 2(3):49–66, Nov. 2015.

[37] Intel Corporation. DPC++. `https://spec.oneapi.com/versions/latest/elements/dpcpp/source/index.html`, 2020. [Accessed Oct. 24, 2020].

[38] Joe Casad and Ben Sander. HIP: CUDA Integration with ROCm. https://www.admin-magazine.com/Articles/Secret-Sauce.

[39] Hartmut Kaiser, Patrick Diehl, Adrian S Lemoine, Bryce Adelstein Lelbach, Parsa Amini, Agustín Berge, John Biddiscombe, Steven R Brandt, Nikunj Gupta, Thomas Heller, et al. HPX – The C++ Standard Library for Parallelism and Concurrency. *Journal of Open Source Software*, 5(53):2352, 2020.

[40] Dhiraj Kalamkar, Dheevatsa Mudigere, Naveen Mellempudi, Dipankar Das, Kunal Banerjee, Sasikanth Avancha, Dharma Teja Vooturi, Nataraj Jammalamadaka, Jianyu Huang, Hector Yuen, et al. A study of bfloat16 for deep learning training. *arXiv preprint arXiv:1905.12322*, 2019.

[41] Brian W. Kernighan and Dennis M. Ritchie. *The C Programming Language*. Prentice Hall Professional Technical Reference, 2nd edition, 1988.

[42] Mikhail Khalilov and Alexey Timoveev. Performance analysis of CUDA, OpenACC and OpenMP programming models on TESLA V100 GPU. *2021 Journal of Physics: Conference Series*, 1740, 2020.

[43] Andreas Knüpfer, Holger Brunst, Jens Doleschal, Matthias Jurenz, Matthias Lieber, Holger Mickler, Matthias S. Müller, and Wolfgang E. Nagel. The vampir performance analysis tool-set. In Michael Resch, Rainer Keller, Valentin Himmler, Bettina Krammer, and Alexander Schulz, editors, *Tools for High Performance Computing*, pages 139–155, Berlin, Heidelberg, 2008. Springer Berlin Heidelberg.

[44] Alex Krizhevsky, Ilya Sutskever, and Geoffrey E Hinton. Imagenet Classification with Deep Convolutional Neural Networks. *Advances in Neural Information Processing Systems*, 25:1097–1105, 2012.

[45] Kubernetes Documentation. DaemonSet. `https://kubernetes.io/docs/concepts/workloads/controllers/daemonset/`.

[46] Gregory M Kurtzer, Vanessa Sochat, and Michael W Bauer. Singularity: Scientific containers for mobility of compute. *PLOS One*, 12(5):e0177459, 2017.

[47] LLVM. Abstract Syntax Tree. `https://clang.llvm.org/docs/IntroductionToTheClangAST.html`, February 2022.

[48] LLVMDocs. Compiling CUDA with clang. `https://llvm.org/docs/CompileCudaWithLLVM.html#compiling-cuda-code`, February 2021.

[49] LTTng. barectf. `https://barectf.org/docs/barectf/3.0`. [Online; accessed 31-August-2021].

[50] LTTng. The LTTng Documentation. `https://lttng.org/docs/v2.13/`. [Online; accessed 03-September-2021].

[51] Marko Luksa. *Kubernetes in Action*. Simon and Schuster, 2017.

[52] M. Heroux and J. Willenbring and S. Shende and C. Coti and W. Spear and L. Peyralans and J. Skutnik and E. Keever. E4S: Extreme-scale Scientific Software Stack. In *Virtual CollegeVille Workshop on Scientific Software - Developer Productivity*, 2020.

[53] Sébastien Marcel and Yann Rodriguez. Torchvision the machine-vision package of torch. In *Proceedings of the 18th ACM International Conference on Multimedia*, pages 1485–1488, 2010.

[54] Dirk Merkel. Docker: Lightweight Linux Containers for Consistent Development and Deployment. *Linux Journal*, 2014(239):2, 2014.

[55] Microsoft. Debug Adapter Protocol. `https://microsoft.github.io/debug-adapter-protocol/`. [Online; accessed 01-September-2021].

[56] NVIDIA. CUDA Toolkit Documentation, v11.5. `https://docs.nvidia.com/cuda/index.html`, October 2021.

[57] NVIDIA. CUDA Kernel Execution Configuration, 2022.

[58] OpenACC-Standard.org. The OpenACC Application Programming Interface Version 3.2, 2021.

[59] OpenMP Architecture Review Board. OpenMP Application Programming Interface Version 5.2. https://www.openmp.org/wp-content/uploads/OpenMP-API-Specification-5-2.pdf, 2021.

[60] OpenMP Language Committee. OpenMP Application Programming Interface, Version 5.1, November 2020.

[61] OTF2 Developer Community. Open Trace Format Version 2 (OTF2). https://doi.org/10.5281/zenodo.4682684, April 2021.

[62] Adam Paszke, Sam Gross, Francisco Massa, Adam Lerer, James Bradbury, Gregory Chanan, Trevor Killeen, Zeming Lin, Natalia Gimelshein, Luca Antiga, et al. Pytorch: An imperative style, high-performance deep learning library. *Advances in Neural Information Processing Systems*, 32:8026–8037, 2019.

[63] Sameer Shende, Nicholas Chaimov, Allen Malony, and Neena Imam. Multi-Level Performance Instrumentation for Kokkos Applications Using TAU. In *IEEE/ACM Protools Workshop at SC19*, November 2019.

[64] Sameer Shende and Allen Malony. The TAU Parallel Performance System. *International Journal of High Performance Computing Applications*, 20(2):287–311, 2006.

[65] SLURM. SLURM Workload Manager Version 21.08. `https://slurm.schedmd.com/documentation.html`.

[66] Gilbert Strang. *Introduction to Linear Algebra*. Wellesley-Cambridge Press, Wellesley, MA, fourth edition, 2009.

[67] Bjarne Stroustrup. *The C++ Programming Language*. Addison-Wesley Professional, 4th edition, 2013.

[68] Sylabs. Singularity: Deploying Performance Intensive Workloads Easily and Securely. `https://sylabs.io`, 2022.

[69] Christian Szegedy, Vincent Vanhoucke, Sergey Ioffe, Jon Shlens, and Zbigniew Wojna. Rethinking the inception architecture for computer vision. In *Proceedings of the IEEE conference on computer vision and pattern recognition*, pages 2818–2826, 2016.

[70] Dan Terpstra, Heike Jagode, Haihang You, and Jack Dongarra. Collecting performance data with papi-c. In *Tools for High Performance Computing 2009*, pages 157–173. Springer, 2010.

[71] Dan Terpstra, Heike Jagode, Haihang You, and Jack Dongarra. Collecting performance data with PAPI-C. In Müller M., Resch M., Schulz A., and Nagel W., editors, *Tools for High Performance Computing 2009*, pages 157–173. Springer, 2010.

[72] Theia. Eclipse Theia - C/C++ Extensions. https://github.com/bohemondcouka/theia-cpp-extensions.

[73] Advanced Micro Devices ROCm Developer Tools. ROC-Profiler. `https://github.com/ROCm-Developer-Tools/rocprofiler`, 2021. [Online].

[74] Advanced Micro Devices ROCm Developer Tools. ROC-Tracer. `https://github.com/ROCm-Developer-Tools/roctracer`, 2021. [Online].

[75] TraceVizLab. Installing Trace Compass. https://github.com/tuxology/tracevizlab/.

[76] Christian R. Trott, Damien Lebrun-Grandié, Daniel Arndt, Jan Ciesko, Vinh Dang, Nathan Ellingwood, Rahulkumar Gayatri, Evan Harvey, Daisy S. Hollman, Dan Ibanez, Nevin Liber, Jonathan Madsen, Jeff Miles, David Poliakoff, Amy Powell, Sivasankaran Rajamanickam, Mikael Simberg, Dan Sunderland, Bruno Turcksin, and Jeremiah Wilke. Kokkos 3: Programming model extensions for the exascale era. *IEEE Transactions on Parallel and Distributed Systems*, 33(4):805–817, 2022.

[77] Vampire 9.1. Vampire Performance Optimization. https://vampir.eu.

[78] Aravind Vasudevan, Andrew Anderson, and David Gregg. Parallel multi channel convolution using general matrix multiplication. In *IEEE 28th International Conference on Application-specific Systems, Architectures and Processors (ASAP)*, pages 19–24. IEEE, 2017.

[79] Sudharshan S. Vazhkudai, Bronis R. de Supinski, Arthur S. Bland, Al Geist, James Sexton, Jim Kahle, Christopher J. Zimmer, Scott Atchley, Sarp Oral, Don E. Maxwell, Veronica G. Vergara Larrea, Adam Bertsch, Robin Goldstone, Wayne Joubert, Chris Chambreau, David Appelhans, Robert Blackmore, Ben Casses, George Chochia, Gene Davison, Matthew A. Ezell, Tom Gooding, Elsa Gonsiorowski, Leopold Grinberg, Bill Hanson, Bill Hartner, Ian Karlin, Matthew L. Leininger, Dustin Leverman, Chris Marroquin, Adam Moody, Martin Ohmacht, Ramesh Pankajakshan, Fernando Pizzano, James H. Rogers, Bryan Rosenburg, Drew Schmidt, Mallikarjun Shankar, Feiyi Wang, Py Watson, Bob Walkup, Lance D. Weems, and Junqi Yin. The Design, Deployment, and Evaluation of the CORAL Pre-exascale Systems. In *Proceedings of the International Conference for High Performance Computing, Networking, Storage, and Analysis*, SC '18. IEEE Press, 2018.

[80] Virtual Institute of High Performance Productivity. ScoreP Measurement Infrastructure for High Performance Codes. https://score-p.org.

[81] Michael Wagner, Andreas Knüpfer, and Wolfgang Nagel. Enhanced encoding techniques for the open trace format 2. *Procedia Computer Science*, 9:1979 – 1987, 12 2012.

[82] Samuel Williams, Andrew Waterman, and David Patterson. Roofline: An Insightful Visual Performance Model for Multicore Architectures. *Communications of the ACM*, 52(4):65–76, 2009.

[83] Keren Zhou, Laksono Adhianto, Jonathon Anderson, Aaron Cherian, Dejan Grubisic, Mark Krentel, Yumeng Liu, Xiaozhu Meng, and John Mellor-Crummey. Measurement and analysis of GPU-accelerated applications with HPCToolkit. *Parallel Computing*, 108:102837, 2021.

www.ingramcontent.com/pod-product-compliance
Lightning Source LLC
LaVergne TN
LVHW060400080326
832902LV00046B/4623